ENTREPRENEURSHIP DEVELOPMENT IN INDIA

ENTREPRENEURSHIP DEVELOPMENT IN INDIA
Emergence from Local to Global Business Leadership

Noboru Tabe

Somu Giriappa

KALPAZ

ISBN : 978-81-7835-989-2
₹ 990

First Published 2013

Published by

Kalpaz Publications
C-30, Satyawati Nagar,
Delhi-110052
Ph. : 9212142040
E-mail: kalpaz@hotmail.com

Laser Typesetting : Rudra Computer Graphics, Delhi
Printed at : G. Print Process, Delhi

Cataloging in Publication Data—DK

Courtesy: D.K. Agencies (P) Ltd. <docinfo@dkagencies.com>

Tabe, Noboru.

Entrepreneurship Development in India : Emergence from Local to Global Business / Noboru Tabe, Somu Giriappa.
p. cm.
Includes bibliographical references (p.) and index.

ISBN 9788178359892

1. Entrepreneurship—India. 2. Business Enterprises—India. 3. Technological Innovations—Economic aspects—India. 4. Industrial policy—India. I. Giriappa, S., joint author. II. Title.

DDC 338.040954 23

Dedicated To

The Fond Memory of
Dr D S Chandran Devanesan
Gandhian Entrepreneur and First Indian Principal, Madras Christian College

While the sun illuminates the earth, man ruminates basking in tillage
Humans to pursue their legends with passion and grit
Removing the barriers that stand blocking their prowess
Which moulded our stay as sire and ward four and thirty ans ago in high tees?

We dedicate this to his love and passion for community service,

Made continual by his spouse and all other follower geese!

...S.G.

Contents

Foreword

This book, co-authored with *Dr. Somu Giriappa* has been a long time in the writing.

My interest in the future growth of entrepreneurship had grown up in the pursuits of my futuristic optimism in the perspective dimension of India's growth. While I stayed at *Indian Statistical Institute*, Calcutta (now Kolkata) from 1960 to 1962, I found myself reasonably sympathetic of the prevailing *Dirigisme Dogma* with a futuristic optimism in the future of the country. This feeling was largely due to my personalized acquaintance with Professor *P.C. Mahalanobis,* an architect of Indian planning, while staying at his guest house,ISI. He and his colleagues were the sources of my futuristic perspective. What I saw beamed in the mind of emerging group of modernizer cum-entrepreneurs in industry were also full of emotionally justifiable optimism.

My first book, *Indian Entrepreneurs at the Cross Road: a study of business leadership*-Tabe,1970 -was written at this point of time, when India was about to move on to a controlled change for economic growth. It took just three decades by the time '*India was unbound'* from the development ideology, popularly so far known as "a socialistic pattern of society". **(Gurucharan Das (2002), *India Unbound*).**

As I frequented my visit since the nineteen nineties, I began to adhere to 'reasoning', rather than 'feeling' on a path toward an entrepreneurial dynamism that was what I saw *thus far* depressed in the mind of human mirror in the days foregone.

I met the multitude of local entrepreneurs to sprout and enchant in the soil of India and a few number of global entrepreneurs to bloom as well. My interest in attempting a revisit to new type of Indian entrepreneurship with global outlook was soon welcomed upon my encounter with my former graduate student, from *Madras Christian College,*Chennai,who agreed to work together in writing a update of my earlier book.

Our study design, framework, and materials were shared together and discussed from time to time via internet communication medium, so that each and all of the draft manuscript were shared between us as a unified paper. Our joint work in drafting of chapter-wise paper commensed as early as two thousand ten and completed in early two thousand thirteen.

I was happy to learn from *Somu Giriappa*, co-author of the manuscript that *Kalpaz Publications,* Delhi, a noted publisher of the academic literatures showed interest in the publication of our book. We are grateful to the publisher for the publication of the book and also have a high word for the expertise and editorship of their staff that contributed profusely to a refined and beautiful editing of the book.

Lastly, but not the least, we appreciate the kind gesture in an effort by *Ai UEMURA*, a Japanese artist at *Musashino Art University*, Tokyo who produced two beautiful echings to adorn the frontispiece, 'Look South' and 'Wheel of Change' respectively. *Wheel of Change* is meant for innovativeness in entrepreneurship, while *Look South* for the V-shaped movements across the Himalaya's Mountains. The reader of the book may find the title of etching relevant to what the authors wanted to imply in the text.

The drama is unfolding !

Look South !

Invent in thy future fortunes!!!

In concluding the Foreword, I can not help but mention sad news of *Dr. Somu Giriappa*, a co-author of the book,who passed away on the 27th of March, 2013, just before the manuscript went to the printer. A brief narrative will help the reader know our story of learning and human bondage that we endevored to enshrine during the past half a century, and between India and Japan.

In Memory of :

Our Eternal Joy of Learning and Human Bondage !

Ah, it's spring and time for *Sakura* merriment in Tokyo,

Those cherries were about to bloom en masse with extreme beauty.

On this moment, sad news of his death reached me,

Fading away cherry blossom as soon as they sprout and enchant
That the spirit of life of eternal joy, know our worth,
I would say our relation blossomed at *Tambaram*,
Madras Christian College and *Mangalore University*
In our scholarly pursuits half a century ago.
Our collaborative work flourished to new heights culminating
In the publishing of a book on entrepreneurship.
But *Somu* is no longer with me. *Somu* would say,
'I wish my teacher cherry blossoms for ever',
As I would ponder over the blossom at my garden
To the eternal joy of learning and human bondage.

The good soul from the land of mangoes graced my family and me At *Tambaram* half a century ago.

As I would say, ***thus far, no farther,*** *Somu* gifted me with his shadows of learning and human bondage that never extinguish from my memory.

May his soul rest in peace! Shine my family and me forever!

Noboru Tabe,
Professor Emeritus
Meiji Gakuin University,
Tokyo

Preface

Coping with discontinuous change resulting from 'creative destruction' is the task of the entrepreneurs and keeping in step with these changes demands innovativeness. Catching up with global changes can be managed as long as the time context is known. Strategic time is so crucial in introducing radical changes, otherwise global business leadership will be a distant strategy. Nonetheless, keeping always in step with the changing environment, when change is abrupt and unexpected, will remain a challenge.

It was only after the emergence of innovative entrepreneurship that the world has been witnessing spectacular growth in per capita income and economic welfare. But for the innovators, the world would have been enmeshed in the 17th century *dirigiste* and mercantile conundrums. In the age of *laissez faire*, not only big corporations, but small and medium enterprises, institutions and public authorities also participate in the entrepreneurial culture and vie for global business leadership. In this, the US had been the lead goose, Japan following the lead and itself becoming the lead goose subsequently, to be followed by Korea, China, India and other countries. In this way, the 'V' formation has facilitated the standardisation of business methodologies and emerging leadership in focal areas. Not only the geese lay golden eggs, they fly to farther lands to spread the message of innovation and leadership. Sometimes, a lead goose may depart from the regular route to be a radical innovator in its own way.

Learning, when fortified with innovative culture, results in the emergence of entrepreneurship in any respective field of study and application. Once diffused and assimilated, it is the local entrepreneurial culture that ultimately pervades into global business scenario. Consequent on the economic liberalisation in the 1990s and the growth of privatisation, India has emerged a global leader in many business areas, in spite of its multitude of developmental bottlenecks and lack of sophisticated industrial revolution. It is now in a position to be a lead goose, especially in sectors like information technology, biotechnology and automotive industry.

Looking at the pace with which countries like Japan, Korea, Taiwan, China, India and the rest of Asia has spearheaded in entrepreneurial and business model building, it seems that Asia has the potential leadership to change the global business scenario in the future. ***Look South*** (with due apologies to Westward Ho!) is a message that may be implicated in the study of evolutionary changes of India's entrepreneurship. Socio-historical studies in the past had dampened off a possibility of appreciating potentials of local entrepreneurship, while economics of entrepreneurship often reflects a historical atavism, once adopted by the Western experiences and adapted to the countries in growing phases like India. The book begins its initial deliberation by reviewing in a nutshell, major theoretical premises behind the related discipline of entrepreneurship studies, in so far as are relevant to the present-day study. The motive for this book came from the interest shown on the first author's 1970 book on Indian entrepreneurs. We have tried to incorporate the views of multitude of authors on entrepreneurship by suitably boxing them into what we have construed as the emerging areas of entrepreneurship with special reference to India. The case studies and the profiles of the entrepreneurs have been adapted from various websites.

This book that concentrates on India's experience in a wider spectrum of time manifests itself as a revisit to the importance of entrepreneurship in streaming type and pattern of national development of a country. Through zigzagged path that India had undergone in the past, the entrepreneurs, though small in number but globally competent in capability, are pushing the country to a front in global business leadership.

There is a clue in the drama that tells a story to catch a missing link within a fast changing structure of opportunity in a world technological domain. The IT software, biopharmaceuticals and others are the one that established sovereignty in technology domain in the world. Only entrepreneurial capability accounts for the lead flying goose to pave the way. 'Look south' is a way for the respective innovation.

Each country can enjoy advantage *in opportunity structure* in industry with the appropriate entrepreneurship intent. So does a country like India that is highly embedded with potential entrepreneurial ability in the most innovative technology domains and in many sectors of human activities like medicals, ecological and what else. The country has now reached a point of no return where its global business leadership is bound to lead, not only the country, but also the world for a sustained growth and stability. This is the message of optimism for India and the world. The authors have benefited a great deal of intellectual insights from the current scenario drawn out of the past entrepreneurial history of Japan, India and Korea. Japanese experiences in early Meiji period tell the story in which strong motive for public service, coupled with moral way of life in private life was the prime factor that led major entrepreneurs in newly evolving industries to catch up and supersede the then advanced economies. India's experience in contemporaneous scenario of early 20th century highlights symbolic premises of entrepreneurship to vie its soil for a strong fortification against foreign dominance and in this, J. N. Tata was a man of public goods for the soil. To cite a current scenario, the founder of Korean Steel was also a man of public goods who led the country to rise from the ashes after the devastation of Korean War. We share those and other country's experience in Asia as a common compass in gauging the range of historic applicability into the current scenario of evolving entrepreneurship in Asian perspectives. Lastly, but not the least, we appreciate the kind gesture in an effort by Ai UEMURA, a Japanese artist who produced two beautiful etchings to adorn the frontispiece. *Wheel of Change* is meant for innovativeness in entrepreneurship, while *Look South* for the V-shaped movements across the Himalaya's Mountains. The reader of the book may find the title of etching relevant to what the authors wanted to imply in the text.

The drama is unfolding! Look south! Invent in thy future fortunes!!

Noboru Tabe and Somu Giriappa

Introduction

A set of three scientific exploration, viz., *'What it is'*, *'How it is'*, *'Why it is'* is a univocal question one has to answer, before any attempt by scientist is made in research field of the unexplored. This is, in my retrospect, what Professor *P.C. Mahalanobis, as* a scientist and an architect of Indian planning loved to say. (*Talks on Planning*, ISI, Calcutta, 1961). We follow his approach in the writing by asking ourselves for three basic questions that, in its final analysis, constitute a framework of the book :

1.'What is Entrepreneurship': theory, evolution, and experiences

A metaphorical narrative may serve the purpose to answer the question, viz. 'what is entrepreneurship'. To cite a country experience in a historical context, the early Meiji Period (1868) marked a start-off phase of rapid industrialisation in Japan, when the multitude of *a man of public service and of simple private life* had mushroomed in every corner of the land. They were the ultimate inputs of entrepreneurship to laying the firm foundation of *industrialism* on the soil of underdeveloped country. Recognising this salient features of entrepreneurship prevalent in non-Western region like Meiji Japan, Johannes Hirschmeier, S.V.D. (*The Origins of Entrepreneurship in Meiji Japan,* Harvard Univ. Press, 1964) answered the question by defining those Japanese entrepreneurs as a type of man who was motivated by the spirit of *Confucianism*, being functioned as equivalent to *Protestant ethics* (Max Weber, 1930). His analysis may be called 'a Paradigm of Equivalent Function' in entrepreneurship. The same analogy may be appropriate in search of a determinant of subjective and motivational elements inherent to entrepreneurial behaviour in a different historical and cultural context. To recollect, who was an individual entrepreneur that highlighted the turn of the century by planting *Industrialism* in the barren land of Jamshedpur, West Bengal, He built a steel plant, the first of its kind in Asia years before Meiji Japan introduced steel technology from the West to vie its soil for a strong fortification against foreign dominance. In this, *J.N. Tata was 'a man of public goods'* for the soil. (D.E.Wacha, The Life and Works of J.N.Tata, Madras, 1914)

Who was 'a man of seed-bed' in Korean steel industry that plowed and seeded down a war-stricken land after the Korean War and cropped the fruits of entrepreneurial development, thus enjoying subsequently the top-most supremacy in world steel production? (Enos and Park, 1988; Lall, 1985). Who were those 'bureaucrat entrepreneurs' of China, that succeeded in an attempt to enjoy economic and social benefit arising out of the industry transfer from Japan. The steel industry was a case among the many. (Zhang and Duysters, 2010).

A look at those and other country experience may leads one to believe that entrepreneurship *is an evolving phenomenon*, if one is careful enough to learn from the recent experiences of industrial growth in Asian region. (Wong, 1988).

Chapter one elaborates on the different theories of entrepreneurship from economic, managerial, sociological and psychological perspectives and assesses various models of entrepreneurship such as occupational choice, dis-equibrium, trading off between risk and returns, symmetric information, besides describing various types of entrepreneurs. (McClelland,1951; Tabe,1970; Porter,1986)

Chapter two explains the evolution of entrepreneurs in India with reference to pre-colonial, colonial, independence and recent periods, focusing on the current business prospects of various business communities. (Tabe, 1970; Tripathi,1971)

Chapter three, in addition to showcasing the Chinese and Korean entrepreneurship development singles out the experience of POSCO Steels of South Korea and Tata Steels of India with regard to entrepreneurial growth.

The experiences of China, Korea and India show that entrepreneurial activity flourishes but each country exhibits differences in terms of access to information, privacy rights and the role of the state. (Westphal, et al, 1985; Ungson et al, 1997). The chapter concludes describing the achievements of the three Tata scions.

2. How is entrepreneurship'; selected growth, family business and business groups, and small business

Each country can enjoy advantage in *opportunity structure* in industry, with the appropriate entrepreneurship intent. Once the structure is fortified with corresponding dynamism in the entrepreneurial activities concerned, technology has its own way to augment a linkage effect over the sphere of entrepreneurial activity concerned. While this is popularly accepted as an inter-industry linkage, a potential area of application and developement in knowledge- generating sector is fast expanding its sphere and extent of the impact in India. A country like India is the best example in the world that tells a story to catch a missing link within a fast changing structure of *opportunity* in world technological domains. The growth of information technology and recent developments in bio-pharmacy and bio-agriculture are the case of selective growth in India.

In furthering growth and stability of information and human welfare activities, current scenario of India's progress in family business and groups, and small business is worth examining, at this junction of our analysis, so that very meaning of entrepreneurship development is understood from the India's experience of this century.

Chapter four recounts the growth of information technology in India and how the IT entrepreneurs have been able to advance the sector to global heights. (Rossini and Kenney, 2002; Athreye, 2005; D'Costa, 2008). The growth of software industry in Bangalore (NASSCON-McKinsey, 2005) and Hyderabad (Nirnajana Rao, 2009) is assessed, besides showcasing the profiles of the noted IT entrepreneurs and companies of India.

Chapter five discusses developments in bio-pharmacy and bio-agriculture segments, besides bio-energy and international collaboration in the field of biotechnology, especially in pharmaceuticals. (Frew et al, 2007)

Barriers that impede innovation and discovery like weak entrepreneurial skills, lack of public-private partnerships, risk averse nature of industry, lack of venture funding, lack of venture capital system and streamlining the regulatory process are explained. The biotech firms like Dr. Reddy's, Wockhardt Ltd., Nicholas Piramal India Ltd. and Ranbaxy are showcased, besides some of the noted entrepreneurs in the field. (Fan and Watanabe, 2008)

Chapter six enumerates the growth of major family business and business groups in India like the Tatas: Reliance Group (Reliance

Industries and Reliance ADA); Aditya Birla group; ITC Limited, The Bajaj Group; Bharti Airtel; The Godrej Group; The Adani Group; The Wiplo Group; The Hero Group; The Escorts Group and the M.P. Birla Group. The chapter concludes by assessing the prospects of Indian business groups. (Dutta, 1997; Pistrui, 2006; Gopalakrishnan, 2009)

Chapter seven showcases the growth of entrepreneurship in small and medium enterprises with special reference to Indian automobile industry. The growth of entrepreneurship in the sector is assessed in terms of technology and information–based growth of entrepreneurship. (Lakshmanan et al, 2007) Besides explaining the different measures of encouraging entrepreneurship in India, the chapter summarises a few cases of budding entrepreneurial ventures in Andhra Pradesh, Karnataka and Tamil Nadu, as sources from the existing studies. (Kondaiah, 2007; D'Costa, 2011; FAO, 2008)

3. 'Why entrepreneurship'; social benefits, multiple dimensions, innovativeness

Entrepreneurship may have supply-side or demand-side perspective. The former focuses on the availability of suitable individuals to occupy entrepreneurial roles (Thornton, 1999). On the other side, the demand-side perspective suggests a number of ways to examine the context of organisational founding, such as the generation of new ventures by organisational hierarchies. Individuals and organisations affect and are affected by their context. It is this aspect of interactive process in entrepreneurship that religious doctrine provides the cultural justification needed to shape the economic behaviour of individuals that lead to the rise of capitalism. (M.Weber, 1904).

Recognising recent exposure of the new genre of *social entrepreneurs,* it is high time to examine the supply-side perspective by looking at: firstly, who they are having the non-profit objectives, and secondly, how culture and personality can empower individual entrepreneurship, and finally, why their chances of success are determined by the structure of their networks. We are optimistic of the future of newly emerging genre of social entrepreneur. As a change agent in the social sector of the economies, he or she is 'a man of social value' (not just private value) who ***pursues*** new opportunities to serve the mission, ***engages*** in a process of continuous innovation, adaptation, and learning, and **acts** boldly without being limited by resources currently in hand.

Chapter eight discusses various types of entrepreneurship and developments that have been accomplished in social entrepreneurship (Raman, 2010); ecological entrepreneurship (Krishna et al, 2000); public entrepreneur-ship (Schneide and Teske,1992); institutional entrepreneurship (Pacheco et al, 2010) ; and women entrepreneurship (Sinha, 2003); citing case studies wherever necessary.

Chapter nine explains the different types of innovations, focusing on radical innovations that have transformed the modern world, showcasing through the *flying geese theory*. (Kaname Akamatsu, 1961; Kiyoshi Kojima, 2000; Terutomo Ozawa, 2009). The *lead goose theory* spearheading innovations and regional agglomeration in Asia is explained, wherein India takes the lead from Japan. Business opportunities in different countries are compared with reference to recent developments in the IT sector and the development of intra-premiership is also discussed. (Hamel, 2002) The predominance of software industry in innovativeness is elaborated (Krishnan et al; 2003; Athreye, 2002)

Chapter ten recounts entrepreneurship in retrospective by comparing the recent Global Competitiveness Index; Global Entrepreneurship Development Index in different countries and India's status. The chapter summarises the earlier chapters with reference to some vital questions to be answered and an assessment of entrepreneurship and scope of Indian entrepreneurship.

4. 'Entrepreneurship ahead' : a challenge, radical innovator, local culture

Our analysis of entrepreneurship as constituted in ten chapters will carry with it three important implications and hence convincing messages to any readership for the book.

Message one: *a Challenge*

Coping with discontinuous change resulting from 'creative destruction', (A. Schumpeter,1950) is the task of the entrepreneur and keeping in step with these changes demands innovativeness. Catching up with global changes can be managed as long as the time context is known. Strategic time is so crucial in introducing radical changes, otherwise global business leadership will be a distant strategy. Nevertheless, keeping always in step with the changing environment, when change is abrupt and unexpected will remain *a challenge.*

Message two : *a Radical Innovator*

It was only after the emergence of innovative entrepreneurship that the world has been witnessing spectacular growth in income and economic welfare. But for the innovators, the world would have been enmeshed in the 17th century *Dirigisme* and mercantile conundrums. In the age of *laissez faire,* not only big Corporation, but small and medium enterprises, institutions, and public business leadership. In this, the US had been the *lead goose*, Japan following the lead and itself becoming the *lead goose* subsequently, to be followed by Korea, China, India and other countries. In this way, the 'V' formation has facilitated the standardisation of business methodologies and emerging leadership in focal areas. Not only the geese lay golden eggs, they fly to farther lands to spread the message of innovation and leadership. Sometimes, a *lead goose* may depart from the regular route to be *a radical innovator* in its own way. (Varadarajan, 2011)

Message three: *local entrepreneurial culture*

Learning, when fortified with innovative culture, results in the emergence of entrepreneurship in any respective field of study and application. Once diffused and assimilated, it is the *local entrepreneurial culture* that ultimately pervades into global business scenario. Consequent on the economic liberalisation in the 1990s and the growth of privatisation, India has emerged a global leader in many business areas, in spite of its multitude of development bottlenecks and lack of sophisticated industrial revolution. It is now in a position to be a *lead goose*, especially in sectors like information technology, biotechnology and automotive industry.

Overall Message : *Look South*

Looking at the pace with which countries like Japan, Korea, Taiwan, China, India and the rest of Asia have spearheaded in entrepreneurial and business model building, it is most likely that Asia has the potential leadership to change the global business scenario in the near future to come.

Look South (with due apologies to Westward Ho!) is a message that may be implicated in the study of evolutionary changes of India's entrepreneurship.

Noboru Tabe,
Professor Emeritus,
Meiji Gakuin University, Tokyo

1

Conceptualisation and the Process of Entrepreneurship

1.1 Introduction

In 'Doing Business 2013', India has been ranked 132 out of 185 countries, wherein it takes 27 days with 12 procedures to start a business and even more to close an enterprise. Looking at R&D expenditure, the country lags behind many countries, suggesting that the development of entrepreneurship is stunted and is subject to many restrictions. Yet, India has emerged in business leadership in few selected sectors and this book discusses these emerging fields as indicators of the growing technological and entrepreneurial advantage of the country. With the advent of technological and digital revolutions, the concept of entrepreneurship has undergone a radical change from the traditional view of risk taking to the modern dilemma of 'innovate and perish'. At the same time, it has emerged as the fulcrum of development in every field of human endeavour, ushering in different types of entrepreneurship in every field of activities. Entrepreneurship has become a dynamic phenomenon, wherein risky and innovative decisions regarding allocation and utilisation of resources have to be undertaken by entrepreneurs for their success. An optimal mix of different types of resources of money, time, knowledge and skills, physical energy and social capital makes the enterprises resourceful, creative, innovative and socially relevant. However, as pointed by Kaufman Foundation (2012), which is corroborated by Global

Entrepreneurship Index of 2012, the rate of entrepreneurship has shown a decline in recent times that requires refurbishment to sustain the tempo of development generated so far.

Entrepreneurship development follows a 'V' formation of the flying geese, in that unlike others, entrepreneurs are always in flight, scourging for new grounds, abandoning old homesteads, sometimes reviving them, characterising new paths for the would-be entrepreneurs, breaking new avenues, fighting potential threats and emulating the lead goose, in turn to be a new lead goose in the formation process. What we witness in the case of the geese turns an apt description of the behaviour of the entrepreneurs and this book makes an attempt to deliberate on the multi-faceted entrepreneurial process as to what is its origins, how the theory has been conceptualised and why the study is of crucial interest in understanding the very process of socio-economic development through the lead sectors. When the entrepreneur makes use of own or others' money (a crucial resource in business) to acquire the other four resources and buy time-saving devices to gain more time, he or she undertakes various types of entrepreneurial ventures and models, paving way for different characterisations of entrepreneurship. Entrepreneurship, in addition to catalysing socio-economic development, has transformed many enterprising people into self-employed business tycoons, enabling the economies in the process to generate value by identifying and exploiting new products, processes and markets (OECD, 2008).

The word 'entrepreneurship' is derived from the French words 'entre' (between) and 'entreprendre' (one who undertakes), thus, meaning one who undertakes an opportunity-based and interactive business enterprise. It was actually the French economist Richard Cantillon (1755), who defines entrepreneurship as any type of self-employment, wherein entrepreneurs buy at certain prices in the present and sell at uncertain prices in the future, thus, bearing an element of uncertainty. According to Jean Baptiste Say (1964), another French economist, the entrepreneur is an agent who combines all means of production and finds in the value of the products, the fruits of the entire capital he employs and the value of the wages, the interest and rent which he pays, as well as profits belonging to himself. The thread was continued by Frank Knight (1921), an American economist, in his uncertainty conceptualization, followed by Joseph Alois Scumpeter (1934), the Austrian economist, who gave the concept a modern innovative interpretation. According to Peter Drucker (1985), the entrepreneur is a change agent aiming at exploitation of opportunities, while Peter Kilby (1971) views an entrepreneur as an imitator of innovations, which aspect describes the behaviour of those in developing economies. Pinchot (1983) and others consider an entrepreneur as an 'intrapreneur', one who innovates within an organisation. Thus, the domain of entrepreneurship has been largely dominated by economic thinking and it was only after Hoselitz (1952), McClelland (1961) and Drucker (1985) that social and managerial interpretations became widely prevalent. In recent times, the other variants of applied entrepreneurship in the fields of social, institutional, public and ecological on the one hand and that related to small and medium enterprises, women and other have been analysed. Further, the very formation of business groups itself has become a major entrepreneurial action, wherein intrapreneurism plays a crucial role in fortifying the entrepreneurial venture.

Conceptualisation of entrepreneurship was not a major developmental exercise in developing economies, despite the important role played by it in the overthrow of feudal economies and rise of capitalism in the first world. The first paper that looked at the issue of entrepreneurship and the development of poor economies was probably by Leff (1979) who identified poor institutions as impediments to the emergence of entrepreneurship. Yet, it was not until the works of Baumol (1990, 2002) and North (1990) that significant theoretical insights emerged about the relationship between the quality of institutional environment and the type of entrepreneurship. These studies have remained as important arguments about why growth of entrepreneurship may be sub-optimal in the developing countries.

Some of the studies that have attempted to analyse the growth of entrepreneurship, mostly in the developing countries include Kilby (1971) for general introduction; Lamb (1955) for growth of business enterprises; Berna (1959), Medhora (1965), Rungta (1970) and Tripathi (1971) for growth of entrepreneurship in India and Watanabe (1970) for growth of small scale entrepreneurship in Japan. Tabe (1970), for example, published a book on 'Indian Entrepreneurs at the Cross-roads.' We intend to carry forward some of the arguments of the book, by focusing on the growth and impact of entrepreneurship on economies like India in the transformation process towards realising the fruits of both traditional and modern-day elements of entrepreneurship. Though the concept can be viewed in respect of many disciplines, this work concentrates on business leadership. We propose to undertake the work in the light of the 'flying geese' theory, pinpointing on the role played by some of the Indian enterprises and entrepreneurs in evolving from local survivalism to 'global' competitive advantage and leadership.

1.2 The 'Flying Geese' Concept

In the spring, when we see geese heading north for the summer or south in the fall, flying along in V formation, we might be interested in knowing why they fly that way. It has been observed that as each bird flaps its wings, it creates uplift for the bird immediately following. By flying in V formation, the whole flock adds a higher percentage of flying range (synergy) than if each bird flew on its own. Business groups which share a common direction and sense of community can get where they are going, quicker and easier because they are travelling on the thrust of one another. Whenever a goose falls out of formation, it suddenly feels the drag and resistance of trying to go it alone and quickly gets back into formation to take advantage of the lifting power of the bird immediately in front. If the entrepreneurs have the sense of geese, they will stay in formation with those who are heading in the same direction as they are. When a lead goose does not gain any energetic advantage from its position, it will drop back after a time; in this case, another bird takes the lead. Though the flock members do not do this on any regular rotation, larger and stronger birds may be in the lead for a greater percentage of the time. When the lead goose gets tired, he rotates back in the wing and another goose flies point and it is advantageous to take turns doing hard jobs, with people or flying geese. These geese honk from behind to encourage those upfront to keep up their speed. The entrepreneur has to be careful what others honk from behind. When a goose gets sick or is wounded by gunshot and falls out, two geese fall out of formation and follow him down to help and protect him. They stay with him until he is either able to fly or until he is dead and then they launch out on their own or with another formation until they catch up with their group. Like the geese, the entrepreneurs have to stand by each other, protect (compete with?) one another and sometimes create new models who seem to be going in their direction. Agglomeration and interaction take place with the lead goose, followed by the early goose, the late goose and lastly by the followers. At around 2000 metres above, the flock may break into circular formation just in time to avoid collision. Sometimes the birds may be in a circular form so as to frighten any predators too.

According to the flying geese theory (Ozawa, 2009), the US, the lead goose, was taken over by Japan as the lead goose in another set-up. Korea took the cue and in turn became the lead goose in the next transformation stage, to be followed by countries like China and India. When China was the lead goose, Vietnam and Myanmar became the followers. The Japanese economic miracle had impacted on its East and Southeast Asian countries through direct investment and as a model of development in the 1980s. Vernon's (1966) *product cycle theory* is similar to it and as a matter of fact the *flying geese theory* has been incorporated into the western product cycle and growth theories.

Japan, a late comer to development, could catch up with more advanced countries through an integrated process of moving from imports through import substitution to one of exports. In the process, production of labour-intensive goods had moved away from Japan (the leading goose) to the Asian tigers of South Korea, Taiwan, Singapore and Hong Kong and then to the Association of South-East Asian Nations countries and certain parts of China, resulting in dynamic changes of the underlying comparative advantages in the region (Kojima, 2000). Flying geese-like industrial transfers has been related to the characteristics of the life cycle of products, which had impacted on the essence of innovations and comparative advantage, leading to agglomeration amongst these countries. When advanced countries upgrade their industrial structure from labour-intensive to capital-intensive industries, the late comers can take over the industries abandoned by the former and receive foreign investment to develop them. However, changing directions of comparative advantage and forms of the *flying geese theory* are not the same amongst small and large economies. This is because a small economy is characterised by the homogeneity of its resource endowment and industrial structure and once its comparative advantage changes, the economy as a whole enters a new stage of development. In contrast, a large economy is characterised by heterogeneity in its resource endowment and industrial structure among different regions. While some regions move to a new stage of development, the development stage of others might remain unchanged.

The flying geese paradigm has been characterised as a catching-up process behind a leader (Japan) and the transnational paradigm of development. This was first presented in the early 1930s by Kaname Akamatsu (1961) and revived in the 1970s and 1980s by Kiyoshi Kojima and Terutoma Ozawa. The theory stresses interactive growth through innovative learning among the economies operating at different stages of growth. Policy makers need a clear understanding of the process that offers both inter- and intra-industrial routes towards upgrading of technology. Interactive growth becomes efficient when countries cluster cooperatively in a regional hierarchy, reaping economies of synergy and benefiting from comparative.

In this, we will have to paraphrase Schumpeter's (1961) views on global competition, an extension and diffusion of new knowledge under conditions of rivalry. Schumpeter does not see economic development as a smooth movement, but a process of jumps with fluctuations, wherein the business cycle is built within the process of economic development. Economic development is driven by innovation and innovative entrepreneurs emerge side by side with old enterprises and try to take their place and eventually replace them. The changes in development conditions caused by the competition between the new and old enterprises take the form of a business cycle ('creative destruction'). As a result, many new enterprises follow and imitate the innovation of the early enterprises, resulting in a boom. Because the boom is pushed partly by the late comer enterprises, which are progressively less qualified in innovation and the old enterprises' struggle for survival, the economic crisis eventually coming to an end, in turn followed by recession.

During times of economic crises, opportunity for creative destruction emerges, wherein, production factors can be recombined and old patterns of growth replaced, while new technologies decimate old technologies and productivity improvements contribute to economic growth (Cai, 2008). Innovative entrepreneurial learning is facilitated by multinationals foreign direct investment and other activities that accompany technology, managerial skills and access to export markets, a powerful catalyst for industrial upgrading and development. Borrowed growth is the finance mode of interactive growth, the benefits and risks varying with the development stage, institutional set-up and policy. Growth stages fundamentally and structurally determine external imbalances, but short-term, situational and coincidental macroeconomic factors magnify the imbalances between nations. These two causes should be distinguished, since the latter alone is amenable to immediate adjustments in fiscal, monetary and exchange rate policies. The Asian countries got the basic right and created an environment where the growth of private investment and investment in human capital succeeded (Ozawa, 2009). This included a relatively low degree of inequality, high productivity growth in agriculture, relatively efficient (corruption-free) public administration and market-enhancing instead of market-distorting interventions (like export goals and some protection for home markets). It also included macroeconomic stability, investment in human capital, in particular primary and secondary education, a functioning price system, a stable, though not necessarily market-oriented financial sector and selective instead of massive interventions, like selective credit allocation or export promotion. Market failure through asymmetric information in the financial sector and underdevelopment of the banking sector was overcome by special measures like long-term financial allocation by the state and the foundation of specialised public industrial banks.

Changes in economic and industrial structures are the by-products of crises in the business cycles and the acceleration of technology transfers among the regions resulted in an initial virtuous circle of accumulation, initiated by Japan, wherein cheap credit had played an important role, but later turned to be a vicious circle of debts forcing companies to collapse. The prolonged existence of the *zombie* companies led to lost decades for Japanese growth in the 1990s and 2000s, thus diminishing the appeal of its economic model. In spite of being the lead goose, Japan never succeeded in developing an international currency (if it had, the 1988 Asian financial crisis would not have taken place?) and all the Asian countries had to be linked to the US dollar. In this market-driven *dirigiste* change, the Schumpeterian entrepreneurship characterises the sky wherein the geese have their methodic and blissful flight.

In the case of Korea and Taiwan, American influence and aid have been stressed as factors explaining rapid catching-up process. However, though the US aid was important for Korea in the 1950s, its growth miracle began when aid was less important in the 1960s. Also in terms of the economic system, American influence was quite limited by domestic political factors. For ASEAN countries, the lead was by Singapore, where a new category of incentives was created for those firms leaving Singapore and moving to other ASEAN countries, which can create a counterpart category (Ozawa, 2009).

True to the flying geese perception, India had taken the lead from not just the US and Japan, but all other lead geese in becoming innovative and entrepreneurial. According to Boston Consulting Group (2012), the Tata group is the only innovative Indian company to find its place in the world's top 50 innovative companies, led by Apple, Toyota, Google, Microsoft and others. Tata Nano has been the most innovative people's car introduced in India in recent times. In iron and steel industry, mergers and acquisitions and technological innovations have enabled Arcelor-Mittal and Tata-Corus to become global leaders. In information technology sector, the emergence of Tata Consultancy Services, Infosys and Wipro as global outsourcing companies has pushed India to the forefront of global IT leadership. The achievement of Indian biotech firms like Ranbaxy, Cipla, Dr Reddy's and Biocon have resulted in India taking up the leadership in many a pharma sector. There are many more such instances prodding Indian innovativeness on to global standards and with greater economic reforms, the country is set to emerge as one of the leading innovative nations in the near future. True to the flying geese, innovative entrepreneurs lead the other stock, sometimes in a radical way too, thus strengthening the pace of socio-economic dynamism.

1.3 A Prelude to Entrepreneurship

According to Lal and Clement (2005), in the West, economic development had resulted in the establishment of individual property rights and encouragement of growth of private capital and competition. Enterprises thrived because individuals pursued Smithian self-interest animalism of survival and wealth accumulation. The instinct to survive under competitive pressures resulted in the growth of innovations and productivity increases, which eventually led to both increased accumulation for businesses and wider choices and lower prices to the consumers. However, capitalism has created a greater degree of inequalities in income and wealth, while private decisions have not led to socially desirable outcomes, especially in the case of developing countries due to market imperfections, as a result of which, appropriate government interventions become essential for sustained economic development and emergence of innovative entrepreneurship (Krueger, 1993). Some of the newly independent colonialised countries which had been deprived of the industrialisation process began to adopt many models of economic growth, planning being one such, based on the experience of the former Soviet Union (Panagariya, 1994). These developing countries invested in basic socio-economic infrastructures like education and health to promote literacy and to ensure an adequate supply of technical manpower to facilitate production of goods and services towards autarky. Industrialisation was attempted mainly through import substitution, whereby imports were being increasingly replaced by domestic production. Many countries like India, in a state of transition, are planning to move away from a subsistence-oriented and inward looking local economy to a surplus seeking and outward looking global economy. Such a move is possible only through the emergence of entrepreneurship stock in every sector towards exploiting the market opportunities and innovating new products and services to achieve global competitive advantage.

The context in which entrepreneurs bear initiative, achievement, motivation and visioning has a hold on what they deliver. When these factors are directed towards realising surplus or value addition in a market environment over a period of time, the entrepreneurs as lead geese, balance out imperfections in the market (Gopakumar, 1995) in pursuit of wealth, which becomes the reward they obtain for the risks undertaken. Hence, exploitation of opportunities would require the entrepreneur's creative ability to evaluate situations in terms of unmet needs, identifying markets or gaps for which products are evolved and the search for creating and consolidating competitive advantage.

The system of entrepreneurship that evolved in the US has been quite successful, having considerable relevance to other technologically advanced countries like Germany and Japan, in line with 'flying geese' theory. Though the role of individual or institutional entrepreneurship to assume the role of followers is different in developing countries, the diffusion of innovations would take a similar path as in the developed economies. Resources are already in full use in the latter and any further increase in productivity has to result only through innovative technologies. For example, in the US, ultra new technologies in many fields have been generated by entrepreneurial small and large firms alike. On the other hand, in countries like India, infrastructure, value system and cultural issues have a sway over entrepreneurial development. Any innovation to succeed needs to be accepted by social system and cultural ethos and it can be argued that acceptance by the mass in itself is a kind of social innovation. In some contexts, self-employment itself may be an indicator of entrepreneurship, if characterised by innovativeness. Where economies are more concerned with achieving basic necessities (a la Maslow), it is entrepreneurship (provided with necessary incentives from the state), which has the power to develop and sustain the system over a period of time.

1.4 Theories of Entrepreneurship

Definitions of entrepreneurship have emphasised a broad range of activities including the creation of organisations (Gartner, 1988), the carrying out of new combinations (Schumpeter, 1934), the exploration of opportunities (Kirzner, 1973), the bearing of uncertainty (Knight, 1921) and bringing together of factors of production (Say, 1964). Cantillon was the first economist to define an entrepreneur as an agent who buys means of production at certain prices to combine them into a new product. He classifies economic agents into landowners, hirelings and entrepreneurs and considered the entrepreneur as the most active among these agents, connecting the producers with customers. Say improves Cantillon's concept by adding that the entrepreneur brings people together to build a productive base.

Frank Knight (1921) emphasises the entrepreneur's role in bearing the uncertainty of market dynamics, though they are required to perform such fundamental managerial functions such as direction and control. Knight introduces the dimension of risk-taking as a central theme of entrepreneurship and holds that uncertainty is a crucial factor of production, where the function of an entrepreneur is to anticipate future events. The entrepreneur earns profit as a reward for taking such risks, the characteristics of a successful entrepreneur being a thorough understanding of the industry, good goose skills and foresight on demand and supply changes and the willingness to act on such risky foresights. This success depends not merely on possession of these skills, but also on the economic and environmental conditions in which the entrepreneurs attempt their endeavours. Based on this precept, entrepreneurship has been termed as the fourth factor itself instead of organisation, coordinating the other three factors.

Economic development takes place when a country's real gross domestic product increases over a period of time, wherein the contribution of entrepreneurs becomes very crucial. Development implies that carrying out of new combination of entrepreneurship is basically a creative activity and according to Joseph Schumpeter (1934), an entrepreneur is one who perceives the opportunities to innovate and carry out new combinations. Schumpeterian entrepreneur is one who possesses characteristics of innovation, foresight and creativity. Entrepreneurship takes place when the entrepreneur creates a new product, introduces a new way to make a product, discovers a new market for the product or finds a new source of raw material and finds new ways of creating new organizations. Schumpeter (1950) stresses the fact that these attributes unaccompanied by the ability to innovate would not be sufficient to account for the emergence of entrepreneurship.

Schumpeter (1950) equates entrepreneurship with the concept of innovation applied to a business context, exhibiting what he calls as a creative destruction system of development. Schumpeter's definition emphasises the combination of resources and therefore, managers of already established business are not entrepreneurs. He contends that the defining characteristic of entrepreneurial ventures is innovation. By finding a new production function in an existing resource, a previously unknown means through which a resource could produce value, the entrepreneur is innovating in product design, organisation of the firm, marketing devices or process design. Innovation is what separates the entrepreneur from others (including self-employed) who undertake closely related endeavours. The dynamics of the process can be vastly different depending on the institutional context and level of development within an economy.

However, his theory ignores the entrepreneur's risk taking ability and organisational skills and places undue importance on innovation. Further, it applies mostly to large-scale corporations, but economic conditions force small entrepreneurs to imitate rather than innovate, as pointed out by Kilby (1971). This entails successful imitation by adapting a product to a niche market in a better way rather than attempting at original product innovation. Schumpeter's innovating entrepreneur characterises an enterprise with R & D and innovative traits, which the developing countries lack most. Further, Schumpeter remained silent about as to why some economies had more entrepreneurial talent than others.

Penrose (1959) opines that entrepreneurial activity involves identifying opportunities within the economic system and managerial capacities are different from entrepreneurial capacities. Harvey Leibenstein's (1968) entrepreneur fills market deficiencies through input-completing activities. Entrepreneurship involves activities necessary to create or carry out an enterprise where not all markets are well established or clearly defined and in which relevant elements of production function are not completely known. Extending this line of argument, Israel Kirzner (1973) argues that an entrepreneur has to recognise and act upon market opportunities; he is essentially an arbitrageur and in contrast to Schumpeter's viewpoint, manoeuvres the market towards equilibrium. Kirzner opines that spontaneous learning and alertness are two major characteristics of entrepreneurship which resulting in the transformation of spontaneous learning into conscious knowledge, motivated by the prospects of gain. Kirzner considers the alertness to recognise opportunities as characteristic over and above innovation in formalisation of entrepreneurship. The entrepreneur finances the venture by borrowing money from a capitalist and uses the funds for his entrepreneurial venture, paying back the capitalist, including interest and retaining the pure entrepreneurial profit to him.

The Entrepreneurship Centre at Miami University of Ohio (Smith et al, 2005) defines entrepreneurship as the process of identifying, developing and bringing a vision to life. The vision may be an innovative idea, an opportunity or a better way to do something. The end result of this process is the creation of a new venture, formed under conditions of risk and considerable uncertainty. Entrepreneurship is often viewed as a Kirznerian function which involves the exploitation of opportunities which exist within a market system. Entrepreneurs usually are considered to bear risk while pursuing opportunities, associated with creative and innovative actions. Entrepreneurs undertake managerial roles in their activities, but routine management of an ongoing operation is not considered to be entrepreneurship. An individual may perform an entrepreneurial function in creating an organisation, but later is relegated to the role of managing it without performing an entrepreneurial role. In this sense, many small-business owners and self-employed persons would not be considered as entrepreneurs.

The Harvard School (Smith et al, 2005) concept of entrepreneurship comprises of purposeful activities that develop profit-oriented businesses in interaction with their internal situations or with the economic, political and social circumstances surrounding the business. This approach emphasises organisation or coordination activity and the sensitivity to the environmental characteristics that affect decision making. Despite its stress on the human factor in the production system, the Harvard tradition never explicitly challenges the equilibrium-oriented neo-classical theory. This is challenged by the neo-Austrian School, which argues that disequilibrium, rather than equilibrium is the likely scenario and as such, entrepreneurs operate under fairly uncertain circumstances. The essence of entrepreneurship consists in the alertness of market participants to profit opportunities. A typical entrepreneur is an arbitrageur (as Say remarks), the person who discovers opportunity at low prices and sells the same items at high prices because of inter-temporal and interspatial demands.

Arthur Cole (1959) defines entrepreneurship in the Harvard tradition, wherein individuals must create new business enterprises in order to be considered entrepreneurial. Cole's entrepreneur is a builder of profit-minded organisations. Shapero and Sokol (1982) argue that all organisations and individuals have the potential to be enterprising. They contend that entrepreneurship is characterised by an individual or group's initiative, resource pooling, autonomy and risk taking. Their definition includes all types and sizes of organisations with a wide variety of functions and goals.

Peter Drucker (1985) puts forward the view that Schumpeter's type of innovation can be systematically undertaken by managers to develop business and non-business organisations. By combining managerial practices with innovativeness, businesses create a model of entrepreneurship that results in the institutionalisation of entrepreneurial practices. Drucker contends that entrepreneurship is something that can be strategically employed by any organisation at any point in its existence, whether a start-up or a firm with a long history towards growth of businesses. According to him, entrepreneurship involves increase in value or satisfaction to the customer, wherein the entrepreneur always searches for change, responding to and exploiting it as an opportunity. According to him, innovation is the essence of entrepreneurship which creates values from resources. For example, mineral oil was considered worthless until the discovery of its use. Similarly, purchasing power was considered an important resource by an innovative entrepreneur especially when instalment purchase was invented.

Entrepreneurship is the practice which has a knowledge base and is not confined only to big businesses and economic institutions. Entrepreneurship behaviour rather than personality trait is more important to enhance the spirit of entrepreneurship and its foundation lies in the concept and theory rather than in mere intuition. Druckerian entrepreneur may not be a capitalist or an owner. A banker who mobilises money and allocates it in areas of higher yield is very much an entrepreneur though he is not the owner of the money. Following this line of argument, Harvey Leibenstein (1968) considers entrepreneur as a gap-filler. The three traits of entrepreneurship include recognition of changing market trends, developing new goods or processes in demands but not in supply and determining profitable activities. Entrepreneurs have the special ability to connect different markets and make up for market failures and deficiencies. In a similar way, Mark Casson (1990) holds that entrepreneurship is a result of favourable economic conditions. The demand for entrepreneurship arises from the demand for change, which includes taxation and industrial policies, availability of raw materials, access to credit and information, availability of technology and infrastructure and marketing opportunities.

While Baumol (2002) argues that institutions regard incentives for rent-seeking as opposed to productive entrepreneurship that lead to growth, Douglas North (1990) identifies the endogeneity of institutions and economic activities in entrepreneurial development. Entrepreneurial ventures adapt to the activities and strategies in exploiting opportunities and overcome the limitations in business environment through formal and informal institutional networks. Poor private property protection and capital market institutions are the two aspects that hinder entrepreneurial growth in developing economies. One predominant effect of poor private property protection is corruption which may increase the transaction costs of undertaking businesses.

1.5 Socio-cultural and Psychological Approaches

The sociological theory of entrepreneurship holds that social culture is the driving force of entrepreneurship, wherein the entrepreneur becomes a role model in tune with the role expectations of the society, based on religious beliefs and customs. According to Max Weber (1930), religion is a major factor in entrepreneurship and the stress on spirit of capitalism highlights economic freedom and private enterprising, wherein capitalism thrives under conditions similar to the protestant work ethic that depends on the values of right combination of discipline and an adventurous free-spirit. Weber makes a distinction between the spirit of capitalism and the spirit of adventure, wherein the former is influenced by the strict discipline and the latter by free flow of impulse, both factors influencing entrepreneurial culture. He emphasises that entrepreneurial energies are exogenous and result through religious beliefs and the spirit of capitalism can be cultivated only when the mental attitude in the society is favourable to capitalism. The spirit of capitalism combined with profit motivation results in the creation of business enterprises. In fact, this theory was best suited the colonial rulers, who wanted to encourage European entrepreneurship in the colonies.

Hoselitz (1952) explains that the supply of entrepreneurship is governed by cultural factors and culturally minority groups are the catalysts of entrepreneurial and economic development. In many countries, entrepreneurs have emerged from a particular socio-economic class, which is true in India also. He emphasises the role of culturally marginally groups like Jews and the Greeks in medieval Europe, the Chinese in South Africa and Indians in east Africa in facilitating economic development.

McClelland (1961) contends that people have three motives for accomplishing things, namely, the need for achievement, need for affiliation and need for power, need for achievement promoting entrepreneurship. Entrepreneurs are people who perform things in a better way and make decisions under uncertainties. The desire to perform peculiar actions overpowers monetary or other incentives. The need for achievement (n-Ach) is responsible for economic development and greater the development of n-Ach, the more likely would be the growth. McClelland state that traditional beliefs may not underperform an entrepreneur, but the motives may be internalised towards achievement through appropriate training and mentoring. He documents that in many economic systems, socio-cultural history has contributed to the effective performance of the entrepreneurial class, the focus being shifted from the act to the actors.

In his psycho-social theory, Hagen (1962) relegates economic variables to a minor role, emphasising on psychological aspects of personality for the emergence of entrepreneurship. Hisrich (1990) identifies characteristics of entrepreneurs, wherein the childhood family background and education level, personal values and motivations and role modeling effects and other support systems become responsible for the emergence of entrepreneurship. Another way of explaining the characteristics of entrepreneurs has been through personality trait and demographic approaches (Robinson et al, 1991). In the trait approach, the entrepreneur is assumed to be of different personality types, wherein particular characteristics explain the differences in endowment of entrepreneurship. Different demographic particulars like family background, birth order, role model, marital status, age, education level of parents and self, socio-economic status, previous work experience and work habits enable profiling of typical entrepreneurs, with the assumption that individuals with similar backgrounds would have similar characteristics. The approach presumes that by identifying demographic characteristics of known entrepreneurs, it will be possible to predict the nature of entrepreneurship in unknown situations (Robinson et al, 1991). However, the approach does not predict who will or will not be an entrepreneur merely on the basis of knowledge of one's birth order, level of education, or parental heritage. Also, demographic characteristics being static in nature, cannot explain a dynamic phenomenon like entrepreneurship.

Though poor institutional environments provide obstacles which reduce the profitability of economic opportunities, effective entrepreneurs devise ways and means to overcome the hindrances. However, absence of capital market institutions may hinder the emergence of entrepreneurship, since they may make the risk of starting a business quite high (Johnson et al, 2000). In the context of scarce capital and large initial scales of production to compensate for missing intermediate markets, firms are able to derive the advantages of risk pooling and cross-subsidy to overcome financial problems. This aspect may induce them to undertake larger risks, which of course is very essential for technology-oriented entrepreneurship. Further, their role in the formation of business groups in emerging economies has been stressed by Khanna and Palepu (2000). As has happened in many East and South Asian countries, firms have adopted technology-based entrepreneurship to guide their economies.

Hansemark (1998), employing a population-ecology model to analyse the concept of entrepreneurship, seeks to predict the probability of births and deaths within a population of firms within a given industry niche, considering the environment rather than the person in determining organisational survival. Recent studies following this approach are focused on the presence, characteristics and changes in a population or organisation in an ecological context provided by the environment (Reynolds et al, 2005).

1.6 Discovery and Opportunity Theories of Entrepreneurship

The discovery theory (Alvarez and Barney, 2007), called the individual-opportunity (I-O) nexus postulation, focuses on the existence, discovery and exploitation of opportunities and their influence of opportunities on development. According to the I-O nexus, opportunities are objective and exist whether or not individuals recognise them. Entrepreneurs are unique and risk-bearing and opportunities are derived from the attributes of an industry or market within which an entrepreneur is functioning. If an entrepreneur understands the attributes of a particular industry properly, he or she will be able to anticipate the kinds of opportunities that may arise in that industry. For example, the primary opportunity in any start-up industry is to exploit economies of scale in order to consolidate the business vertically or horizontally. Contrasted to this, the primary opportunities in mature industries would be to modify products and engage in process innovations so as to improve product quality and achieve lower costs. Understanding entrepreneurial opportunities becomes important because the characteristics of an opportunity influence the very value that they create.

Entrepreneurship involves differences in individuals characterised by the ability to recognise opportunities and entrepreneurial alertness is a receptive attitude and an emotional state with a pre-disposition for action, which is currently overlooked by opportunities in a market. Pursuant to Kirzner, entrepreneurial alertness is not a deliberate search, but a constant scanning of the environment by exploiting market imperfections not previously recognised. Risk-bearing is a necessary part of the entrepreneurial process which may be mitigated by opportunities. The assumption of information asymmetry is based on neo-classical economics which assumed that information about technologies, demand and other market determinants are known to be available, but may be costly to acquire. The entrepreneur acquires the information at a lower cost than other economic actors, leading to the generation of profit. Any element of price, invention, or information has within it many opportunities and individuals discover them, though not creating the same. While it is not known when the opportunity is discovered that it will be successful, owing to the nature of the discovery, it can be estimated what will be the nature of outcome.

The creation theory (Alvarez and Barney, 2007) focuses on the creative qualities of the entrepreneur and how an enterprise is established. Similar to the opportunity theory, a major assumption of this theory is that opportunities are created through decisions to exploit potential opportunities. Further, this theory suggests that it is difficult to separate the ex-ante and ex-post conceptualisation of opportunities.

Opportunities are created by economic actors and whatever be the source of opportunities, it is their existence that is responsible for profit generation. The creation theory argues that under conditions of uncertainty, the attributes of an industry are not known and knowledge about industry structure cannot be used to anticipate opportunities, which have to be created and refined through a process of hypothesising what they could be.

The above cited works rarely examine entrepreneurship explicitly, or ask how the modern problems of development may affect the ability of entrepreneurs to operate effectively within the context of developing economies. The presence of underdeveloped financial markets, poor protection of property rights and weak contract enforcement inhibit entrepreneurs in these countries to miss the opportunity wagon. However, most entrepreneurship research today implicitly assumes that there is no difference between the entrepreneurship being carried out in the most developed nations and that carried out in late comer and developing economies. An important effect of poor private property protection is corruption, which may increase the costs of doing businesses. Johnson et al (1999) argue that businesses in transition economies generally circumvent this problem by relational contracting and access to informal networks alleviate the shortcomings of the environment. The resources of the firm are seen as relevant as in developed market economies, where also entrepreneurs with good generation of ideas may lack the resources required for successful launching of new ventures.

1.7 The Entrepreneurial Process

Since entrepreneurship refers to the process of organising, operating and assuming risk to start new business ventures, its success may indicate as to the outcome of that process, as evidenced from the extent to which the venture meets the needs of its stakeholders and the entrepreneurs themselves. The factors for success may vary from one entrepreneur to another and the success is greater when the stakeholder needs are met continuously over a period of time. Bygrave (2004) characterises the entrepreneurial process as one of idea generation and screening, followed by innovation, implementation and formation and growth of the company. The success of the process would be through the interaction of social networks, risk taking, vision, leadership and organisational effectiveness, involving opportunity identification and effective allocation of resources to achieve the business.

Entrepreneurs go through three stages in the process of starting their ventures, the first being the concept formation stage, where ideas are generated, identifying the opportunities and innovations and formalising the start-ups. In the second stage, resources are pooled together to launch the new business and in the third stage, the organisation itself is actually created. Many entrepreneurs may fail when they are unable to strike an effective balance between management and the strategies that consolidate the new ventures. They may eventually reach a point where these obligations cannot be fully met, in which case they will have to delegate some of the management tasks to others team members, keeping the leadership tasks to themselves. Greiner (1972) points out that entrepreneurship growth is similar to life cycle, each stage evolving over the other, but assumes a revolutionary phase of growth in the subsequent stage.

Creativity involves not only generating multitude of alternatives, but also discovering hidden possibilities and new avenues (Shane and Venkataraman, 2000). An entrepreneur gets an idea for a new business either through a deliberate search or a chance encounter. The pursuit of that idea depends on alternative career prospects, family background, friends and role models, state of the economy and the availability of resources. Existing entrepreneurs may exert influence on would-be entrepreneurs and hence role modelling assumes importance. Potential entrepreneurs come into contact with their role models primarily at home and/or at work and family responsibilities play a crucial role in new start-ups. As Timmons (1994) remarks, Darwin was preceded by Wallace in publishing his theory of evolution and Poincare formulated a theory of relativity at the same time as Einstein did, while the integrated circuit was invented first by Jack Kilby at Texas Instruments and then by Robert Noyce at Fairchild. Alexander Fleming discovered penicillin by chance but never developed it as a useful drug and it was after ten years later that Ernst Chain and Howard Florey highlighted Fleming's mould. Entrepreneurs like Thomas Alva Edison, Alexander Graham Bell, Henry Ford, Steve Jobs, Bill Gates and other innovators have propagated products that had immense impact on the world's lifestyles. According to Edison, success is 'one per cent inspiration and 99 per cent perspiration'. The extent to which the potential of an idea is realised depends upon how well the entrepreneur completes its screening and testing so as to meet the varied needs of the existing and potential consumers. Thus, besides developing an idea, its implementation and building a successful business that pre-empt entrepreneurship.

As unemployment is a major problem in many countries, emphasis on employment generation has been a major focus of entrepreneurship through provision of self employment, wherein entrepreneurs perceive profitable opportunities for investment (Shane and Venkataraman, 2000). In addition to an innovative idea and leadership qualities of the entrepreneur, success in any entrepreneurial venture involves building a team with complementary skills and talents. Entrepreneurs exploit opportunities to their advantage, while others see in them contradictions (Timmons, 1994). Entrepreneurial process requires taking strategic decisions at the right time by accumulating dynamic skills, know-how, experiences and contacts. Knowledge sharing is a part of their jobs and may be integrated into their actions, wherein the shared organisational culture enables them to determine the perception of a situation and how to react to it. According to Timmons (1994), entrepreneurship generates and consolidates something from practically nothing. Entrepreneurs have a personality trait that is different than others and self-motivation and n-Ach differentiate successful entrepreneurs from those who fail. Business knowledge, self-confidence, technical and communication skills and courage are the other qualities of successful entrepreneurs. However, one of the major problems is in the realm of allocation of scarce resources, as could be discerned in the decision of how best to utilise small advertising budget or limited computer resources. Entrepreneurial success is directly related to the ability to cope with limited resources and how the ambiguities of uncertainty are tackled.

According to Casnocha (2011), entrepreneurs are of different types, slow, moderate or most successful. Home-run slow-movers want to change the world in a big way and are not thrilled with incremental success, serial entrepreneurship not appealing to them. These sluggers would make a single business in making it flourishing and are not amenable to early exits. Fred Smith of FedEx may be a good example of a slugger. Entrepreneurs, who initiate successful start-ups, are hitters, who like the on-base hitters, become content to achieve success in small ventures on a regular basis, rather than all in one go. For example, Rene Lacarte, the founder of PayCycle and Bills.com, has launched a series of online payment businesses (Casnocha, 2011). Fact finder entrepreneurs seek details before making decisions. Follow-through entrepreneurs think in a linear manner, where step one leads to step two and so on. The companies operate by productivity methodologies like Six Sigma, rewarding employees for continuous process improvement. Implementers are innovative by nature, allowing them to work with their ingenuity. On the other hand, successful entrepreneurs work hard to build their organisations, starting from the beginning (Casnocha, 2011) and even the best ideas become profitable only when the entrepreneur goes through necessary steps in the build-up process.

Apart from the above mentioned personality types, contributions by Pinchot (1985) and others identify intracorporate or intrapreneurship in the emergence of entrepreneurial process within organisations, showing how new businesses can be created within large corporations. Corporate entrepreneurship employs internally generated innovations from employees. Burgelman (1983) shows how traditional enterprise has to be transformed into new business through internal corporate venturing that stem from the conceptual, pre-venture, entrepreneurial and organisational stages. The process of corporate entrepreneurship includes pure venture capital, new venture development incubator, idea creation centre and employee project modelling, besides institutionalisation of innovations. Siti-Maimon's (1993) exopreneurship is a part of corporate entrepreneurship, enabling acquisition of ideas from external sources. Acquisition of innovations that are outside the organisation is inducted into the firm through franchising, strategic alliance, external capital ventures or subcontracting. In the case of technological enterprises, an entrepreneur who is technology savvy, creative, innovative, dynamic and dares to be different and takes the unexplored path, being very passionate about the work is called a technopreneur. Technopreneurship is not a product but a process of synthesis in moulding the future of an individual, an organisation or the nation. Failure is a learning experience, a stimulator to look things differently and move on to the next opportunity. Technopreneurs undergo an organic process of continual improvement and, trying to redefine the dynamic technological and digital economy.

1.8 Entrepreneurial Models

Entrepreneurial models discuss about the choices available to the entrepreneurs in the areas of necessities, information exploitation, opportunities and skill development. The occupational choice model

(Lucas, 1978) states all individuals need not be entrepreneurs and those who opt for entrepreneurial action have different characteristics when compared those who do not. The model effects division of labour in such a way that an entrepreneurial class emerges, while others choose alternative actions best suited to them. For, as Lucas argues, individuals differ in terms of their innate entrepreneurial capabilities and the most-abled choose the path of entrepreneurship. There may be marginal entrepreneurs, who are just indifferent between entrepreneurship and paid employment. Lucas also shows that it is the most able entrepreneurs who lead the largest firms. Entrepreneurs employ the market-cleared workforce and capital. Under various assumptions, Lucas shows that as accumulation of capital takes place, economies (as happened in the advanced countries) may encounter a shift of labour force from entrepreneurship to paid employment, in which case, the average firm size increases, small-scale entrepreneurs being replaced by larger corporations. However, this replacement does not occur because of entrepreneurs are being driven out of the market by unfair competition, but as the average wage rate increases, it results in paid employment being more attractive to owners of small enterprises forcing them to quit voluntarily.

In the Holmes and Schmitz (1990) model, the economy is in a permanent flux of disequilibrium. As individuals have to encounter new opportunities, forced by external technological factors, they may differ from each other as to the probability whether their new ventures will survive or not. Holmes and Schmitz investigate the circumstances under which entrepreneurs decide to continue operating the existing ventures or to transfer them to others in order to release their time and resources in exploring new opportunities. They show that the least able entrepreneurs will only manage existing firms, while the most able ones specialise in setting up new enterprises. Those with intermediate ability manage the businesses or replace them with higher quality ventures transferred from able entrepreneurs. The model extends the ideas of Schumpeter and Kirzner about opportunity recognition and provides a basis for understanding why some individuals are portfolio entrepreneurs, while others become serial entrepreneurs or simply rely on buying businesses created by others.

Kihlstrom and Laffont (1979) model builds on modelling Knightian entrepreneurial choice as a trade-off between risk and returns. It is assumed that risk aversion is common and the least risk-averse individuals choose entrepreneurship and run large firms.

Entrepreneurs provide income compensation to workers and in turn, are rewarded in receiving residual profits. The model explains the co-existence of firms of different sizes and when there is a welfare loss caused by lack of risk-sharing and therefore, a wrong number of individuals become entrepreneurs from a social welfare standpoint. When this leads to too few effective entrepreneurs, the issue can be sorted out by domestic entrepreneurs who may compete with more efficient foreign entrepreneurs. Efficiency losses of this kind are best addressed by creating risk-sharing mechanisms, like in a stock market.

The Stiglitz and Weiss (1981) model assumes that because of information asymmetry, entrepreneurs are better informed about their projects than banks, which have to offer the same debt contract to all loan applicants. They posit that projects and entrepreneurs differ from each other in terms of risk, with some entrepreneurs operating risky and others relatively choosing safe investment projects. Because of this, projects that may become undesirably risky from the viewpoint of the banks cannot be detected at the time loans are provided. This induces the banks to under-invest in entrepreneurial activities.

Hayward et al (2006) propose a hubris theory of entrepreneurship, wherein many new ventures are created in the background of high venture failures. When more confident players start ventures, they act on over-confidence in deciding on allocation and use of resources. This over-confidence affects how they interpret information about their past and current ventures. Entrepreneurs with greater socially constructed confidence tend to deprive their ventures of resources, thus leading to failures.

The model of de Meza and Webb (1999) treats entrepreneurs as different from each other in terms of expected returns, where able entrepreneurs have the greatest probabilities of success. Ability is unobserved by banks, which have to offer a pooled interest rate. This makes the ablest entrepreneurs to end up cross-subsidising the least able, which inducts individuals with socially inefficient investment projects into new ventures. They show that neither credit rationing nor under-investment may be effective in this set-up, similar to Kihlstrom and Laffont. But there may be over-investment when too many entrepreneurial projects are undertaken, because of cross-subsidisation. Everyone could be made better off, if the least able entrepreneurs are discouraged from becoming entrepreneurs and by making credit more expensive, only the ablest entrepreneurs will be willing to pay for it.

Evans and Jovanovic (1989) develop a model of borrowing constraints, which assumes that the wealth limits of entrepreneurs are constrained by the amount of funds they can obtain. Entrepreneurs learn from a series of probabilistic events that ensue forth from the market and adjust their beliefs and market strategies based on new information. Able entrepreneurs survive and grow, while the less-abled exit the market. Newer and smaller firms will have higher and more variable growth rates and also higher exit rates than older and larger firms.

Similar to Schumpeter's, Klepper (1996) showcases the nuances of new firm entry and exit rates and seeks to explain the distribution of innovations and market concentration as industries evolve. He also explains why the importance of major product innovations and new firm entries slow down as industries age and the increasing importance of process innovations in later stages of industry's life cycle. Schumpeter's insights are developed, wherein patent competition induces established firms to fight against each other in the discovery of new innovations yielding monopoly profits, while rendering previous products obsolete. But as Bianchi and Henrekson (2005) point out, this competition does not capture the essence of Schumpeter's entrepreneur, who is termed as an extraordinary individual responsible for innovation. Instead, the focus is on firms that devote resources to large-scale routinised R&D activities.

The contribution by Lazear (2002) contends that entrepreneurial selection and performance are guided by a balance of skills held by individuals, rather than by specialised expertise. Lazear claims that entrepreneurs are jacks of all trades rather than specialised experts, as are generally found in wage and salary work. Accordingly, if entrepreneurs have balanced skills sets, then trades like art (which requires disparate skills including artistic talent and business management) may be less likely to be engaged by entrepreneurs, than say, insurance, where the required skill set is more homogeneous. When technological progress demands additional skill requirements, this may decrease the number of suitably competent individuals and entrepreneurs. However, technological change might also improve individuals' ability to acquire better skills.

There is a growing recognition of the importance of human capital in the growth of entrepreneurship. Moskowitz and Vissing-Jorgensen (2002) observe that entrepreneurs may earn returns similar to that accruing from publicly traded equity, but with a riskier profile.

Human capital is not at risk when one becomes an entrepreneur, because future labour earnings are unaffected by the risk of the current venture. Hence, the risk of total net worth (including the present value of human capital) is much lower than that of financial wealth. Parker and Van Praag (2004) propose an extension of credit rationing model to unify the human capital and borrowing constraints. They predict that more highly educated entrepreneurs will face lower borrowing constraints, favouring human capital with direct and indirect effects on entrepreneurial action. The direct effect is the rate of return to education and the indirect effect is on enhanced performance through lower capital constraints. The combined rate of return for the entrepreneurs exceeds the average rate of return for employees, suggesting that highly educated individuals may become successful entrepreneurs.

Krugman (1991) argues that knowledge spillovers diffuse easily without national boundaries, but there are advantages due to geographical proximity, promoting technical spillovers and other economies into entrepreneurial ventures. These include networking, technical know-how, trust, co-operation and social capital, the combination of which facilitates exploitation of new opportunities. Audretsch and Lehmann (2006) show that knowledge and technology-based new ventures have a high propensity to locate close to universities in order to acquire knowledge spillovers. The spillovers may contain a greater proportion of tacit knowledge, which is not codified and hence can cross national boundaries more easily. Use of hazard analysis shows that, greater the geographic proximity of new ventures to universities, the quicker the progress of the venture from start-ups to stock market listings.

Birch (1979) highlights the superior job creation performance of small firms and claims that during 1969-76, small firms employing fewer than 20 workers generated 66 per cent of all new US jobs and firms with less than 100 employees accounted for 82 per cent of net job gains. The implication is that the small firm sector has been the primary engine of job creation. Bernhardt (2000) challenge this claim and argues that larger US manufacturing firms have created and destroyed most manufacturing jobs and there is no clear relationship between net job creation rates and employer size. However, it has been found that the share of jobs accounted for by small enterprises has increased since the early 1970s in most developed economies (OECD, 1998).

1.9 Resume and Conclusion

Since innovation is basic for growth of entrepreneurship, the need to encourage entrepreneurship might arise if small firms are more innovative than large firms. According to Acs and Audretsch (2003), small firms contributed around 2.4 times as many innovations per employee as large firms did. They also note that innovation in small entrepreneurial firms has different causes than those in large firms, responding to the availability of skilled labour. Carroll and Khessina (2005) estimate that lower marginal income tax rates are significantly and substantially associated with both small firm growth rates and investment expenditures.

For a balance between knowledge generation by scientists and knowledge exploitation by entrepreneurs, state intervention assumes an important role in promoting entrepreneurship as a growth-enhancing strategy. The crucial question is whether new firms are best suited to exploit knowledge spillovers or whether the existing firms can do well through intrepreneurship. Nonetheless, entrepreneurship can stimulate competition, create innovation and jobs and generate positive externalities, thereby reducing poverty and discrimination. If credit rationing and under-investment exist, free market conditions will generate too little entrepreneurship. Therefore, governments have to intervene to correct market failures and increase involvement in relevant entrepreneurship models. Everyone can be made better off, if governments tax interest-bearing deposits to make capital more expensive. In sum, entrepreneurship would generate benefits to the economy by intensifying competition and promoting innovation and knowledge spillovers, thereby mitigating social exclusion. However, a comprehensive cost-benefit analysis has not been widely used to evaluate government's entrepreneurship policies, where entrepreneurial learning process has been very crucial for characterising many aspects of industry.

While personal initiative and purposeful behaviour can be viewed as an entrepreneurial effort, many such initiatives may end up as failures. The successful entrepreneur characterises achievement motivation (McClelland, 1961), which facilitates the creation and development of archetype enterprises in competitive environments. Individuals with high n-Ach seek and assume high degree of personal responsibility, set challenging but realistic goals, work with concrete feedback, research their environment and choose partners with expertise to promote their work (Kanungo and Bhatnagar, 1978). Such characterization of high n-Ach people contribute to successful completion of actions and achievement orientation assumes a cognitive and behavioural tendency, oriented towards ensuring enterprise creation, survival and growth. Schumpeter (1950) regards entrepreneurs as persons who are not necessarily capitalists or having command over resources, but as those who create new combinations of the factors of production and the market. In the process, as countries transform through stages of traditional society, preconditions for take-off, take-off and drive to maturity and the age of high mass-consumption (a la Rostow). While these stages are a way of characterising development of modern economies, they also identify critical events that may take place in developing economies.

While Rostow focuses on the age of high mass-consumption, Porter (1990) follows recent developments in the economics of innovation and provides an approach by identifying three stages of development, consisting of a factor-driven, followed by an efficiency-driven and then by an innovation-driven stage. The factor-driven stage is characterised by high rates of self-employment in the agricultural sector (Porter et al, 2002). Countries in this stage compete through low-cost production methods or manufacture of low value-added products. This experience does not create knowledge for innovation nor help in utilising the knowledge for generating surplus. To move into the second efficiency-driven stage, countries must increase their production efficiency and educate the workforce to adapt to the subsequent phase of technological development, where the preconditions for take-off play a crucial role. The drive to efficiency describes the first transition, predominantly institutional in nature. To compete in the efficiency-driven stage, countries must have efficient productive methods and enabling the corporations to exploit economies of scale. The efficiency-driven stage is marked by declining rates of self-employment and capital and labour play crucial roles in productivity increases through endogenous development.

The transition to the innovation-driven stage is characterised by increased activity by the knowledge seekers and knowledge assumes the role of major input in the production process. In this stage, the focus shifts from institutions (important in the first two stages) to entrepreneurs in possession of new knowledge, who decide to start new enterprises based on expected net returns. The knowledge-driven stage is biased towards high value added enterprises, in which entrepreneurial activity becomes very crucial for development.

According to Sala-I-Martin et al (2007), innovation accounts for only about five per cent of economic activity in factor-driven economies and rises to ten per cent in the efficiency-driven economies. However, in the innovation-driven stage, when opportunities are exhausted in both factors and efficiency, innovation accounts for 30 per cent of economic activity, mainly because of technology. An S-shaped relationship (Acs and Szerb, 2010) between entrepreneurship and economic development develops, owing to the fact that in the transition stage, the role for entrepreneurship is minimal. In the process of transition from the efficiency-driven to the innovation-driven stage, entrepreneurship plays a crucial role, its growth increasing at an increasing rate, depending upon the types of incentives provided by the system and then levelling off as economies become fully developed.

1.10 Chapter Outlines

The book consists of 10 chapters. Chapter 1 introduces the concept of entrepreneurship, including the different theories, models, entrepreneurial types and process, besides reviewing the relevant entrepreneurial literature. Chapter 2 discusses the origin and development of entrepreneurship in the pre-colonial, colonial and post-independence eras of India. The chapter concludes that India is still in the transitional phase as evidenced by global entrepreneurship monitoring reports. Chapter 3 focuses on the rudimentary characterisation of innovative entrepreneurship in India, showcasing the experience of Tata Steel, cued from the Korean Posco example. The two major innovative initiatives of Tata Steel in respect of cold rolling mill and the merchant mill are described. Apart from iron and steel, India's foray in information technology is then deliberated along with the noted achievers in the field like, Tata Consultancy Services, Infosys, Wipro, Mahindra Satyam and Hindustan Computers. Chapter 5 extends the IT gain into biotechnology too where India has had a remarkable growth in terms of global competitive advantage and innovativeness. The chapter concludes with profiles of noted biotech firms like Dr Reddy's, Wockhardt, Nicholas Piramal and Ranbaxy.

Chapter 6 picturises the activities of important business groups in the country, starting from the Tatas, Reliance, Birlas and Bajaj to the less known but emerging groups. Indeed, it is the family businesses that determine the corporate culture and governance in the country. This chapter profiles some of the biotech business leaders. Chapter 7 focuses on the entrepreneurial development in small and medium enterprises with the example of automotive industry. The institutional support programmes available for the development of SMEs and their innovativeness has been dealt with, citing some case studies in Andhra Pradesh, Karnataka and Tamil Nadu. Chapter 8 introduces various developments in the field of modern entrepreneurship with respect to social, ecological, public and institutional and women entrepreneurship with brief case studies and examples. Chapter 9 showcases the innovative emergence of India in select fields, after comparing entrepreneurial growth in some countries.

Chapter 10 extends the comparison and reviews the growth of entrepreneurship, considering the global competitiveness index, global entrepreneurship assessment and global entrepreneurship development index. The assessment shows that India has to go a long way from the factor-driven stage to accomplish the innovation-driven stage of development.

2

The Evolution of Entrepreneurship and its Development in India

2.1 Introduction

Entrepreneurship *per se* has had its growth in India only after the economic reforms in the late eighties and its development in the past relied mainly on family business skills, mentoring across generations, understanding cultural ethos and exploitation of technical know-how. Inheritance played a major role in skill development and the conversion of skills into technological transformation paved the way towards routine entrepreneurship. Post-liberalisation and globalisation have imparted into the growing middle class, a huge potential for the growth of entrepreneurship. The know-hows learned and refined over generations would lead to a sustained development path, wherein these would be converted into innovations With this background, coupled with a increasing supply of engineering and information technology talent, management acumen and R&D facilities, India has become a major outsourcer of knowledge services from all parts of the world, thus enabling emergence of a new class of nouveau entrepreneurship. However, the adventurous entrepreneurs who progress on the corporate ladder face several problems during their entrepreneurial journey. Further, the venture capitalists who invest in India are risk-averse and are unwilling or unable to offer the right investment at the right stage. Under these circumstances, it may be profitable to understand the history of entrepreneurship, so as to postulate its future growth prospects.

This chapter documents different works on the evolution of entrepreneurship in India during the pre- and post-independence periods and summarises the essentials of entrepreneurship in the traditional Indian society as evidenced by the first author (Tabe, 1970) in his earlier work. The post-independence experience regarding the growth of entrepreneurship in the country and the various factors involved in the process, as showcased by the global entrepreneurship monitor are also reviewed in this chapter.

2.2 Business Enterprising in the Past

Whereas western culture tends to encourage the drive to achieve (McClelland, 1961) as essential for entrepreneurial activities, the Indian culture consists of a compound of beliefs, which in many ways counter entrepreneurship development. For example, Indians believe that being passive and content with the status quo is healthier for the inner soul than striving to improve materially. Work in itself is not valued for it, but is accomplished with involvement for propitiating superior goal (Sinha, 1990). According to McClelland (1965), employees in India perform their work mostly as a favour to their employers and energy and creativity (incorporated into entrepreneurial behaviour in the context of different cultures) are redirected towards aligning oneself with the *status quo* (accepting destiny). As Kahar (1978) explains, people are more sensitive to emotional affinity in the workplace than towards work and productivity.

A positive correlation has been established between self-efficacy and task performance (Bandura, 1982). The external locus of control has been reinforced by the caste system, which has hindered class mobility over centuries. Gadgil (1959), Medhora (1965) and Weber (1958) have observed that the caste system and its series of obligations reinforce the practice of following family occupations rather than undertaking new ventures. In the past, entrepreneurs mostly belonged to communities in which caste divisions were not rigidly observed (Nafziger, 1971).

Max Weber (1930) has pointed out the negative elements in the Hindu value system, presupposing that the single value system was all-pervasive, influencing not only the followers of that religion, but also those of other religions. The Indian community internalised these values and translated them into daily behaviour, these values remaining insulated against external pressures. However, it is difficult to identify a single Hindu value system and it is doubtful whether the

Jain ethics which, according to Weberian argument, approximated Protestant ethics would have inculcated the spirit of enterprising among the Jains. Jainism, with its stress on *aparigraha* (non-attachment), *ahimsa* (non-violence), *aasteya* (non-stealing) and *brahmacharya* (non-sensuous pleasure), can be termed neither less ascetic nor less other-worldly when compared to Hinduism (Tripathi, 1971). Tripathi points out that business behaviour of the Jains varied from their faith. However, it may be generalised that the behaviour of businessmen anywhere in the world alludes to the view that their business ethics and values do not necessarily conform to their personal ethics or religious values.

The emergence of entrepreneurial culture in the pre-colonial period relates to local innovations, in which, the primary unit of work culture system was the village, a community of elders (Gupta, 2008). Historically, the village system favoured a crafts form of entrepreneurship, wherein each village had different occupation-based community groups, each specialising in a particular class of crafts or services. While the behaviour of the mercantile class was not at all entrepreneurial in the modern sense, the occupational barriers as prescribed by religious customs was not broken by the non-mercantile classes. Further, they lacked an effective communications system, which is essential for the spread of entrepreneurship, conditioned by the existence of innumerable systems of currency (Tripathi, 1971). The combined effect of the prevalent educational system, reinforcing the occupational structure and business, held in low esteem failed to blossom up entrepreneurship. Kautilya's belief that a businessman was a thief but was not called so was the commonly held view (Tripathi, 1971).

McClelland (1961) notes that entrepreneurial response, distinct from adventure or gambling, consists of moderate risk taking, but enmeshed by a combination of achievement motivation and expectation of rewards. By this account, low expectancy of reward, more than anything else, explained the business behaviour and occupational structure of pre-colonial India. The success of British merchants was due to superior British technology and managerial skills. In the process, the agency houses were established in the presidencies, were supportive of British firms in London, facilitating remittances of money to England, but their activities flourished even after the East India Company lost its monopoly of trade in 1813 (Tripathi, 1971).

Tripathi (1971) recounts that Virji Vora of Gujarat and Dwarkanath Tagore of Bengal were associated with the British merchants either as lenders to East India Company or involved in joint ventures, but there is nothing to suggest that the enormous profits they earned were utilised either for diversification of activities or for manufacturing products. Those who participated in these joint ventures were ideologically close to the British culture, either by personal contact or by education. Traditional businessmen, safe in their money-lending and trading business and with little contact with new values, abstained from entering into more challenging fields, such that, the partnerships were confined to the confines of agency houses or free merchants. In the early part of 18th century, the Jagat Seths of eastern India thrived mainly on money lending, thereby amassing huge wealth. They supported the English in their economic and political activities and were a decisive force, when the British occupied Bengal in 1757. Thus, the traditional mercantile classes dominated business and commercial activities till 19th century, but they introduced no qualitative changes in business practices with low entrepreneurial calibre. There is no evidence to suggest that occupational division, sanctioned by the caste system, underwent any changes in business till the modern times (Tripathi, 1971).

During the colonial period, indigenous crafts faced an adverse environment (Gupta, 2008), when the rulers facilitated in creating many opportunities for global entrepreneurship. However, the revival of local traders specialising in international markets is documented in the work of Ranchhodlal Chhotalal of Ahmedabad, when he took a position as a clerk in the colonial government in 1842. Chhotalal obtained cost information from London and decided that a local cotton textile mill would be a profitable venture. He identified a British investor and a local banker who were each willing to finance 50 per cent of the necessary funding and his success motivated the local Hindu and Jain traders to set up their own mills (Oonk, 2007).

The established business groups responded to the new opportunities by diversifying their activities and entered into foreign collaborations to explore less familiar businesses. Owing to changes in the material environment, the value system allowed easy entry of non-business classes into business ventures. Since the European demand for Indian goods was high, and that for European goods domestically was limited, the balance of trade always remained in favour of India (Tripathi, 1971). In spite of the restrictions imposed by several

European countries against the export of bullion from their respective colonies, the companies had to import the same into India to finance their operations. Although colonialism provided ample opportunities for the emergence of Western entrepreneurs in India, colonial government did not facilitate expatriate enterprises or metropolitan industries (Hopkins, 1987). Goswami (1985) finds that the growth of *marwari* businessmen in eastern India began well before independence and that the political history of colonialism was only mildly connected to business history. Entrepreneurship flourished among ethnic minorities which formed special links with colonial administration, as in the case of *parsis* in 19th century (Dobbin, 1996). The Jains have been a trading community, not because of entrepreneurial spirit, but rather because trading was an occupation that kept them free from conflict with the demands of their religious practices. However, the *marwaris* (also known as *banias*) specialised in domestic trade, complemented those of English entrepreneurs (Medhora, 1965).

The colonial regime differed from that of its exploitative regime of the past (Jones and Wadhwani, 2007). As a result of British free trade policies, traditional Indian handicrafts had to compete with Lancashire textile mills. By the interwar period, India became protectionist, including against British imports. It can be said that the impact of colonialism provided a channel for domestic entrepreneurs to acquire foreign technology and make an entry into international markets (Tripathi, 2004). Entrepreneurs, not white or rich, were less qualified to pursue new opportunities. During the 1800s, the British discriminated against those business classes that competed with their entrepreneurs in international commerce, thus, forcing many of them out of business. During the same period, local firms with established reputations were duped by British partners, an action which led to more exits from the business sector); also, the lack of indigenous entrepreneurship was a result of discrimination of the rulers (Nafziger, 1971). When we evaluate the policy of 'tryst with destiny' after independence, which did not encourage big private enterprises in the beginning, only small and tiny enterprises were allowed to be established in the private sector. Further, the occupational structure, sanctified by the caste system, did not change radically. There was no major innovation in the field of agriculture or any other sector of the economy. Social and occupational mobility was increasingly difficult and commercial activities became a monopoly of the *vaishya* sect. World War I halted supply of finished consumer products from

Britain and the shortage of many products created an increased demand for railways to speed up transportation needs of the British in the war, resulting in the subsequent British expansion. This demand offered an opportunity to Tata's new iron and steel factory to be established (Oonk, 2007).

2.3 Overview of the Traditional Indian Society and Entrepreneurship Development

This section purports to summarize the views of the first author as in his 1970 book on entrepreneurship in the traditional Indian society. Tabe (1970) finds that in the traditional Indian society, the interest rates charged to different castes varied from two to five per cent, which indicates the absence of economic factors in entrepreneurship development. Further, interest rates varying among the different business communities led to economic separation, where small business communities were divided along religious and social classes. In spite of this separation, the *parsis* were able to create the Tata business combine and there were no other comparable Hindu business combines. Ray (1992) emphasises on the enterprising spirit of the *parsis*, who were 'highly Britonised and the Gujaratis, cold-hearted and selfish.' Indeed, the *parsis* have grown into the richest class of entrepreneurs in India through their participation in opium and yarn trade with China and were able to control businesses in Bombay by the mid-19th century, which enabled them to develop into leading business community.

Unlike the conservative Gujaratis of Ahmedabad, Gujaratis of large cities were diligent and adventurous and following the example of the *parsis*, were venturing into new business combines. The 'clever and sensitive' Bengalis, owing to their affinity with the colonialists were able to amass wealth and start new businesses. Calcutta (the first trading capital of East India Company) and Bombay (the trading capital of India in later days) had wide differences in their functioning. In the former, capital was raised within a particular business group, based on the credit standing of a small number of capable entrepreneurs, who controlled their enterprises under the prevalent managing agency system. In the latter, each business group developed itself into a trust based on family ties, which aspect has greatly diminished in importance in recent times.

Big cities provided prospective businessmen the opportunities for their growth and determined the nature of domestic consumption depending on the quantum of import of British goods. The British way-of-life became common amongst the high-income groups, with its own demonstration effect. As the cities expanded, factory system of production was adopted, leading to different modes of commodity consumption, as distinct from the traditional ways in rural areas. While the city-made goods were available everywhere, the artisanal products were consumed mainly in the rural areas. The factory products and the rural traditional products in a way performed different roles (Morris, 1967). However, the picture is fast changing with the impact of urbanisation and industrialization which are changing the rural consumption habits very much. However, the retarding caste system has resulted in a high proportion of people (especially in rural areas) living below poverty line.

The towns of Navsari (in the hinterland of Bombay and a *parsi* stronghold) and Murshidabad (in the hinterland of Calcutta and *marwari* stronghold) can be compared in respect of consumption differences (Tabe, 1970). Navsari was a cotton centre, while Murshidabad was a silk trading centre. While the kinds of products supplied by handicrafts industry varied according to castes, their distribution and consumption were on caste lines. In Navsari, the *parsi* entrepreneurs effected the substitution of traditional products by new products which were cheaper as a result of large scale production.

Murshidabad had many silk centres and it was a major East India Company commercial centre, that Lord Clive compared that town to London and declared that if the rich inhabitants wanted to expel the Europeans there, they could have done at any time they wished (Tabe, 1970). However, the present day Murshidabad presents a dilapidated and a deprived rural caricature owing to its neglect. On the other hand, a village named *surely,* which was in the same district as that of Murshidabad was able to adapt to the colonial demands and prospered by indigo trade. M.G. Ranade (1898) points out the absence of individual rationalism, prevalence of personal tie and lack of competition in Indian society as contrast to the west. The social inertia resulted in inflexibility in the supply of factors of production according to him.

Tabe (1970) analyses the structure of opportunity available for entrepreneurial development in India from 1854 (when the first cotton mill was established) to 1914, interwar period and from 1940 to independence. The occurrence of economic opportunity took place that it almost coincided with the changes in the political situation and industrial policy of the government. The *marwari* community of Calcutta controlled the economic activity of east India. They were regarded as 'northern imperialists', being disliked by the locals. The *marwari* group of Calcutta had developed from the merchant class of Rajputana, *marwari mahajan*. After using Murshidabad as their base, they slowly penetrated into Calcutta. The *marwaris* and the *banias,* the other business class grew into powerful communities. As they extended their influence, they came into close contact with the imperialists in both economic and political activities. However, the alien culture and profit-seeking attitude of the *marwaris* earned the wrath of local politicians and public.

Entrepreneurial activity was mainly confined to particular communities, which were restricted by caste belongingness. The factors that enabled the entrepreneurs to carry on their businesses included intuition and the ability to utilised the opportunities. They were termed a 'political merchants' in view of their connection with the colonialists. The motives and profit seeking activities were entirely different from those in the post-independence period. If a comparison is made of the value standards of Japanese businessmen in the Meiji period with their Indian counterparts, it seems that the system that prevailed among the Zaibatsu business combine was characterised by protestant ethical functions and public interest orientation. They turned to recruitment and promotion by ability and merit as a management technique to survive (Lockwood, 1954). This will explain why the entrepreneurial system emerged in Japan quite early, when compared to that of India.

The Birla combine of the *marwari* community is characterized by solidarity of family ties and has been mainly involved in the production of consumption goods. Its proposal for construction of a steel plant was rejected by the government in 1954 which resolved that only government can undertake new steel plants. B.M. Birla had explained to the estimates Committee of the Parliament that the negotiations for British aid was satisfactory and that the costs would be lower than that under any government venture of similar type.

The nationalism movement resulted in a fresh natioanal motive, wherein the entrepreneurs were expected to carry out their activities in tune with the existing public interest provided for by the new dispensation and they were to see to it that their activities will further the interest and promote the prosperity of the business combines they belonged to. This has to be contrasted from the 'pro-colonial motive' of enriching both the enterprise and the society by availing of opportunities created by the colonialists.

Many business combines of today had their origins in the 17th century. These castes achieved their growth by associating themselves with the Portuguese, Dutch and French business houses operating in important trading centres. After the British domination, these merchants continued their activities entering into close association with British capital. Hence their profit-seeking interests were in contradiction with the national spirit of the intellectual class. That the entrepreneurs had deliberately separated their economic and political activities to enable their communities to prosper is significant when compared to that of industrialised countries.

2.4 The Post-Independence Period

India's economic development strategy after independence was based on the Mahalanobis model, which provided an emphasis on mining and manufacturing sectors for the production of capital goods and infrastructural development, the services and household goods sectors being given a low preference (Lal and Clement, 2005; Nayyar, 2008). The model, with a view to mitigate the prevailing unemployment problem in the country, gave less importance to factory goods sector owing to its demand for higher capital intensity. Due to low per capita income, the required higher levels of savings had to be generated mainly by restrictions on consumption expenditures. Therefore, the government propagated a progressive tax system to generate a higher savings rate and also to restrict undue increases in income and wealth inequalities. This strategy involved diversion of resources into their most productive uses, wherein investment by public sector was undertaken in strategic sectors like railways, air transport and national defence, while the private sector was required to contribute to India's economic growth as envisaged by the planners. Not only did the government determine where enterprises could invest in terms of location, it also identified what businesses could produce and sell at what prices. Jawaharlal Nehru, the first prime minister of independent India, opined that entrepreneurs had to focus on nation building rather than selling products or competing with each other, because he felt that it did not directly contribute to the cause of self-sufficiency (Lal and Clement, 2005).

The licence raj period was characterised by a regulatory framework of hindrances and compensation, resulting in the public sector assuming command of major investments, while the small scale sector was content with minor investments (Gupta, 2008). Many business communities were benefited directly or indirectly because of the public sector undertakings, since the latter offered critical infrastructures and capital goods, while small enterprises were ensured of supply and demand linkages. To regulate the larger private sector initiatives, the law required approvals for both establishing new manufacturing units and for expansion of capacity. The large private enterprises were to obtain licences in whatever domains, through whatever means they could. This period witnessed restructuring of many enterprises; for instance, the Birlas turned onto a quasi-public company with major shareholdings and extending into many businesses like metals, textiles, cement and fertilisers. Because of the licences problem, many Birla companies became highly fragmented. For example, Indal, the copper company, owned both a copper smelter and a fertilizer business.

Under the regulatory regime, *kisan* or farm entrepreneurship and *jawan* or defence entrepreneurship thrived. Farm entrepreneurship was the basis of green revolution, whereby India was able to mitigate the famine of the mid-1960s. In this endeavour, the state extended support to farm R&D and financing, while the US-style extension networks improved the capacity of farm entrepreneurs to make the nation self-sufficient in food grains (Gupta, 2008). The state supported borrowing of defence and allied informatics, transportation and space technologies from abroad and developed the local versions by extending support to private entrepreneurs. In both the cases, small entrepreneurs were encouraged. The licence raj regime had trained many professionals through public sector firms, government R&D laboratories and technical colleges. This led to the emergence of two forms of entrepreneurship namely, hardware dealers and designers and software developers. The opportunity was to find out creative short-term work and then achieve capacity building. While many small entrepreneurial firms began importing and assembling Korean and Taiwanese computer kits by exploiting market niches, the large entrepreneurial firms hired professional talent to build their capacity to compete on designs. As a result of such initiatives, a wide range of industries began to offer custom designs and complex solutions in many areas.

To ensure that nation building character was enforced by business enterprises, Nehru made it mandatory that every entrepreneur had to receive a certified nation building licence from the relevant licence officer (Lal and Clement, 2005). He promulgated a rule that only two to three companies could be granted a licence within the same industry, thus constraining healthy competition amongst the industries. However, Nehru's vision of industries being located all over India, rather than in select industrial clusters was not yet realised fully. Therefore, he passed laws requiring entrepreneurs to obtain a location permits before their start-ups. In order to avoid monopolies, Nehru stated that companies should obtain licences to expand their production capacity. To prevent money laundering within companies, Nehru made it mandatory for the excise and licensing officials to visit and audit every firm each year in order to ensure quality assurance (Lal and Clement, 2005). All these resulted in the need for entrepreneurs to obtain multiple licences but the underpaid government officers, in charge of licensing, resorted to bribery and corruption.

This type of strategy resulted into a direct government participation in production and selling of products and services and regulation of private sector activities. As the economy was protected from foreign competition through use of both infant industry argument and a binding foreign exchange constraint, imports were restricted to essential goods necessary for the development of the economy or to the maintenance of minimal living standards. As regards exports, they had to play a limited role in development, thereby minimising the prospects of global competition. As a result, India became an inward-looking closed economy, resulting in a protected, highly-regulated and public sector-dominated economic environment.

Due to state domination of the economy, the country faced not only problems in its overall approach to development, particularly in the area of industrialisation, but also had to encounter an increased level of corruption (Ahluwalia, 1985). Finally, like any other developing economy, India faced a number of sectoral imbalances, with shortages in some and surpluses in others. Businessmen bribed government officials not only for the right to enter a particular line of business, but also to prevent others from entering into that line. Government officials effected payoffs to politicians to obtain premium government positions that would allow them to easily contact enterprises to seek illegal income and wealth (Wade, 1990). The complex system of government controls, including price ceilings, along with the resultant corruption, meant that decision making was arbitrary and the transactions were non-transparent. Price controls and control of ownership of private capital by both Indian and foreign businesses, coupled with high individual and corporate income tax rates and high customs and excise duties, led to similar outcomes like that from price ceilings, thus increasing the level of corruption and higher transaction costs.

The size of the government grew substantially as it played an increasingly larger role in the economy in such areas as investment, production, retailing and regulation of the private sector. During 1950s and 1960s, the government established public sector enterprises in production and distribution of electricity, petroleum products, steel, coal and engineering goods and also part of banking and insurance sectors. After 1970, in order to increase foreign exchange earnings, it designated exports as a priority sector for active government assistance and established a duty drawback system, programmes of assistance for market development and cent per cent export-oriented entities to boost exports. Later, the government liberalised imports, wherein the proportion of commodities, not subject to licensing, increased from five per cent in 1980-1981 to about 30 per cent of total imports in 1987-88 (Pursell, 1992). However, the partial removal of quantitative restrictions was accompanied by a steep rise in tariff rates. Under these circumstances, enterprises had to obtain a government licence even to meet foreign business delegates in other countries (Lal and Clement, 2005). This type of business environment offered no incentive to invest in technical innovations so as to reduce production costs or improve product quality. As a matter of fact, India was branded as a stagnant economy with the 'Hindu rate of growth' of 2.5 per cent for long, wherein entrepreneurial development was also stunted. It was only after the economic reforms in the 1990s that outward growth became prominent with privatisation and globalisation moves. India's gross domestic product (GDP) grew at an average rate of 6.3 per cent from 1992-93 to 2000-01 (Acharya, 2001); further, inflation and fiscal deficit levels declined appreciably (Bhalla, 2000). Foreign exchange rate management led to improved financing of the current account deficit and higher foreign exchange reserves. Both GDP and per capita income have been registering higher growth rates from 1990 onwards.

2.5 The Current Scenario

Economic liberalisation resulted in the inflow of foreign direct investment and technology, resulting in many new globalised enterprises and strengthening of the already established business groups. Many MNCs influenced local entrepreneurship and transferred older technologies and product designs, while product diversification propelled increased consumer choice. They offered higher salaries and compensation to attract experienced employees. Alongside, the survivalist form of entrepreneurship became widely prevalent as many were forced to contend with the establishment of micro-enterprises, which had limited life span and produced only opportunistic products. For example, if a paint factory underperformed, the entrepreneur opened a paint shop and if that too failed, he moved into real estate business, thus providing a way out to the previously existing resources and opportunities. Some of the grassroots entrepreneurial ventures, which have emerged along with modern type of entrepreneurship, require mention. Aravind Eye Hospital, for example, with a mission to provide quality healthcare to the needy has grown to be the largest provider of eye care services in the world. On average, it treats two free patients for every one fee paying patient. It charges only $20 per eye surgery, compared to $2000 in the US and has a success rate comparable to that of the US, while still generating 40 per cent operating margins (Neumann and Greenberg, 2012). The essence of grassroots or micro innovation is visible in the life of Jagani, a man who dropped out of his village school at the age of ten due to financial hardship (Gupta, 2008). During this time, the bullocks in his village had little fodder in a drought-affected region, the farmers worrying about how to cultivate their fields. Jagani hoped to rectify this problem with the use of the powerful Royal Enfield Bullet motorcycle. Jagani modified the motorcycle by replacing the rear wheel with a $450 cultivating device, having attachments for tilling, weeding and sowing. After completing the necessary modifications, Jagani sold his product for much less than other cultivating devices, costing up to $6,000 (Neelakantan, 2005). Similarly, one Agrawat saw women drawing water from a well with a rope and noticed that the bucket would fall into well if the rope slipped. Hence, he added a lever so that the bucket would stay in place, making it easy for women to draw water. Chitagopakar and Harshangi developed a modified stick for the visually challenged that can sense obstructions with different alarm signals. Saidullah developed a bicycle that not only travels on land, but can also float on water. This helps people easily cross over ponds and rivers (National Innovation Foundation, 2005).

However, with the advent of the internet, 'glocal' multinationals have thrived both in India and in other countries. Similarly, others have used new technologies and global markets for making local impacts. For instance, an illiterate masseuse, Indu Sharma in Mumbai, bought a cell phone to expand her business. In the US and Europe, most tractors use high horsepower, given the large farm size there. After observing the difference between Indian tractors and the US and European tractors, Mahindra and Mahindra has expanded its parts warehouse and assembly production in the US and the UK to source advanced features so as to make 75 per cent of the Western tractors. A new dealer network in the US and Europe and a new hobby farmer segment (farmers who work on farms during weekends and holidays) were created using lower horsepower models. This resulted in a 40 per cent market share in that segment. Similar global presence is evident in the success of *patel* business community, which owns 60 per cent of the low-end hospitality market in the US and also the Palanpuri Jain community, which owns 50 per cent of the world's rough diamond trade (Godrej, 2005).

With the opening up of new opportunities, a small but growing percentage of engineering and management personnel started many entrepreneurial ventures. Many firms began hiring professionals to construct capacity building for participating in national automation projects. And the state extended necessary help to link these professionals with MNCs, while offering a captive infrastructure support to others. Closer alliances with the US firms allowed the Indian entrepreneurs to outsource higher cost systems analysis and design works. However, the low-skill programming, involving short-term client interactions, was retained onsite in the US. This strategy transpired into the starting up of many ventures in entertainment, media, transportation, hospitality and other infrastructures. The internet gave rise to several Indian portals with specialised offerings, start-ups and 'casualpreneurs', those with full-time day jobs who created India-centric web products in their spare time using internet advertising (Rao, Niranjan, 2009).

The growth of entrepreneurship in the bio-tech industry is documented by McKinsey Consulting in respect of clinical trials sector. In the West, if there is a disease, firms search for new chemical entities (NCEs) for cure and then patent them. In India, many entrepreneurs use software capabilities to scan for all non-patented NCEs and patent what they discover, then licensing them to Western firms for further analysis. Many entrepreneurs are also venturing into modifying NCEs and discovering new forms and new drug delivery systems. Hepatitis B was priced by the US drug companies at $50 per day dose, but Shantha Biotech has developed the drug with less than

$1 million investment over a five year period and has marketed it for $5 per day dose (Varaprasad, 2011).

A pattern of entrepreneurship, distinct from early Japanese and Chinese styles appears to be emerging in India. The Japanese model of entrepreneurship was based on the use of globally discarded materials and manpower. The Chinese model has been based on the cost-effective use of earlier generation's global machinery and methods. The emerging Indian model is based on the making of the next generation's products and services accessible to the grassroots (Gupta, 2008) and creating new products and services by leveraging the intellectual properties of the grassroots. It may not be feasible to fix knowledge paradigms in the communities as the tendencies of poverty, terrorism, migration and other exogenous factors may have acted as bottlenecks (Prahalad and Hammond, 2002).

As Gupta (2008) points out, the potential of diverse families and community groups resulted in a type of cultural entrepreneurship. Once this is achieved, the community might be involved in specific value-adding activities, generating value-adding entrepreneurship. Extension networks may then be established to deepen the participation of the members of the community, through targeted support leading to extension entrepreneurship. Several communities across international boundaries may be linked together for mutual exchange, in which case glocal entrepreneurship would result. This will strengthen knowledge and build the capacity of the communities to solve grassroots problems, resulting in the emergence of grassroots entrepreneurship. In this regard, India may be adopting what Bagchi (2005) underlines the development and exchange of culturally-embedded grassroots know-how, requiring an institutional framework with an acknowledgement of the rights of communities to the grassroots intellectual properties towards innovative entrepreneurship.

In 2006, OECD initiated a new Entrepreneurship Indicators Programme in order to globally generalise the determinants of entrepreneurship and the Global Entrepreneurship Monitor Report of 2002 evolved the Total Entrepreneurship Activity (TEA) measure to evaluate the nature of ventures generated in different countries based on the contributions of the ventures on sales, consumption and employment indicators (Acs and Szerb, 2010). When ventures are evaluated to succeed by the use of the measure, they will attempt to reduce the negative effects of failures, which took place hitherto. However, TEA's limitation is in evaluating the quality of ventures started or the different measures initiated for such creation (Sala-I-Martin et al, 2007). India was second amongst all nations in the TEA and after several years of data, India appears to have a TEA level rather close to the world average. India is ninth in the Global Entrepreneurship Monitor (GEM) survey of entrepreneurial countries (Sala-i-Martin et al, 2011). It is among 28 countries in necessity-based entrepreneurship, while it is fifth from the lowest in opportunity-based entrepreneurship. Liberalisation and the information technology boom have been the significant factors, leading to a wave of entrepreneurship in the country. While China's growth has been achieved by a heavy influx of foreign direct investment, India has followed more on the development of institutions that support private enterprises, by building a stronger infrastructure for that facilitation. Its present corporate and legal systems operate with greater efficiency and transparency. The government has established many entrepreneurship development programmes by providing training and crucial infrastructures to develop industries, including rural and small scale sectors, as would be discussed later. In the latter case, one type of innovation that may work in a country like India is grassroots innovation.

In the current scenario, even though there are many sources of finance, access to credit is one of the major problems faced by the entrepreneurs, especially in the start-up stage. In spite of liberalisation, the entrepreneur has to deal with many regulatory and compliance issues, as shown by World Bank's Doing Business, where India ranks very low in starting a business. Availability of skilled and technical manpower is another issue which has to be tackled. As a matter of fact, the real human capital component of household workforce and policy makers has been very small, as has been shown by their productivity yield, yet these sectors obtain a great quantum of subsidies.

Except in telecommunications (where the proportion of population possessing mobile handsets is much more than the proportion of people having hygienic sanitation), other physical road, air and ports, energy infrastructures have to be greatly developed to induce effective entrepreneurship in these fields. Inadequate infrastructure has been identified as a major problem by the Global Competitiveness Report of different years. However, there are many opportunities for growth of small business enterprises, if only necessary credit and market facilities are provided. Entrepreneurship has to be looked as both innovative in order to globally compete and also provide productive employment to the large force of unemployed and underemployed workforce.

2.6 Conclusion

With reference to innovative and growth consequences of entrepreneurship, some scholars have mistakenly cited India's religion as an impediment to innovativeness and growth (Weber, 1930). They contend that the caste system hinders social mobility and Hindu spiritualism inhibits pursuit of material growth (Anstey, 1952; Morris, 1967). Many empirical studies indicate a low level of innovativeness amongst the entrepreneurs, showcased by the fact that most of them are less likely to develop new products or new production methods (Shivani et al, 2006). However, entrepreneurial development has resulted in an increased rate of self-employment, according to National Sample Survey and Central Statistical Organisations. During 1993-2004, the average income for the bottom 20 per cent of the population grew by ten per cent. This is nearly at par with the 12 per cent for the top 20 per cent of the population in rural and urban areas. Both population strata have high rates of self-employment. However, although many areas are experiencing an income growth, fixed-income groups experience it the least (Shivani et al, 2006).

Turner (2007) dismisses India's recent dynamism as a temporary phenomenon, attributing the growth to the returning Indians who have held leadership positions elsewhere and to those who have access to leading edge technologies and exposure to global operations or to the US-born children of Indian immigrant hi-tech entrepreneurs. However, the long-term changes in entrepreneurial innovativeness are now recognised as a function of the work culture system, besides economic, political, legal, financial, logistical and social structures that characterise a society (Morris, 1998). Work culture system includes the rules of the game that influence the allocation of entrepreneurial resources between productive activities such as innovation and unproductive activities such as rent seeking or organised crime (Baumol, 1990).

In understanding the fate of entrepreneurship formation in developing economies, we have to look beyond environmental conditions and the technological capabilities of firms which though important, are not sufficient in explaining the technology of entrepreneurship. The Indian software and biotechnology sectors provide a good example of recent efforts in the emergence of leadership in entrepreneurship. Political and policy issues may come in the way of institutional change in the form of vested interests, distributive conflicts and collective action on the part of many business groups in response to the ensuing reforms.

An optimistic view of the importance of entrepreneurship in developing economies comes from Hatten and Ruthland (1995), who point out that in the presence of uncertainty about a country's capacity to produce competitively, imparting appropriate social values mostly assist in discovery of economies of scale. However, as in the case of externalities, this would subject entrepreneurship in the underinvestment bracket. Therefore, the state policy has to induce investment in entrepreneurship, while at the same time, avoiding excessive diversification once such investment has taken place. Indian engineers who had migrated to the United States in the eighties have found it a haven for entrepreneurial pursuits and have become highly successful in their respective fields. They started high technology companies in Silicon Valley, focusing on solving critical market problems. Many of these Indian entrepreneurs, after making fortunes in their market segments, started helping entrepreneurs back home in establishing many start-up companies. Individual entrepreneurs who have a comparative advantage and conduct low budget experiments can play a critical role in developing not only large scale enterprises, but also small-scale complements, many of them being unique for a developing economy. Large companies may have an advantage in acquiring and implementing modern technologies to build new organisations. Recently, sectors like automobiles, iron and steel, telecommunications, pharmaceuticals and agriculture have provided the best example for the emergence of small entrepreneurs, which we will discuss in some detail in later chapters.

3

Development of Entrepreneurship in Iron and Steel Industry

3.1 Introduction

As pointed out in 1.8, development and innovativeness would imply the evolution from a resource-based to a knowledge-based economy (Porter et al, 2002), which characterises the modern entrepreneurial process. At the lowest levels of economic development, production is based on mobilisation of different factors of production. At the factor-driven stage, international competitiveness is based upon low factor costs and the adequacy of minerals and other raw materials. As countries move to the next stage of industrialisation, economic growth becomes more capital intensive and thus investment-driven. The third, innovation-driven stage is one of technology generating economy and countries reaching this stage, start innovating at the global technological level at least in some sectors. Transformation to this stage requires not just developing the ability to generate new knowledge, but also in commercialising by entrepreneurs, who create new businesses and in turn new businesses create more jobs, intensify competition and increase productivity (Porter et al, 2002), certain sectors assumimg the role of lead geese.

Globalisation means more than just participating in global markets and a global corporation may embrace a culture that emphasises international leadership and ownership. For example, Nokia realised that it could not become a global enterprise all by itself, hence went for a merger with Siemens and now has a diverse leadership cadre. Without liberalising the economic and legal infrastructures, several bottlenecks may arise in the ability of the corporations to become global. In the wake of the recent financial crisis, many countries have started to focus on their own problems and will pull back from the global economy. In countries like the United States, major forces behind entrepreneurial success have been availability of capital and the ability to fail, whereas in India, it is almost impossible to shut down a company because failure is still a stigma. In modern business, Schumpeterian innovations play an important role in inducing the V formation of entrepreneurs. The chapter outlines the Korean experience of Pohang Iron and Steel Company and the growth of entrepreneurship in that country, besides documenting the activities of Tata Steel in respect of innovation and intrepreneurship development.

3.2 Types of Innovations

Innovations are essential for global leadership and when we look at the 50 top innovations in the world during 2011, radical innovations accounted for the bulk and some of the radical entrepreneurs are found in the electronics industry. Innovations may be general purpose, which change the way of thinking and doing, incremental (continual improvement resulting in improved creativity) and radical (typical creative destruction) innovations. Schumpeter (1950) identifies radical innovations as new products or processes that are far superior to the existing ones technologically. Technologically strong firms invest in the creation of radical innovations to increase their market share but at the disadvantage of their competitors. Radical innovations cannot be copied easily because they require a high scientific and technological capability that limits the acquisition by late-comers (Varadarajan, 2011). Product and process innovations may include continuous product and process improvement, process revolutions, service innovations and strategic innovations like the lean production method and the implementation of new technology for improving supply chain management. These innovations also represent new products or services, such as the iPhone, without changing business models. Strategic innovations include new products or services but with new business models such as Segway rentals or web-based applications (Varadarajan, 2011). Finance innovation relates to business models, networks and alliances for innovations such as Dell's personal computer business and supply chain management.

Managerial innovation relates to innovative approaches to managing manpower, technology and resources. Sometimes, even small firms become innovative and grow into becoming lead geese.

Fundamental innovation is a creative idea that leads to a revolution in thinking. Such innovations are based on extensive research and are knowledge-driven, theoretically proven, leading to follow-up research and development. Examples of such fundamental innovations include Einstein's theory of relativity, electricity, penicillin, the telephone, wireless communication, the transistor, computer software, UNIX and the internet (Varadarajan, 2011). The platform innovation leads to the practical application of fundamental innovations like personal computers, silicon chips, cellular phones, digital printers, Microsoft Windows, databases, Linux, iPad, drug delivery devices, satellites and the space shuttles. A derivative innovation is a secondary product or service derived from a platform innovation which includes new server-client configurations based on a new network architecture or operating system for a cellular phone. A variation innovation is a tertiary-level innovation that requires less time to develop and is a slight variation of the next-level products or services based on a derivative innovation. Variation innovations in cell phone include various colour covers, ring tones, camera features and additional software-based optional features (Varadarajan, 2011).

When we characterise entrepreneurs as general, incremental or radical based on the type of innovations they make, the radical innovators in electronics industry bear the accolades. It all started in Japan following the lead of the US goose (Ozawa, 2009), flourishing in electronics, textiles and automotive industries. Conglomerates like Toyota, Honda and Nissan have had radical innovations in respect of battery, hybrid and fuel cell electric vehicles, with the aim of increasing the understanding technologies of shift process, which were not only incremental but also radical, illustrated by their position in the competitive race. Japanese firms in industries such as automobiles, consumer electronics, precision equipment, semiconductors and various hi-tech components have been successful in international markets. In spite of the country's economic malaise from the 1990s, many Japanese firms continue to be world leaders in various product areas like hybrid automobiles, machine tools and various hi-tech components.

In this connection, it may be useful to know the plight of once-leading leaders, as in the case of disc industry. Christensen (1997) points out how in the disc drive industry, technology changes have sustained new product performance improvement. One type of technology sustained the industry's rate of improvement in product performance (total capacity and recording density) and ranged from incremental to radical architecture. The industry's dominant firms always led in developing and adopting these technologies. The other type of technology disrupted (a la Schumpeter) or redefined performance and consistently resulted in the failure of the industry's leading firms. It is the disruptive technologies that toppled the industry's leaders. The most important disruptive technologies (architectural innovations that shrunk the size of the drives from 14-inch diameter discs to diameters of 8, 5.25 and 3.5 inches and then from 2.5 to 1.8 inches) were technologically straight forward. The companies generally packaged known technologies in a unique architecture and enabled the use of these products in applications where magnetic data storage and retrieval previously had not been technologically or economically feasible.

Further, the purpose of advanced technology development in the industry was always aimed at sustaining established patterns of improvement in order to reach higher performance levels and higher margin domains. Many of these technologies were radically new and difficult, but they were not disruptive (Christensen, 1997). The customers of the leading disc drive suppliers led them towards these achievements. As a result of this, sustaining technologies did not cause failure. In the third pattern, despite the established firms' technological strength in leading sustained innovations, from the simplest to the most radical, the firms that led the industry in developing and adopting disruptive technologies were entrants to that industry and not its incumbent leaders. The question posed by Christensen is: why was it that firms that could be considered as aggressive, innovative and customer-sensitive could ignore or attend belatedly to technological innovations with enormous strategic importance? The problem was that established firms were unable to confront successfully the downward vision and mobility. Finding new applications and markets for these new products had been a capability that these firms exhibited upon entry but then apparently lost. Perhaps the leading firms were held captive by their customers, enabling attacking entrant firms to topple the incumbent industry leaders each time a disruptive technology emerged (Christensen, 1997).

Notwithstanding this failure and the catch-up process of North American and Western European countries in the past centuries, the rise of the newly industrialising countries of Asia then by present-day emerging economies is characteristic of radical first and second generation innovations in the typical Schumpeterian sense of creative destruction. The emerging countries have been able to absorb and creatively adapt international technological knowledge and achieve accelerated growth from a global diffusion of technology. These have had access to new technologies without bearing all the costs and risks of investment. Such technological adoption goes beyond mere imitation and is an example of creative and innovative entrepreneurial behaviour.

3.3 The Genesis of Innovative Entrepreneurship

Innovative entrepreneurship is based on factor sequences or personal traits like risk taking, achievement motivation and human capital. Both male and female entrepreneurs in India score rather low on risk-taking propensity measures (Rutten, 2006). This low risk-taking propensity serves as an explanation for the historical preference in India for service ventures, which have lower initial capital outlays and shorter breakeven periods compared to manufacturing start-ups. For, as Veen (1976) highlights, structural impediments include market imperfections for venture capital and the non-supporting institutional environment for industrial investment. However, as Streefkerk (1985) and Chandra (2009) document, several artisans, blacksmiths, masons and carpenters, set up small industrial workshops and gradually became industrial entrepreneurs. Such studies discredit the assumption that a low risk-taking propensity is an impediment to industrial entrepreneurship in the country.

McClelland (1961) identifies the n-Ach as key to entrepreneurship and notes that high achievers are motivated by an enduring desire to succeed and to exploit opportunities, by taking advantage of favourable trade conditions. Indian entrepreneurs have low levels of achievement motivation (McClelland and Winter, 1969), but recent studies show fairly high levels among men entrepreneurs, while it is moderate among women entrepreneurs (Shivani et al, 2006). This low level among women entrepreneurs may be associated with a lack mentors and role models to assist them in the acquisition of technical and conceptual skills. However, small group bondage is more common among women than men and women tend to be more assertive when denied fairness. Rather than being only achievement motivated, women tend to build and mobilise support networks for achieving success.

The Swedish firm Kairos Future (*Times of India*, 2007) reports that Indian youth (16-29 year olds) are the happiest in the world and these youth show optimism about their future and their society's future. Work comes as top priority for them, followed by a good career and higher status, which prioritises entrepreneurship growth.

Human capital is another factor strengthening entrepreneurship through technical, human and conceptual skills (Nafziger and Terrell, 1996). Hosseini (1990) observes that the presence of the most able work force can be of little use if the individuals are not sufficiently motivated to work hard. Leeuwen (2007) shows that India has lagged behind in human capital during the 20th century, making it difficult for entrepreneurs to adopt new technologies and for politicians to support new technology-based entrepreneurship without causing social unrest. This chapter considers the example of Indian iron and steel industry as an example of innovative growth, following the examples of South Korea's advanced iron and steel industry, which was a late-starter when compared to (say) Tata Steel.

3.4 Steel Entrepreneurship Development in Korea

Decimated by Second World War, the Korean economy experienced tremendous change from the beginning of the 1960s during its transformation into a modern industrial country (Surie and Torras, 2007). In 1962, Korea promulgated its first economic development plan projecting rapid economic growth, followed by many plans. Exports and increased investment under government-private partnership programme contributed to the rapid growth of the economy. Education received a relatively large share of total investment and Korea achieved nearly universal adult literacy, universal primary education and enrolment rates grew rapidly at all levels above the primary level by 1960. Throughout the decade, resources were allocated to industries with relatively low capital intensity. During the 1970s, the rate of growth of fixed investment (12.7 per cent) outgrew GNP growth (eight per cent). During 1962–1991, the ratio of gross investment to GNP rose from 0.10 to 0.32. By 1999, value added in industry, as a percentage of GDP has been 35.9 per cent (Enos and Park, 1987).

The Korean government, after realising the need for backward integration into heavy industry, began to attract Japan's sunset industries in chemical, petrochemical and iron and steel industries (Enos and Park, 1987). The government mandated that companies have to be internationally competitive in scale and cost with a condition that entrepreneurs had to provide capital for at least 40 per cent of the total investment. It established rules for selecting technology supply and foreign loans and played a crucial role towards industrialisation by directing allocation of resources to entrepreneurship. Among the many challenges entrepreneurs faced in initiating such projects, lack of capital, technology, skilled workers and managerial capabilities and political risk, which could result in policy changes such as nationalization of industries or strict government control, have been important.

Owing to high capital investment required, only large companies and the government could participate in the field of industrialisation. With foreign reinforcement of capabilities, the government began to promote entrepreneurship in the mid-1990s by providing better opportunities for financing small and medium enterprises. In addition, some large companies also began to reduce delays in payments to small firms providing them with more financial stability (Shim and Steers, 2001). The government offered incentives to Korean and foreign firms willing to invest in the new areas and granted tax privileges for a five year period. The government also made substantial investments in harbour facilities, water supply systems and roads for these industrial complexes (Enos and Park, 1987).

Korea acquired technology mainly through licensing rather than through foreign direct investment to strengthen local capabilities. The case of Pohang Iron and Steel Company Ltd (POSCO), which began as a government owned enterprise (initially with $5.8 million investment) but later privatised, highlights the role played by the government in incubating technological capabilities (Westphal et al, 1985). POSCO was founded in 1968 as the first integrated iron and steel mill with a modern, large-scale and continuous production system. Construction of the plant began in 1970 with a capacity of one million tonnes per annum of crude steel. In the first stage of expansion, completed in 1976, steel capacity was increased to 2.6 million tonnes; in the second stage, completed in 1978, it increased to 5.5 mt and in the third stage, completed in 1981, to 8.5 mt. In 2004, POSCO became the world's fifth largest producer of crude steel (Surie and Torras, 2007).

When the former South Korean general Park Tae-joon, the founder of POSCO passed away in December 2011 at 84, he had left a vast steel empire in the world, including India. He built the first blast furnace at POSCO in 1974 in Pohang, south-eastern port city, with the full-fledged aid from Yawata Iron and Steel Company of Japan. He was the first dynamic entrepreneur who introduced steel industry at the instance of that country's president, where neither technology nor capital was available at that time and the country was largely an agrarian economy with very little steel production of a few hundred thousand tonnes only. Being a graduate from Waseda University, Japan, majoring in mechanical engineering, Tae-joon learnt from Japanese experience the feel of economic nationalism of 'steel is the state'. He foresaw an immediate future of Korean steel industry to take the lead which China later followed, thus giving credence to the 'flying geese' theory. In the iron and steel innovation cycle, the US was the lead goose, soon followed by Japan, which was followed by Korea and later China. A young goose which was nurtured by the Japanese goose, now would nurse a newly-born goose China in 1980s to fly up. Currently, China is number one steel producer, followed by India's Arcelor and POSCO.

Owing to challenges of a shortage of capital for financing large scale projects and lack of technology, a consortium named Korea International Steel Associates was formed to raise capital for POSCO. However, the consortium was dissolved in 1969, because of its inability to raise funds. Subsequently, agreements were signed with the Japanese for loans totalling $123 million and all major technology and facilities (Enos and Park, 1987). The Japanese contract specified the provision of help with planning and consulting, purchasing and construction, planning and execution of the construction and construction management system, and on-site assistance for start up and operation. Amsden (1989) documents the challenges faced during construction of the first stage facilities, such as delays in the laying of concrete, necessitating two month long emergency works to compensate. However, POSCO's employees worked round the clock and their efforts to learn built capabilities and established a tradition of early project completion. Initially, the major products of POSCO were hot rolled steel used for structural purposes, high tensile steel being developed in 1975.

As local engineers learned from the effort to absorb the technology, reliance on foreign technical assistance was reduced. By 1981, POSCO depended solely on the Japan Group for the master engineering plan. Also, the Pohang University of Science and Technology (1986) and an R&D centre were established to build science and technology capabilities and disseminate skills by establishing links between academia and industry. Emphasis on learning continued and POSCO engineers succeeded in absorbing the technology of making high carbon steel and high tension steel. Higher value-added products such as cold rolling coils and sheet, galvanised coils and sheet, as well as low-sulphur clean sheet and steel plate were included and further expansions were undertaken in the 1980s (Enos and Park, 1987). A strategy of exporting to other developing countries strengthened capabilities and helped to finance growth.

POSCO entered the global market by obtaining ISO 9002 certification and listing on the New York, London and Korean Stock Exchanges. In 1999, the company began to globalise operations by launching corporate-wide process innovation and Six Sigma initiatives to generate an improved quality culture. Information technology utilised to speed up operations and implement activity-based management. The company was privatized in 2000, achieving ISO certification for its cold rolled steel quality management system, without reliance on external specialists. The company focused on knowledge management through continuing education and R&D efforts. Collaborations with the Pohang Institute of Science and Technology (POSTECH) and the University of Pittsburgh materialised in establishing a Graduate Institute of Ferrous Technology at POSTECH in 2006. In the same year, POSCO was ranked third among global steel producers by the International Steel Institute. Similar developments in other manufacturing sectors like automotives, electronic goods and semiconductors have led to successful participation by Korean firms in global hi-tech markets, indicating that building entrepreneurial capabilities by adapting to increasing returns technologies has greatly helped in spearheading development (Murphy et al, 2006).

3.5 The Tata Iron and Steel Industry

From the 1950s, the Indian government pursued an industrial strategy directed towards conserving foreign exchange and producing heavy capital and intermediate goods domestically. The scale and capital intensity required of steel industry necessitated that only large integrated steel plants were established. The Tata Iron and Steel Company (TISCO, now Tata Steel) and later, the government-owned Steel Authority of India (SAIL) were established. In the beginning, India faced the similar problems as Korea in obtaining financing.

Consequently, all the Indian public sector plants were turnkey plants gifted by Russia, the UK and West Germany, the best technology not necessarily being transferred. SAIL was burdened with difficulties in transferring technology, besides poor engineering, failure to take account of weak local raw material characteristics, low capacity utilisation, price controls and poor management, which all contributed to its ineffective performance. Moreover, the government allowed only limited capacity expansion (from 1.3 to two million tonnes in the late 1950s) and modernisation of its aging facilities was possible only in 1983, partly because of the possibility of nationalisation and partly because price controls contributed to low profitability levels (Lall, 1985). In contrast to the industrial policy followed by Korea, favouring large enterprises, Indian industrial policy focused on encouraging small enterprises while containing the growth of large private enterprises. Consequently, India's progress was slow in comparison with other developing countries in the 1960s and 1970s. Its manufacturing value added was $15.6 billion compared to $40.3 billion for Brazil, $23.4 billion in Mexico, $11.2 billion in Argentina, $10 billion in South Korea and $12.8 billion in Yugoslavia (Lall, 1985). Value added as a percentage of GDP in 1999 was 25.9 per cent as opposed to Korea's 35.9 per cent and it remained at 26.6 per cent in India with Korea at 34.6 per cent in 2003 (World Bank, 2006).

From 1974 onwards, the Indian government demanded foreign owned affiliates to dilute their shareholding to 40 per cent, as a result of which about 60 companies closed operations in India. No foreign firms were permitted to enter strategic industries such as computer hardware and were not permitted to undertake turnkey works until the 1980s, leading to reliance on domestic consultants and licensing to gain access to foreign technologies (Lall, 1985). These regulations were to protect indigenous technologies in order to reduce royalty rates and the period of agreement and ensure that technology was absorbed fully to permit the licencee to sub-licence the technology locally. Existing Indian producers (government enterprises included), were protected regardless of efficiency and the market was insulated from external competition, whereas Korean incentives to export resulted in attempts to adapt to global standards and markets.

However, low reliance on foreign technology, together with efforts to focus on indigenous R&D and local enterprises, hindered technological learning to a large extent (Lall, 1985).While India was not a major exporter of capital goods among newly industrializing countries in 1978, the total value of product exports in this category was $421 million compared to $1.4 billion for Brazil and $1.5 billion for Korea (Murphy et al, 2006). However, if exports of technology are considered as such or accompanied by the sale of capital goods, India was among the leaders, in terms of value of exports and the range and complexity of technologies (Heeks, 2010). The departure of foreign computer firms created opportunities for new enterprises in information services and software. After liberalisation was accelerated, foreign competitors were once again permitted, to start joint ventures, licence or import new technologies. By the end of the 1990s, some leading Indian enterprises had expanded overseas emerging as new multinationals. Capability building in various sectors such as trucks, heavy equipment, chemicals and computer hardware led to an expansion of each sector, creating further demand for skills (Murphy et al, 2006). The government continued to promote industry and entrepreneurship by easing regulations. In 1981-82, India produced 1.3 million tonnes of pig iron and 8.8 mt of mild steel and was the 16th largest steel producer in the world. There were six integrated steel plants, one in the private sector (Murphy et al, 2006).

TISCO (according to its website), the largest private integrated steel producer and a good performer in the steel industry because of efforts to indigenize technology, has built its own capabilities in maintenance and backward integration into manufacturing of equipment and R&D. TISCO was founded by Jamsetji Tata in 1907 with technology from USA. The steel industry was granted tariff protection by the British government from 1924 till 1941. In the 1950s and 1960s, Indian steel was much cheaper than imported steels. The import-substituting regime instituted by the 1960s reserved all future steel capacity for the public sector. Therefore, TISCO faced several challenges and the company had to achieve satisfactory performance in order to continue its existence and avoid nationalisation. Price controls restrained local prices and reduced profitability; imports were permitted only when necessary to make up for shortfalls (Lall, 1987).

TISCO, like SAIL also had problems with raw materials but overcame these challenges by retaining its own collieries and installing washing and blending facilities to alleviate the high ash content of coal used in steel production. Instead of relying on foreign equity or licences, TISCO obtained foreign technology in the form of individually recruited experts and equipment. To compensate for difficulties in maintaining equipment and the scarcity of foreign exchange for spare parts, TISCO developed capabilities in project execution by the establishment of its growth shop which began as a maintenance facility for imported machinery and manufacturing spares. To solve production inefficiencies resulting from poor raw materials, process engineering capabilities were developed by making improvements in the raw material and coke oven areas. To substitute expensive imported materials with local materials, TISCO continued to introduce new steels developed from its in-house R&D. Managing input costs was necessary since government price controls prevented firms from capitalising on monopoly. Other capabilities were developed in industrial engineering such as quality control, productivity monitoring, and cost evaluation. In 1983, TISCO launched its first expansion in almost 30 years and began its modernisation process (Lall, 1987).

TISCO modernised further in the 1990s, by importing a new state-of-art blast furnace which was installed mainly by locally organised cross-functional team and learning was transferred to other divisions. Similar to POSCO, the blast furnace project team worked overtime to meet completion deadlines and by the late 1990s, the company focused on quality through continuous improvement, obtaining ISO certification and benchmarking progress against other global players. In 2000, a new cold rolling mill was installed using the same procedure and an internal reorganisation to match new technology and enhance capabilities throughout the value chain was accomplished with the help of McKinsey and Company. Consequently, there was an emphasis on value-added products, accelerating innovation through R&D and patenting. The company then began globalising through increased exports, overseas expansion, acquisition and diversification into information technology based industries. TISCO was ranked the fifth largest steel producer in the world by the International Iron and Steel Institute in 2006. In 2007, TISCO completed the acquisition of a steel company in the UK.

Despite facing a difficult regulatory environment until the 1980s, TISCO emerged as a leader. At each stage of its evolution, new capabilities built through technology acquisition increased demand for new products and skills, which resulted in the emergence of ancillary industries. An example is the manufacture of bearings for trucks, cars and trains, indicating a need for research on increasing returns technologies (Murphy et al, 2006). In Korea, the steel industry was developed entirely by the public sector, the government assuming the role of entrepreneur (Freeman and Duvall, 1984). In contrast, the expansion of the Indian steel industry was hindered by government policies that regulated prices and threatened nationalisation, but import substitution policies helped to build indigenous capabilities. However, both countries considered technology acquisition as an important factor in fostering entrepreneurship. While the timeframe and speed of evolution differed, companies in both countries followed a similar pattern of technological development. Although TISCO was established in 1907, the regulatory environment impeded its expansion and entry into the global economy until the 1990s. POSCO evolved more rapidly because newer technologies were adopted at the outset in the 1970s, while TISCO began modernisation only in the 1980s and was able to catch up in the 1990s. This aspect of innovation is being dealt in some detail in the ninth chapter.

Other industries followed a similar evolutionary path, suggesting that the framework may be widely applicable to other cases. For example, the Indian software industry emerged to provide services to the domestic computer hardware industry (Heeks, 2010) and software firms gained global experience by interacting with international clients (Surie, 2007). Similarly, government investments in science and technology institutions led to the emergence of the biotechnology industry in the1990s, attracting multinational corporations seeking low-cost research capabilities. By the late 1990s, the Indian government had privatised some public companies by increasing entrepreneurial activity in many sectors, including education. Thus, despite late entry into the global economy, India is being recognised as an important location for knowledge-based industries. The success of leading firms also results in cultural transformation, generating interest in entrepreneurship as a career of choice (Stiglitz, 2004). Recently, Tata Steel has been selected by the Japanese Union of Scientists and Engineers for Deming Grand Prize in total quality management for becoming the first integrated steel plant in the world.

3.6 Development of Intrapreneurship

Intrapreneurship involves assuming ownership and operating with an entrepreneurial mindset. In the corporate context, since the individual leading the organisation is not an autonomous entrepreneur, he or she is referred to as an intrapreneur. Renovation at any level cannot occur without this transformation of perspective from employee to psychological owner or intrapreneur. Intrapreneuring is not a path chosen by many, since this requires a lot of ingenuity from tentrepreneur, than would be the case operating with an employee mindset. The importance arises because of innovations being generated across the organisations (as opposed to centralised innovation) as one of the important strategies for long-term success. There is a strong relationship between innovation and employees taking on psychological ownership of the company's growth, thereby manifesting entrepreneurial behaviour (Seshadri and Tripathy, 2006). Since this is accomplished within the framework of a large organisation rather than as an autonomous entrepreneur, it is more appropriate to look at these innovators as corporate entrepreneurs or intrapreneurs (Pinchot, 1985).

Intrapreneurism enables employees to make their innovativeness known to the management, which results in generating new ways for business growth or alternately provides radically different ways of doing existing businesses. Organisations require new ideas to survive and grow profitably and hence, have to find ways to exploit the entrepreneurial potential inherent in the employees. A model of intrapreneurship is presented by Hamel (2002) wherein, apart from the culture of innovation in the organisation that the top management creates, there are three other major components namely, innovation activism implying the crucial role played by autonomous corporate entrepreneurs, innovation as a capability, whereby employees are trained towards innovativeness and innovation as a process, which ensures that ideas are progressively developed from imagination to experimentation, assessment, scale-up and reality. The implicit rule in intrapreneurial innovation is 'make a little, sell a little,' 'low risk experimentation', or 'freedom to fail'. This is visible in 3M, the US-based company that has built its fortunes by harnessing the power of its corporate entrepreneurs (Hamel, 2002).

Cost reduction and enhanced customer focus have been the major objectives of innovation and intrapreneurship. Intrapreneurs seeking to reinvent a company so as to increase efficiency may do so by removing unproductive elements of bureaucratic hierarchy, harnessing the power of technology and proper delegation of authority and power. Another motive may be the need to provide more value to the customer and may develop innovative means of minimising inconvenience to the consumers. They may also enhance the market image of the organisation by providing additional features to its offerings.

Innovating the Cold Rolling Mill

The example of Tata Steel's Cold Rolling Mill (CRM) to manufacture high value cold rolled products for use in the automobile and white goods industry has been cited as a case study of intrapreneurship development by Seshadri and Tripathy (2006). The estimated project cost was Rs. 25 billion with a completion period of 36 months. The company did not have a very strong in-house project implementation team at the time, when the project was initially being conceived and this envisaged an appointment of a project manager. RP Singh, who had earlier occupied several senior project management positions in various public sector steel plants and he joined the company as part of the senior management with a special focus on new projects.

After taking stock of other worldwide CRM implementation processes, Singh was for drastic changes in the implementation of the CRM complex. However, when he put forward his vision to the project team and contractor companies, he was greeted with scepticism and was regarded as a new entrant whose enthusiasm would vanish once reality set in. Many foreign contractor companies had their own doubts. While the initial reactions of the project team ranged from polite amusement to outright disagreement, by July 1998, the 400-strong CRM team fully supported Singh. The mindset in the group went through many stages starting from 'it is not possible,' to 'it is very difficult,' followed by 'it can be done,' 'it is being done,' and finally, 'it has been accomplished.' Singh succeeded in creating a sense of ownership and intrapreneurship among the team members energised by a powerful collective vision of creating a world record in project implementation of the CRM. By June 1999, Tata Steel completed the project successfully under Singh's leadership in a world record time of 26 and half months and at the lowest project cost of Rs.16 billion, while ensuring world-class quality. The steel industry was in a downturn at that time which contributed to achieving the lowest project cost.

The company managed to excel all earlier records set by several other bigs in the industry including Bethlehem Steel of the USA, Posco of Korea, Siam United Steel of Thailand and Baoshan of China in implementing similar CRM projects. Consequent to the liberalisation process, the top management had realised that due to a variety of legacy, it either had to reinvent itself or perish. Although the company was still not ready to face the competitors from overseas, steps were taken to face the new environment. In spite of a competitive market responsible for innovativeness by intrapreneurs, the threat of extinction would induce many companies to choose status quo and gradually undergo a process of 'ossification' (Piramal et al, 2000).

While the possibility of failure to achieve the targets was a reality through the implementation phase, this did not stop Singh and the company from attempting what seemed impossible to most others. Soon after the completion of the CRM project, Singh was entrusted with the responsibility of revamping Blast Furnace-F (Seshadri and Tripathy, 2006). The old furnace had outlived its utility and had to be totally upgraded. Reputed foreign project consulting firms came up with a best estimate of 210 days and a cost of Rs. 5 billion. The Blast Furnace is a set of equipment that forms the heart of any integrated steel plant. The impact of delay in executing such a project is several millions of rupees for the company. Based on Singh's recommendation, the board approved a shut-down period of 155 days, but the team came up with a target of 110 days for the completion at a cost of Rs. 2.1 billion. The foreign consultants felt that this was not a practical target even by western standards.

By the time the Blast Furnace–F project was conceived, Singh had already established his reputation in the company. Singh had earned what Pinchot (1985) termed as 'intra capital' where the intrapreneur earns the right to dream with a heroic vision. After the successful implementation of the CRM and Blast Furnace-F revamp projects, the project management activities at Tata Steel had got into a virtuous cycle. Blast Furnace-G furnace was three times the size of the Blast Furnace-F and the target completion time for this revamp was set at 95 days and the project was completed within this target.

Innovations at the Merchant Mill

We can also disscuss the other innovative venture of Tata Steel, because innovation becomes a necessity for sheer survival. When Nandji Pandey took over as the chief of Merchant Mill (MM) at Tata Steel in 1997, the worker morale was low and the plant that was over 40 years old was in a rundown condition. MM was not on the priority list of the company, through the nineties, the company had launched a major modernisation programme (Seshadri and Tripathy, 2006). As a result, all unviable plants were getting progressively phased out. The company had two Rolling Mills, RM1 and RM2, which supplied feedstock in the form of 75 mm square billets to the finishing plants in the company including to the MM. MM converted these billets into steel rods for construction. RM2 was too far from MM and it was logistically very difficult to supply billets from RM2 to MM. RM1 had to be closed down because it was very old and rundown. The only other source of billets was the Continuous Caster (CC) that produced billets with a square cross-section in two sizes, 100 mm and 127 mm. The foreign collaborators and equipment suppliers who installed MM were consulted regarding the possibility of using 100 mm or 127 mm square billets as raw material for MM. They made it clear that the design of MM would not allow the use of such large-sized billets in the place of the 75 mm square billets for which it was designed. The top management saw no merit in making any further capital investments for a rundown plant like MM. The foreign consultants, therefore, suggested that there was no alternative but to close down the MM and sell off the assets.

As the prospective buyer was being taken around the plant, Pandey informed him that the plant was not for sale and that his team would make it profitable. Pandey set about motivating his team, encouraging them to come up with their best ideas so that they could run the plant using the larger square billets in place of the earlier 75 mm billets without additional capital expenditure. The team came up with several ideas and for a systematic implementation and whatever minor investments were needed, these came from the revenue budget of the mill. The steps taken included frequent and thorough maintenance, changing the design of the hydraulic pushers to take care of the large-sized billets, changing entry and exit guides to the furnace, improving mixing of fuel gas and air in the burners to create better swirling effect and improving the material handling and logistics on the plant. There was a change in the mindset of the workforce, a can-do attitude being imparted into them. The average production of the MM plant was in the range of 300 to 500 tonne per day for several years before Pandey took over. Owing to the many steps taken by him to motivate his team, the production by December 1997 reached 1,300 tonne per day. This was a major turning point for MM and demonstrated the mill that with focus, determination and teamwork, it was possible to make it economically viable. In the case of MM, necessity had literally become the mother of reinvention.

The objective of innovation was to bring in higher volumes without incurring significant incremental investments. This prompted the top management to comment that the capacity of a plant is only in the minds of the people running them and not on the name plate of the plant. The key to the successful turnaround of MM was the vision of the intrapreneur as well as his ability to mobilise the entire team of 400 dispirited workers to rise up to the challenge and work towards turning around the plant by working in an entrepreneurial mode. MM has achieved record production levels crossing 300,000 tonne per annum in the early 2000s, up from about 95,000 tonnes in 1995.

Indian Steel Wire Products Ltd, Jamshedpur was earlier closed for over eight years. Recently, through a court order, it was transferred to Tata Steel as its wholly-owned subsidiary. Pandey's intrapreneurial efforts have borne fruit in this plant also and within a short period of takeover of the company by Tata Steel, it achieved its rated capacity. Whenever there was any significant achievement by anyone in the plant, he made it a point to acknowledge the contribution of the workers who made it possible. For any record that was broken, he would ensure that the achievement was genuinely celebrated through various means such as distribution of sweets to the entire team.

Apart from a face-to-face communication with the workforce, Pandey would also send written messages in Hindi to each one of the members of his team. He also involved the wives of the workers to provide the emotional support to their husbands to achieve higher targets. In this manner, the targets became targets not only for the MM team but also for the families of the workforce. Pandey's intrapreneurial skills lay in making workers closer to the machines, who intimately knew the equipments to innovate in many ways in the rebirth of the mill. When the top management sent messages congratulating him on the progress being made in the plant, he would ensure that individual copies of these messages were given to every member of his team (Seshadri and Tripathy, 2006).

Resource constraints and time pressures would bring out the best in intrapreneurial activities, wherein freedom to induct or remove any member of the team and freedom to select suppliers becomes crucial. This is what Hamel (2002) refers to as an open market for talent. The management needs to recognise, mentor and encourage persons who demonstrate intrapreneurial traits. The management's inconsistent, intermittent or lack of commitment can decimate the intrapreneurial spirit of the employees. Also, a high manpower turnover due to poor human resource policy or a rigid approach by the top management can hurt the intrapreneurial process. Some companies simply lack the courage to accept failures and instead penalise employees for failures. The case of Tata Steel, as a lead goose and the leadership of entrepreneurs like Singh and Pandey provide ample evidence to the contribution of intrapreneurship in rejuvenation of rundown plants.

3.7 Conclusion

The experiences of Korea and India show that entrepreneurial activity can flourish under different circumstances, but each country exhibits differences in terms of access to information, privacy rights and the role of the state. The Korean experience demonstrates the support of the government in private entrepreneurial development towards achieving technopreneurship. Indian business owners on the other hand thrive independently, rarely interacting with government, enmeshed in many bureaucratic procedures. India is a hierarchical society, based on a caste system that dictates status with very little social mobility. However, it is governed by a democratic system that fosters entrepreneurial activity and conflict resolution that tend be decided in favour of private rights, as has been shown by the iron and steel industry case.

India's strong entrepreneurial position is reinforced by the Global Entrepreneurship Monitor report (Sala-I-Martin et al, 2011) of non-entrepreneurial adults, in which the Indian population exhibits higher perceived entrepreneurial opportunities and capabilities, resulting in higher entrepreneurial intentions and eventually higher potential entrepreneurial activity than the Chinese. Entrepreneurial performance may be a subjective concept, depending on the nature of personal expectations, aspiration levels and skills of the individual entrepreneur. While this type of focus may throw some light on personality and traits of entrepreneurs in general, their performance as evidenced by the above profile of Tata entrepreneurs prompts consideration in terms of the number and proportion of successful new enterprises that are established, following their lead.

4

The Emergence of Indian Information Technology Industry

4.1 Introduction

Porter (1990) lists four major factors that contribute to the success of a country in terms of utilisation of resources towards achieving competitive advantage. They are demand and factor conditions, presence or absence of supporting suppliers and the degree of rivalry in the domestic market. Also considered are firm's structure, strategy and the degree of state influence. Porter contends that competitive enterprises can exist as part of a cluster of related industries, and countries that lack natural endowments will invest in the generation of factors like education, training of workforce and improvements in communication systems. India's information technology (IT) sector, another lead goose is an apt example appropriating Porter's demand and factor conditionalities and in establishing competitive advantage in the world market, especially when global economic activity is driven by pervasive information and communication challenges. In this, new market provides many opportunities in making available financial support by both official and private sources and facilitating public-private partnership programmes, besides evolving private sector initiatives for supporting knowledge-intensive entrepreneurship. The *keiretsu* system in Japan and *chaebols* in Korea are examples of highly developed conglomerates with interlocking ownerships and business partnerships that developed in this manner. In addition to minimisation of risk and improved sources of funding, interlocking businesses provide a source of informal information flow, access to a broader pool of skills and resources and when well implemented, a brand name that can be leveraged across all businesses. This chapter explains software development in India, besides presenting the growth of Bangalore and Hyderabad, showcasing the examples of IT services firms like Tata Consultancy Services, Infosys, Wipro, Mahindra Satyam and Hindustan.

4.2 Software Development in India

According to Arora et al (2001), in necessity entrepreneurship, an individual becomes an entrepreneur because there is no other option, whereas opportunity entrepreneurship is an active choice to start a new enterprise based on the perception that an unexploited or underexploited business opportunity exists. Necessity entrepreneurship has little or no effect on economic growth while opportunity entrepreneurship has a positive effect. Software services industry is an example of the latter type. Indian software industry has had a phenomenal growth in recent times, owing to global outsourcing on the one hand and the availability of local knowledge base to exploit the new digital technology. A large section of the domestic software industry consists of resale of software packages developed by the US firms overstating the extent of software available for the domestic market. However, there exists in-house software written by users and many software firms have developed software packages aimed at the domestic market. It may be that weak intellectual property rights are responsible for the failure of Indian firms to develop successful global packages, besides lack of experience in design and marketing. Hence, the activities carried out are essentially maintenance tasks for applications on legacy systems such as IBM mainframe computers, development of small applications and enhancements for existing systems or migration to client-server systems through re-engineering.

Software exports can be divided into three categories based on where the software is developed and how the development is managed and organised (Bala Subramanya, 2007). The first category is onsite consultancy or onsite projects, where the Indian company provides the foreign client software professionals with the particular technical skills asked for. These skills could vary from mainframe related software to specialist expertise in UNIX and WinNT platforms with

JAVA programming skills. The second category of exports has a combination of offshore as well as onsite jobs, wherein the Indian company sends its software professionals to the client's site for requirement analysis or training in a particular system. These professionals then bring back to India the specifications for the software and a larger team develops the offshore software. If the project is large, a couple of Indian professionals remain at the client's site acting as liaisons between the project leaders offshore and the clients. To execute such projects, a firm needs not only skilled professionals, but also a software development process and methodology and an ability to manage software development. Unlike in onsite projects, in offshore ventures, the Indian firm provides technical and managerial expertise as well. The third avenue of software export is in the form of an Offshore Development Centre (ODC). An ODC is an organisational firm established especially for firms based in the US and Europe and for those who like to take advantage of the skilled talent pool and lower wages in India (Bala Subramanya, 2007). The ODC involves an umbrella contract with a long-term agreement on prices for time and materials (usually standardised on a man-hour basis). In this, a large fraction of the project is executed offshore and the Indian firm is responsible for adherence to schedules for delivery.

Software exports from India have grown from $330 million in 1993 to $17.3 billion in 2006, employing around 878,000 professionals (Athreye, 2010). In 2001, entrepreneurial firms accounted for about 38 per cent of sales revenues and 35 per cent of employment in the Indian software outsourcing sector (Athreye, 2005).The share of software industry has been 6.7 per cent of GDP and its share in total exports is about 18 per cent (NASSCOM, 2010).The industry exported 77.5 per cent of its output of software and services during 2008, indicating its heavy reliance on the world market. The US is India's principal market and absorbs about two-thirds of IT exports. However, the dependency ratio (the ratio of the region's share of India's exports to the region's share of world IT services) for North America was 1.4, indicating India's asymmetric relationship with the US (Athreye, 2005). In contrast, the second largest IT market in the world, Japan absorbed only two per cent of India's IT exports, due to lack of diversity in product and service markets and missed learning opportunities by not serving technologically complex markets such as Japan, known for its production engineering and its electronics industry, which demand embedded software going into products such as automobiles.

Japan's total IT market in 2006 was $146 billion (Japan Information Technology Services Industry Association, 2008) but India had a very small share of it, indicating limited engagement of India in the high-value Japanese market. India specializes in customised software and Japan's largest IT segment is customised software services.

India's presence in countries like Japan is weak owing to the attractive US market, closed subcontracting and business practices in Japan, unfamiliar Japanese cultural and language requirements and vice versa, India's technological shortcomings in hardware and Japanese reluctance to conduct international outsourcing in general due to high transactions costs (D'Costa, 2008).The American pull can be seen from the substantial number of IT professionals hired by the US companies. More than one lakh Indian students go to the USA to study annually, the highest number for any country, providing not only billions of dollars in revenues to educational institutions but also highly trained professionals as a sizeable number stay in the USA. In the recruitment of IT professionals with employer-sponsored H-1B visas given out to non-US residents, in 2005, India secured 48 per cent of all H-1B visas, of which 40 per cent was granted to Indians were for the IT industry. According to the US Government Accountability Office, between 2000 and 2009, 46.9 per cent of the total approved H-1B visa holders had India as their country of birth. In L1 visas used by multinational companies to bring staff from subsidiaries to their US parent firm or branches, Indians have become prominent, increasing from 4.4 per cent in 1997 to 43.8 per cent in 2006 (US Department of State, 2009).

The basic outsourced business services was established in the 1970s, resulting in a new form of the model adopted in the 1990s when the offshore content of onsite delivery began to slowly increase. As prices of telecommunications access declined, the offshoring of work became steadily cheaper, utilising the large educated labour force towards a well-established division of labour in software teams due to large scale of operations. With financial liberalisation of the economy, software companies realised advantages of operating in a global market. For example, being an entrepreneurial firm, Infosys was vulnerable to periods of capital scarcity and to keep the potential of future growth, it was the first to leverage its reputation to enter international markets like NASDAQ and the New York Stock Exchange to attract new US customers. In this, the IT service providers had to adhere to corporate norms of US firms like use of more transparent accounting practices and the use of employee stock options to avoid attrition of their staff. Later, another component of the offshore model (application of the software services delivery model to administrative functions of companies) also became institutionalised (Bala Subramanya, 2007).

According to Chaminade and Vang (2008), in respect of competence building, the content of work consisted of multinationals outsource specific tasks to the indigenous SMEs, wherein the former will be responsible for assembling the different modules into the final product. Competitiveness of the local SMEs is mainly based on costs. In the next innovation stage, indigenous firms start providing final products to specific market niches. In some cases, cooperation between SMEs is needed to combine complementary competences. Indigenous firms start using their integration skills, integrating modules, developed by different companies. The focus is on the accumulation of technical human capital and after that, for new skills that are needed beyond technical skills, indigenous firms have to integrate different modules into the final product. As regards social capital, the main linkages are those established between the MNC and the local indigenous company. Social capital is relevant in the innovation stage, where it plays a crucial role stimulating and supporting interactive learning amongst the indigenous SMEs. A new set of horizontal relationships emerge, both formal and informal, particularly in embedded software (Chaminade, 2004) in relation to entrepreneurship. Here, the search and access of new market niches requires strong entrepreneurial services and entrepreneurship is increasingly embedded in software. In the non-innovation stage, the majority of indigenous SMEs do not have direct access to international markets. Their customer is the MNC who sets the standards of the product and has the contacts with the final customers. In the second stage, the direct access to the final customer becomes critical. Local markets can stimulate innovation in the indigenous companies. In this sense, public procurement could be a good instrument to stimulate the SMEs to use their competencies and create incentives for investing more in them. The focus of MNCs in the first stage is direct access to the final customer and public procurement could be a good instrument to stimulate the SMEs to use their competencies and create incentives for investing more in them. In the next stage, SMEs and MNCs could collaborate in the provision of R&D services and traded externalities leading to spillovers and offshore R&D labs and untraded spillovers.

Transnational commitments are crucial in the competence building stage since they contribute to the development of the regional innovation system and the indigenous SMEs by reducing institutional distance which in turn reduces transaction costs. They become relevant in the innovation stage as they reduce the institutional distance and facilitate the direct access of the indigenous firms to the final markets (Chaminade and Vang, 2008).The entrepreneurial software companies tend to be established by technically trained entrepreneurs. They are transparent regarding their operations and performance and all the firms operate in technology-intensive industries, being highly integrated with the global economy. Exports of these enterprises range between 30 to 95 per cent of total sales. Notwithstanding phenomenal increases in venture capital funding, most Indian companies still finance their growth and expansion through internal resources. Another factor is the availability of technically trained personnel including those trained abroad and those willing to return to homeland to start technical ventures.

Enterprises in information technology, biotechnology and aerospace industries have emerged due to the growth of knowledge-intensive entrepreneurship. The first known case of a software product from India was from Tata Consultancy Services (TCS), a subsidiary of Tatas. TCS had always paid attention to instruments in software writing and utilised the opportunity to sell some of these tools as products. Case Packet was launched to good reviews in the technology business press and retailed for about $200,000. Though TCS proved very capable of making products, it did not create the product market. TCS invested in training engineers to learn software languages and management skills and responded to changing technologies by negotiating with the government to exploit new opportunities. In choosing the outsourcing path, the company recognised the potential advantages towards technology upgradation, and in 1975 partnered exclusively with Burroughs in this regard.

A more recent trend is R&D outsourcing in the telecommunication sector. The offshore delivery model has utilised India's advantage of a large and educated labour force, while at the same time making use of development in technologies and advantages of global market for emerging services. The model focuses on improving entrepreneurial energies along a narrow path of proven success. In the mid-1980s, the installed capacity of personal computers increased and companies like Sonata and Mastek introduced software products aimed at the domestic market. Sonata tried to develop software products while Mastek became the first company to use tools to speed up product development for domestic market. However, these product ventures have failed due to the small domestic market and weak intellectual property protection laws (Chaminade and Vang, 2008).

The lack of venture capital support also made the product model a very risky one for entrepreneurial firms to adopt due to the high up-front investment. The stimulus was the spread of distributed computing and the opportunity to write products previously constructed for mainframes around the new technology platform of local area network and interlinked computers. Ramco tried to develop an enterprise resource planning product and CITIL (a spin-off of Citibank, COSL) developed a financial product Flexcube on a pre-existing market product called COSMOS. Subsequently, COSL acquired the full IP rights for the package. Ramco's product Marshall was overtaken by solutions by SAP and other enterprise resource planning producers. It took a long time for the company to produce the basic software infrastructure required for a successful product. While having been in the market longer, SAP was able to transfer to another technology platform quite easily. Ramco Virtual Works Flexcube has emerged as the most successful product developed from India, although its ownership has been changing (Athreye, 2010).

The adoption of tighter intellectual property rights norms in 1995 gave rise to new products in embedded software. Many telecom firms like Texas Instruments, Motorola and Nortel have sourced their research on digital signal processing chips in India resulting in spin-off firms. Two examples are Sasken (previously a joint venture with Nortel) and Ittiam, which hold patents and aim to earn revenues largely through licensing to large firms. Sasken combines outsourced R&D services with licensing and this gives the firm stable cash flows and the ability to develop. Ittiam operates a pure product model and has been endowed with venture capital financing from Silicon Valley venture capitalists. It had filed for 11 patents in the first four years of its existence and the chips are licensed to many client firms.

It may be pointed out that capital market institutions did not understand how to evaluate the financial needs of the emerging software industry. Infosys was refused a bank loan when it was set up in 1981 and had to borrow the start-up money from the wife of one of the founders. Faced with a situation where bank finance was not readily available and venture capital was not forthcoming, software firms were conservative in their cash flow calculations, but experimented with stock exchanges in the USA and in Europe with strict disclosure norms in order to raise money for investments and acquisitions. The compliance of firms to international norms was a means towards improved corporate governance. However, the combined effects of liberalisation and the success of the software industry attracted US venture capital into India after 1993. Dossani and Kenney (2002) show that a significant portion of the increase in funds from 1993-98 was accounted for by the entry of foreign investors after 1995 through investment divisions of foreign banks and venture firms.

Indian Silicon Valley entrepreneurs have encouraged new business plans within India and exploited the new exit routes made possible by the international listings of Indian software companies on foreign stock exchanges. Domestic and foreign venture capitalists invested $774 million in 2003 in India up from $590 million in 2002 (Basu, 2006). An important organ established towards institutional reform has been the National Association of Software and Services Companies (NASSCOM), set up in 1988 with 38 members who collectively accounted for 65 per cent of the industry revenues. Many of these members were small enterprises and the total industry revenue reported according to the Association in 1988 was about $100 million. By 2003-04, the number of members had risen to more than 800, collectively accounting for about 95 per cent of the industry output of $21 billion. NASSCOM operates as a collective body, representing the interests of the software sector with functions of lobbying, advocacy and public relations. The Association has been effective in lobbying for policies favourable to the software industry's continued growth, advocating collective marketing at a time when Indian companies did not have an international reputation for delivering quality service, besides providing information about the industry for both insiders and outsiders. The employment growth of the firms is high and these are efficient in the utilisation of capital for the most productive uses.

The emergence of third party BPO activities in India led by firms such as EXL Services, 24/7, Spectramind, Dakshe-Services and Transworks, which received venture capital funding for their seed capital, has impacted on manufacturing, health care, banking and financial services, pharmaceuticals, engineering and textiles besides others (Athreye, 2010). There is a gradual convergence towards the US model of venture capital institutions, which was initiated and aided by the diaspora of technology entrepreneurs and their Silicon Valley partners. The NASSCOM model of industry-government interaction has been adopted by new sectors relying on domestic entrepreneurship. Examples include the interactions by Association of Biotechnology Led Enterprises and the Automotive Component Manufacturers Association. Offshoring of administrative and technical work mainly involves investments in manpower, office space and infrastructure for communications and data. These investments may be significant but they are in comparison not large and therefore allow firms a much higher degree of flexibility in finding the right offshoring business model (UNCTAD, 2004). This means that services offshoring processes are subject to path dependency than manufacturing offshoring processes, the latter usually involves rather simple tasks and production processes (Andersen, 2008). Very little of this type of offshoring will be subject to the commoditisation and standardisation in the industrialised information chain. Further, the advanced nature of entrepreneurial tasks would demand a process of knowledge transfer from home to host company and vice versa which is fundamentally different from offshoring of manufacturing.

Firms in India largely rely on internal sources and debt capital rather than equity for financing their long-term investment goals. Within the external source of finance, bank borrowings are more important. While this pattern of financing by internal sources may be important for existing companies, new companies may have to depend on external sources. For this, the emergence and growth of the private equity market and the venture capital funding is essential. Athreye (2010) shows that over 70 per cent of the entrepreneurs relied on personal savings for their initial funding needs and about 40 per cent of them continue to rely on the same personal sources for their additional funding, while external sources of bank loans, venture capital and angel investors become very important for expansion of the further scale of operations.

It is interesting to note that equity capital is conspicuous by its absence as a source of funding even at the expansion stage. Both venture capital and angel investing become market-based solutions in the financing of knowledge-intensive entrepreneurship. Venture capital focuses on investing in private, young and fast growing companies, while buyout and mezzanine investing focus on investing in mature companies. Innovative business ideas get their funding from angel investors. If and when their business model works and the enterprises are ready for growth, they approach venture capitalists who usually invest in the company in return for an equity stake. Angels invest their personal wealth as opposed to venture capitalists who mostly work as fund managers. To institutionalise this process of channelling of funding from high net worth individuals to technology-oriented start-ups, the Indian Angel Network was founded in 2006. A typical investment in a start-up is in the range of Rs. one to five million and the exit duration is usually between four to seven years. The returns can vary from 400 per cent to even zero if the investment goes bad. Many enterprises in both developing and developed economies are leveraging e-commerce models as a way to cut overhead costs and increase efficiency. Furthermore, economic progress is becoming increasingly knowledge and information infrastructure and knowledge assets are rapidly becoming wealth creating assets for many developing countries such as India, China and Indonesia. Advancements in e-commerce capabilities, coupled with IT knowledge, have enabled developing countries to build up their competencies in IT technology, besides export success of e-services.

4.3 The Government Initiatives

There are a number of government programmes and institutional arrangements that encourage technology-based entrepreneurship like the Knowledge Commission, which has been set up to encourage innovative entrepreneurship in many sectors. The information about various institutions has been adapted from different websites. The establishment of the National Science and Technology Entrepreneurship Development Board (NSTEDB) in 1982 was an institutional mechanism, with the objective of promoting gainful self-employment among the science and technology manpower in the country and to encourage establishment of knowledge-based and innovation-driven enterprises. The NSTEDB has two major responsibilities of establishing technology parks and incubators for nurturing already existing entrepreneurs. It organises a series of training programmes to initiate freshly graduated engineers and other technically qualified students to learn the basics of entrepreneurship.

Another important programme to facilitate knowledge-intensive entrepreneurship is the Technopreneur Promotion Programme (TePP), launched in 1998 to realise the innovative potential of the entrepreneurs. A major objective of TePP has been to transform individual innovators into technopreneurs. TePP support is provided for in all areas except software development for which there are other avenues of support. It helps the inventors to identify and network with an appropriate R&D or academic institution for guidance, technical consultancy and development of models and prototypes, besides assisting in for filing and securing of intellectual property rights and linking with appropriate source of finances. TePP provides financial support of up to Rs.1 million as a grant-in-aid to promote the idea and a similar amount for the second phase for commercialisation. Technology Innovation Management and Entrepreneurship Information Service (TIME IS), a joint project of NSTEDB, DST and FICCI strives to enhance the entrepreneurial capability and has taken initiatives to provide guidance and assistance to technopreneurs to find technologies, projects, funding options and information about policy environment, incentive schemes and industrial infrastructure. TIME IS facilitates entrepreneurs with online interactive tools and templates for developing project profile, feasibility reports and calculating financial and profitability ratios. The DST-Lockheed Martin India Innovation Growth Programme is a two-year, nation-wide project, created to enhance the growth and development of India's entrepreneurial economy. The programme is wholly funded by Lockheed Martin Corporation and was developed with the assistance of University of Texas and FICCI. Its overall goal is to accelerate the launch of early-stage technologies into the global market place.

Business incubation is a relatively new concept in India and unlike in other BRICS countries such as Brazil or China, the concept is not well developed as a support system for engineering technology-based entrepreneurs. Many incubators are spread throughout the country, into three types depending upon the physical location and ownership, under the aegis of leading institutions of engineering technology and management (IIMs and IITs) or within the Science and Technology Parks or by leading private sector enterprises such as Nirmalabs. The incubation idea has received encouragement, when NSTEDB decided to create an incubation fund with an initial corpus of Rs. 50 million to facilitate the development of entrepreneurship in knowledge-based businesses. The fund is for bridging the financial needs of technology-based entrepreneurs between the time the business venture is floated and the time to attract venture funding.

The TiE network (The Indus Entrepreneurs, established in Silicon Valley in 1992) and the Wadhwani Foundation promote entrepreneurship by organising workshops and seminars nationally and fund various entrepreneurship education-related projects like the National Entrepreneurship Network (NEN). TiE is a network of entrepreneurs, professionals and venture capitalists active in technology-related sectors and has over 10,000 members in nine countries. Every year TiE holds a conference in Silicon Valley attended by numerous stakeholders from the IT industry. Although TiE is not directly involved in funding enterprises, it provides important mentoring services to its affiliates and help would-be entrepreneurs in preparation of business plans, fund raising and strategic guidance. NEN, in encouraging young entrepreneurs towards technology-based entrepreneurship, conducts Entrepreneurship Week India, focuses on public attention on today's biggest opportunities and encourages participants to reflect on their role as leaders and innovators. E-Week's activities are led by NEN members, academic institutions and NEN student entrepreneurship clubs (E Cells).

4.4 Recent Developments in the IT Sector

In India, the pioneering pathway in being a business leader has been made possible by the information technology revolution. The case of Infosys, a global provider of IT consulting and services, is a good example. Murthy led its exponential growth, totalling over $2 billion in annual revenues. Murthy is one of many Indian entrepreneurs who successfully exploited information technology and the internet to establish world class business, amass huge personal fortunes and create well-paid jobs for young and well-trained Indians. Others like Wipro Technologies have become large software companies and the world's largest providers of research and development services. This development was made possible by a convergence of three factors. The first was the emergence of India's technical manpower, which combined with low wages, established a favourable competitive advantage. The second factor was that the licence raj, the system of licences and regulations that were required to set up businesses in India until 1990, which discouraged entrepreneurs since independence, had not anticipated the emergence of the IT industry. The third factor was the emergence of the internet, which became the acclaimed path for India's IT exports. Within a decade, IT service exports grew from virtually nothing to more than $40 billion a year. Service exports have also increased from basic services such as call centres to increasingly sophisticated business process outsourcing. This industry, while building personal fortunes for the successful pioneers, has also become the standard path to affluence for young and well-educated workforce.

In contrast with their Chinese counterparts, most of the Indian business leaders who have come through the pioneering pathway in the IT industry are well educated, technologically savvy and have had some exposure to international business dealings. These companies form the professional pathway for a whole new generation to lead businesses. However, corporate leadership challenges in the India and China are very different (Wong et al, 2005). This is largely because the three pathways function very differently and have influences on emerging business leaders, moulding them to evaluate their strengths and weaknesses as opportunities. Therefore, meeting the challenges of corporate leadership has to begin with an understanding these pathways and their impact. The Tata group, after being refused entry to a hotel reserved for the British in Bombay, built the legendary Taj Mahal Hotel on the water front of that city. Ratan Tata began to professionalize management and moved to invest in the booming IT sector by launching Tata Consultancy Services (TCS), which has since become a global leader in computer software and services. Active overseas, TCS is a leading investor in China's IT sector and an ambitious multibillion dollar plan to invest in Bangladesh was unveiled in 2005. Seizing opportunities opened by economic reform in the 1990s, the Tata group has expanded into financial services to take advantage of rising domestic purchasing power.

The success of the Indian software industry (the lead goose) can be attributed to factors on both the demand and supply sides. Globally, large corporations are under pressure to reduce their costs and yet exploit the potential benefits of advances in information technology. They have moved toward operating models that allow them to concentrate on areas of their core competence and outsource other activities. Indian software companies built on a strong human resource base to create organisational processes to quickly absorb new technologies and improve internal delivery capabilities in a short time to meet customer requirements, at the same time ensuring on-time delivery at an acceptable level of quality. Using cost arbitrage as an entry strategy in an emerging business, they opportunistically expanded their business, building more sophisticated organisational capabilities (Athreye, 2002). Their growth was facilitated by the fact that the software services model would not involve irreversible commitments on specialised resources and that the basic skills required would be fairly generic (Krishnan et al, 2003). The persistent gap between demand and supply allowed for greater experimentation by firms to find the right business model and also prevented a downward spiral in rates (Athreye, 2002).While it cannot be claimed that the software industry is a policy-driven success, it played an important role in the 1990s through the exemption of software industry export profits from income tax and the setting up of Software Technology Parks that allowed companies to have the regulatory benefits of an export promotion zone irrespective of their location. The early employees of the software industry came from scientific research organisations and some public sector enterprises that had good computer infrastructure such as Hindustan Aeronautics or Bharat Electronics. This was due to the fact that these organisations were the ones that had an installed base of state-of-art computers and therefore also had employees who were skilled at working on computers. Subsequently, as the number of computers in the economy grew and so did the number of formal education training programmes, the need for those from the laboratories declined. Companies also created their own training programmes to convert raw engineers into programmers. Though when compared to manufacturing, software development has limited spillovers to the rest of the economy (Arora and Athreye, 2002), its growth has had a number of indirect benefits to the Indian economy.

Software companies were among the first companies to raise capital internationally and to be listed on foreign stock exchanges. They set new standards for corporate governance, adopting US GAAP and became benchmarks for disclosures. They also introduced US-style employee ownership plans (through the creation of stock options) to the Indian corporate environment. Compared to traditional Indian organisations, they are more egalitarian and less hierarchical. Indian software companies also succeeded in converting the made-in India label from a liability to a source of competitive advantage. This has enabled the creation of an IT-enabled services industry centred on business process outsourcing, call centres and other remotely-provided services. This reputation also facilitated the movement of higher-end R&D services like chip design and engineering services to India and some MNCs have also started locating multi-disciplinary research and development centres in India. Prominent among the latter is the

John F. Welch Technology Centre set up by General Electric in Bangalore. Indian software companies have also provided role models for entrepreneurship. Three out of the top five software companies were started after 1980 by individuals who were not from Indian business families. They have, therefore, communicated a message that there is no need of a family business background to be successful in business. Their success and the status enjoyed by their founders have attracted many persons to start new ventures. The maximum impact of this could be seen during the dot.com boom. The software industry has made direct contributions to local governance and the Bangalore Agenda Task Force, an industry-government joint initiative develops the city's urban infrastructure and private foundations have created civic facilities and spread primary education.

The software industry also attracted international venture capital to India and has been responsible for annual flows of more than $1 billion. About 70 per cent of the venture capital coming in to India is estimated to have gone to the software industry (Nigam, 2001). The software industry has used its influence to play a role in creating policy changes such as changing the norms for venture capital, international listing and the acquisition of companies outside India. The software services sector has attracted India's best talent and spurred a tremendous growth of technical education, much of it in the private sector. A sizeable computer and software training industry has also evolved in the shadow of the software industry. The software industry has created more than half a million jobs in addition to providing an entry to hundreds of software professionals to immigrate to the United States. The software industry, with its strong export orientation, has developed limited links with the local manufacturing industry. This is partly a result of the fact that export contracts are much more lucrative for the software industry. However, it is also a result of the limited sophistication of the Indian manufacturing sector's information technology infrastructure. The high cost of domestic telecommunications services (until the recent decline in the wake of telecom industry deregulation) and the low penetration of the internet have also prevented manufacturing companies from taking the benefit of networking their IT infrastructure.

4.5 Bangalore, the IT Hub of India

Software sector is human capital intensive in its production process, when compared to other industries (Balasubramanyam and

Balasubramanyam, 2010). According NASSCOM-Deloitte (2008), India has an estimated share of 65 per cent of the global IT services offshoring segment and around 46 per cent of the global BPO market. Bangalore, the dominant software cluster is a major exporter of software services, with about 34 per cent of national exports in 2008-09 (Software Technology Parks of India, 2011). Bangalore software firms provide advanced IT services and some indigenous firms have started to outsource to other cheaper emerging clusters. In the initial phase many small new firms specialized in the provision of body-shopping services (sending software programmers to the clients to provide maintenance services). Over the years, Bangalore has achieved in promoting hi-tech industries in key sectors like electronics, telecommunication, information technology, precision engineering, automobiles, ready-made garments, biotechnology and food processing.

In 1985, an exclusive electronics city was established in Bangalore and the International Technology Park established later was co-financed by the state government of Karnataka. Bangalore has a range of public sector research and educational institutions (Indian Institute of Science, Indian Institute of Management and Indian Institute of Information Technology), public sector establishments (Indian Air Force and Indian Space Research Organisation) and hi-tech manufacturers (Hindustan Aeronautics, Bharat Electronics and Hindustan Machine Tools). The firms in the industry produce products like application software, system software and programming software, besides exploiting niche markets like software for banks, education institutions and hospitals.

Bangalore is recognised as one of the top ten technopolis and entrepreneurial hubs in the world (Athreye, 2010). It is the only global hub of technological innovation not only in India, but also in South Asia (UNDP, 2001). The availability of highly qualified human resources, along with the proximity of research institutions and hi-tech clusters, has been responsible for the emergence of the regional innovation system in Bangalore. Although the local interaction among the indigenous firms was almost absent, the SMEs developed strong linkages with the multinationals located in the region, particularly during the offshoring and outsourcing periods. The regional advantages provided by Bangalore explain the interest of the US firms in locating their outsource activities in the region. Employee attrition and wage increases has forced the firms to introduce human capital management and other advanced management techniques (Athreye, 2005). This, together with a tendency to codify procedures and improve the transfer of knowledge has increased the organisational capital of the firms and their absorptive capacity towards intrapreneurship.

International Business Machines (IBM) set up its subsidiary in India in 1951 to manufacture accounting machine plants in Mumbai. It soon started sourcing manpower from Bangalore and other locations through this organization. In 1970, the Indian government established a department of electronics, which was instrumental in formulating and implementing a new software export policy in 1972 aimed at providing incentives to firms exporting software services in the form of skilled manpower, besides encouraging investments in software services. However, a shift in the regulatory policy of the Indian government in the late 1970s meant that most foreign companies, including IBM left India, leaving unmet demand for IT products and services as well as a glut of engineering talent (Balasubramanyam and Balasubramanyam, 2010).

This problem ended when Texas Instruments (TI) opened a development centre in Bangalore in 1985 to leverage wage arbitrage and to take advantage of the available talent pool. While sourcing work to Indian service providers was in progress in Bangalore since 1970s, entry of TI with a lab that aimed to produce complete software products offshore sent a strong market signal. TI began with low level software requirements and over the years, began to develop complex R&D tasks, such as the design of the DSP chip. TI setup its own satellite link to improve communications with the US, which helped smaller firms in the region to utilise the excess bandwidth to communicate with clients in the US (Lateef, 1997). It provided the uses of satellite links and leased excess satellite capacity to companies like Wipro and Infosys. It was involved in curriculum development activities and funded laboratories, especially in the Indian Institute of Science, besides being involved in the starting up of Centre for Artificial Intelligence and Robotics, Defence Avionics Research Establishment and Centre for Airborne Systems (Athreye, 2005).

Bangalore became a cluster for scientific and knowledge-intensive activities and Indian employees in US-based companies provided connections or reassurances that led to outsourcing deals with Indian firms (Saxenian, 2006). Motorola established Motorola India Electronics Limited (MIEL), a software subsidiary in Bangalore. Despite the obvious cost advantages, no product division within

Motorola was willing to risk sourcing its software needs from MIEL. However, many multinational development centres were started by Indian managers working in the United States, while MNC centres (IBM, Google Labs, Hewlett Packard) were set up by Indian employees of the MNCs who returned to India and by Indians (Cisco, Oracle) with international management experience who had earlier managed similar projects. In addition to managerial expertise, the Indian diaspora also brought highly specialised skills and knowledge about US clients' practices, market players and technology advances to Bangalore (Balasubramanyam and Balasubramanyam, 2010).

The R&D centres in Bangalore that were engaged in high-level research (as opposed to product design and engineering), employed many US-trained researchers, most of them Indian returnees. In 2002, TI announced a collaborative R&D programme with Wipro, Infosys and Sasken to work on the GSM standard. This co-operation would probably have been impossible if TI had not been serving a captive parent market. Thus, the entry of MNCs grew rapidly throughout the 1990s and most IT companies continued to choose Bangalore for at least one of their subsidiaries. Oracle entered in 1994 and Analogue Devices in 1995, while Philips set up its Innovation Campus in 1996 and Cisco established a development centre in 1998, to be followed by Intel and Hewlett Packard in 1999. Based on general satisfaction and trust accorded to the work being done in India, MNCs began to locate full-fledged knowledge intensive R&D centres in Bangalore (Balasubramanyam and Balasubramanyam, 2010).

Catering to the need for higher-skilled computer scientists, the International Institute of Information Technology was established in 1999. In the late 1990s, demand for software engineers in the US and other industrialised countries increased because of Y2K (year 2000) problem. Many software programmers were hired to convert the date structure in various applications from a two-digit to a four-digit format. Bangalore continued to be a large source of labour during this time as local software engineers were known to be skilled at coding for legacy systems. By 1999, almost half of all engineering colleges and over half of all engineering students in India were located in the southern states. Several firms in the non-IT sector set up centres to develop embedded software for their products (General Motors Technical Centre in 2003 and ABB's IT Lab in 2002). IBM and Microsoft, which had already established Indian development centres, opened research centres in Bangalore in 2005. Other software and hardware companies like Bell Labs (Lucent-Alcatel), Cisco, DELL and Google set up subsidiaries between 2000 and 2007 (Balasubramanyam and Balasubramanyam, 2010).

As Bangalore's reputation grew and business practices were adapted to global standards, entry into its IT cluster became much easier for MNCs, which opened many centres in India by the end of 2006. During 2006-07, MNCs announced new investments of over $10 billion in the Indian IT and ITeS sectors (Balasubramanyam and Balasubramanyam, 2010). Cisco shifted many of its senior executives to the newly established east headquarter in Bangalore. This was achieved to complement government programmes and to reduce information asymmetry. There are different types of software companies ranging from product application to produce sophisticated programmes. Software firms tend to agglomerate in regions that are endowed with pools of trainable labour and required entrepreneurial capability. Factors that were crucial in the emergence of Bangalore as the Silicon Valley of India include the initiative of the Karnataka government in establishing a software technology park in 1977, later fortified by the Software Technology Parks Scheme of the central government, followed by the presence of a large number of science and engineering teaching and research institutions a large number of public enterprises. This was strengthened by the contribution of the Indian diaspora in the Silicon Valley in California and state support for infrastructure and the cultural ambience of Bangalore. There were also several hardware firms in the city, another proximate reason for software firms to flourish in the region. Bangalore has had a history of being host to many industries and another reason has been the availability of a large number of scientists and engineers (Balasubramanyam and Balasubramanyam, 2010). Bangalore is home to a number of firms manufacturing machine tools, electronic equipment and bio-technology products.

However, it has been observed that the links between universities and the software firms are weak because many academic institutions in Bangalore lack a tradition of research and are ill-equipped to be trouble shooters or partners of software firms (Balasubramanyam and Balasubramanyam, 2010). But they do perform a significant service for the software firms since they produce engineering graduates and act as a filter. They save the software firms considerable search costs. In fact, the engineering graduates who are successful in the interviews and tests administered by the software firms may be overqualified for the jobs they are initially required to do. Their academic training in mathematics and engineering may be much more extensive and advanced than that required by the software industry. Software firms like Infosys and Wipro provide the type of training the young graduates need. The cluster has evolved because of proximity of software firms to educational institutions in the city, besides the concentration of skilled labour, suppliers and information in the region.

4.6 The Hyderabad Experience

The state of Andhra Pradesh does not have a strong background and tradition of industrial development, like the neighbouring states of Karnataka and Tamil Nadu in terms of entrepreneurship, technical skills and infrastructure. During 1995-2004, the policy was shifted from the pursuit of equity-centred on the development of agriculture to one of growth-centred on IT. The software sector took birth mostly because of the zeal for spreading IT throughout the state. The World Bank provided $266 million per annum during the late nineties and the DFID provided another £230 million spread over three to four years. Such disbursements by external agencies directly to a state government by-passing the central government in Delhi, attests to the autonomy over policy of the then chief minister Chandrababu Naidu exercised, mostly because of the number of seats his party held in the Lok Sabha. Naidu managed to lure external investors such as Microsoft to establish research centres and a business school in Hyderabad, linked to Kellogg's Business School in the US. He bought the services of the international management consultants to prepare a document titled Vision 2020 outlining the policies to be put in place to promote the development of Andhra Pradesh. The consultants accorded information technology a major role in attaining his objective and he adopted the recommendations of the consultants. The incentives provided for investment in the IT sector included non-applicability of labour laws, non-applicability of pollution control laws and non-applicability of statutory power cuts. Some of the other incentives provided were allotment of land, power tariff rebate for small and medium enterprises, rebate on cost of land, physical infrastructure such as power, water, sewerage and roads and telecommunication infrastructure (Rao, 2008). Bangalore could not obtain much state support as was in the case of Hyderabad.

Hyderabad is known not only for its IT and IT-enabled Services, but also for pharmaceuticals and entertainment industries. Many call centres, business process outsourcing firms, dealing with IT and other technological services were set up in the 1990s making it the hub of BPO firms. Ramoji Film City, the largest film studio in the world is located on the outskirts of the hi-tech city. The progress of a township with state-of-art services called HITEC City encouraged several IT and ITeS companies to set up operations in the city. Hyderabad has also been referred to as the second Silicon Valley of India after Bangalore. There have been widespread investments in digital infrastructure, which include several multinational corporations having established centres. The city offers many software courses and has been selected as the location for India's first Fab City, a silicon chip developing facility, being setup with an investment of $3 billion by the AMD-Sem India syndicate. In Hyderabad, Gachibowli is one of the fastest growing IT hub consisting of Microsoft, Wipro, Infosys, Capegemini, Polaris, Bank of America, Franklin Templeton and others. Because of this development, Andhra Pradesh records for fourth largest revenue from IT exports, amounting to Rs. 240 crore, represent about 24 per cent of the total software exports. The software sector in Hyderabad has registered an impressive growth and its total exports of Rs. 325 billion in the year 2008-09 was surpassed only by Bangalore (Rs. 703 billion) and Maharashtra (Rs. 423 billion). According to NASSCOM (2008), Hyderabad scores over Bangalore and in fact over other software locations in the quality of its infrastructure. Whilst Hyderabad is ranked number one amongst the various locations of software firms in the country, Bangalore ranks number six. It is a known fact that the infrastructure in Bangalore, especially roads and power supply are inadequate. Software, however, is not a transport intensive service and most companies in Bangalore have instituted emergency power supply facilities. The issue has become one of the capabilities of a cluster in generating externalities and promoting human capital development, without dependence on state subsidies. The software sector in the two cities present a case wherein one has been founded and formed by entrepreneurs with a relatively low level of state support and the other with substantial state support. The number of migrants into Bangalore is relatively high and this is mostly due to the software sector. Bangalore has an advantage over Hyderabad in many other respects including the longstanding presence of a number of higher education institutions. The state's comparative advantage seems to rest in agro and science based industries such as pharmaceuticals than in services.

4.7 Information Technology Achievers

This section purports to brief a few of the information technology service providers, who have transformed India's global presence in the IT industry, namely TCS, Infosys, Wipro, Satyam and HCL, the information sourced from their and other websites.

Tata Consultancy Services: TCS is the largest provider of information technology in Asia and second largest provider of business process outsourcing services in India. TCS has offices in over 42 countries with more than 142 branches across the globe. One of its first assignments was to provide punched card services to a sister concern, Tata Steel (then TISCO). It later bagged the country's first software project, the Inter-Branch Reconciliation System for the Central Bank of India. It also provided bureau services to Unit Trust of India thus, becoming one of the first companies to offer BPO services. In the early 1970s, TCS began exporting its services and pioneered the global delivery model for IT services with its first offshore client in 1974. Its first international order came from Burroughs, one of the first business computer manufacturers. TCS was assigned to write code for the Burroughs machines for several US-based clients. This experience helped TCS bag its first onsite project, the Institutional Group and Information Company, a data centre for ten banks, which catered to two million customers in the US and assigned TCS the task of maintaining and upgrading its computer systems. In 1981, TCS set up India's first software research and development centre (Tata Research Development and Design Centre) in Pune. The first client-dedicated offshore development centre was set up for Compaq (then Tandem) in 1985.

In 1979, TCS delivered an electronic depository and trading system called SECOM for SegaInterSettle, Switzerland. It was a complex project undertaken by an Indian IT company. TCS followed this up with System X for the Canadian Depository System and also automated the Johannesburg Stock Exchange. It associated with a Swiss partner, TKS Teknosoft, which it later acquired. TCS pioneered the factory model for Y2K conversion and developed software tools which automated the conversion process and enabled third-party developers and clients to make use of it. In 1999, TCS saw outsourcing opportunity in e-commerce and related solutions and set up its e-business division. During 2005, TCS ventured into a new area for an Indian IT services company, Bioinformatics. In 2008, the company went through an internal restructuring and in 2011, it entered the small and medium enterprises market with cloud-based offerings. As a brand, TCS is the 76th Most Trusted Brand according to The Brand Trust report, 2011.

Faqir Chand Kohli started off as an engineer with Tata Power Company and rose through the ranks to become its deputy general manager. He was in control of TCS in 1969 and shaped its destiny. He was the first to talk about Tandem, first to import an IBM 3090, to maintain that mainframes are not dead and to question the openness of open systems before others. He continues to work on projects that spread computing in the country and in recent years has been focusing on hardware and microelectronics. He is regarded as the father of Indian software industry.

Beginning his career with TCS as a junior engineer, S Ramadorai rose through the ranks and eventually was charged with setting up TCS operations in the US in 1979 in New York, which has since grown to over 40 offices throughout that country. Since taking on the role once, Ramadorai focused his efforts on building relationships with large corporations and academic institutions, planning and directing technology development and acquisitions and overseeing the company's research and development activities. He has played a pioneering role in establishing Offshore Development Centres to provide high-end solutions to major corporations. Under his leadership, TCS set up Technology Excellence Centres that have acquired knowledge, expertise and equipment in specialised technology areas like IBM, SAP, AS400, DEC, HP, Microsoft, Silicon Graphics, Sun and Tandem. Recently, he led TCS in forging new alliances with the American International Group of Companies, Citibank, Microsoft, Oracle and widening existing relationships with banks and insurance companies. Ramadorai spearheaded TCS quality initiatives, taking sixteen of its Development Centres to Software Engineering Institute's CMM Level 5, the highest performance assessment. TCS also attained the distinction of being the World's first company to have all Centres assessed as operating at Level 5 of People-CMM.

Infosys: Infosys Limited, formerly known as Infosys Technologies Limited is a global services company headquartered in Bangalore and is the second largest IT concern with more than one lakh employees. Infosys is ranked 28th globally in the list of IT services provision. It has offices and development centres in 33 countries and offers software products for the banking industry (finacle) and business process management services, besides many end-to-end business solutions. According to Forbes magazine, sales and earnings of Infosys compounded at more than 70 per cent a year after its listing on the Bombay Stock Exchange in 1993. In 2000, President of the United States complimented India on its achievements in hi-tech areas citing the example of Infosys along with Wipro and Satyam Computers. Infosys invested $100 million on establishing a 20,000-seater campus in Shanghai. In 2001, it was rated Best Employer in India by Business India and as best employer to work for in 2000, 2001 and 2002 by AON. In 2007, Infosys received over 1.3 million applications and hired fewer than three per cent. Infosys was the only Indian company to win the Global Most Admired Knowledge Enterprises award for 2003, 2004 and 2005 and has been inducted into the Global Hall of Fame. In 1996, Infosys created the Infosys Foundation operating in the areas of health care, social rehabilitation and rural uplift, education, arts and culture.

Since 2004, Infosys has embarked on a series of initiatives to consolidate and formalise its academic relationships worldwide under the umbrella of AcE-Academic Entente. Its Global Internship Programme, known as InStep, is one of the key components of the Academic Entente initiative. It offers live projects to interns from the universities around the world. InStep recruits undergraduate, graduate and PhD students from business, technology and liberal arts universities to take part in an 8 to 24 week internship. InStep interns are provided career opportunities with Infosys. In 1997, Infosys started the 'Catch them Young Programme' to expose the urban youth to the world of information technology by conducting a summer vacation programme, aimed at developing an interest and understanding of computer science and information technology. In 2002, along with Wharton School of Business, it started Wharton Infosys Business Transformation Award, which recognises enterprises and individuals who have transformed many businesses, leveraging information technology. Infosys developed a corporate R&D wing called Software Engineering and Technology Labs (SET Labs) in 2000 to carry out applied research for the development of processes, frameworks and methodologies to effectively capture customer requirements and to iron out common critical issues during a project lifecycle.

Nagawara Ramarao Narayana Murthy acquired a degree in electrical engineering from Mysore University and later studied computer science at the IIT, Kanpur. The Infosys legend began in 1981 when Narayana Murthy dreamt of forming his own company, along with six friends. Though he did not have any seed money, his wife Sudha then an engineer with Tatas had saved Rs. 10,000. The second break came with the liberalization process in 1991. While working in France in the 1970s, Murthy was strongly influenced by socialism and it was his belief in the distribution of wealth that made Infosys one of the first Indian companies to offer employees stock-option plans. Infosys now has many employees who are dollar millionaires. Sudha Murthy heads the Infosys Foundation, which channels Rs. 50 million into charity every year. Infosys is the first Indian company to be listed on the NASDAQ.

Nandan Nilekani had been the chief executive officer and managing director of the Infosys and along with Narayan Murthy, was one of its co-founders. He has served as a director on the company's board since its inception in 1981. The study at IIT Mumbai transformed Nilekani from a small town boy to a confident mature man. After graduating in electrical engineering from IIT Mumbai in 1978, Nilekani joined Patni Computers, working under Narayan Murthy. Three years later in 1981, he along with Murthy and five others founded Infosys. While Murthy stayed in India, Nilekani shifted to the US to take care of its interests there. In 2006, he became one of the youngest entrepreneurs to join 20 global leaders on the prestigious World Economic Forum Foundation Board. He figures among one of the 100 most influential people in the world by Time Magazine. In 2005, he was awarded the prestigious Joseph Schumpeter prize for innovative services in field of economy, economic sciences and politics. In 2006, Nandan Nilekani was conferred the Padma Bhushan. He left Infosys in 2009 to serve as the chair of the Unique Identification Authority of India. He co-founded India's National Association of Software and Service Companies as well as the Bangalore Chapter of The IndUS Entrepreneurs.

Wipro: Wipro Technologies division was established in 1980 as a subsidiary of Wipro (Western Indian Palm Refined Oil). The company logo still contains a sunflower to reflect their original business. During 1970s and 1980s it shifted its focus and began to look into business opportunities in IT and computing industry. Wipro was the first company which marketed the first indigenous homemade

PC in 1975. It is headquartered in Bangalore and is the third largest IT services company and employs more than two lakh people worldwide. Wipro is ranked 31st globally in 2011 in the list of IT service providers. It is 9th most valuable brand in India according to an annual survey conducted by *Brand Finance* and *The Economic Times*. It provides outsourced research and development, infrastructure outsourcing, BPO and business consulting services. The company operates in IT services, IT products, consumer care and lighting. By 2000, Wipro Technologies emerged as the largest publicly listed software exporter in India and the first software services provider to be assessed at Level 5 in the world. Wipro won the Golden Peacock Innovative Service Award for effective service delivery using state-of-art technology in 2001.

Wipro was awarded SVG1, the highest rating in Stakeholder Value Creation and Governance Practices by ICRA. It was awarded the India Manufacturing Excellence Award for its factory in the large enterprises category by Frost and Sullivan and ASTD BEST Award for 2005 by the American Society of Training and Development. Wipro's Global Command Centre won the Marico Foundation and Business World's Innovation for India Award in 2006. The conglomerate was rated as the number one Network Integrator and number one Network Security Services Provider by Voice and Data Magazine. The majority of Wipro BPO business comes from the US, followed by Europe.

Azim Hashim Premji is chairman of Wipro Technologies and is an icon among Indian businessmen. Premji was studying electrical engineering in Stanford University when due to the sudden demise of his father; was called upon to handle the family business. He took over the control of his family business at 21. At the first annual general meeting of the company attended by him, a shareholder doubted Premji's ability to handle business at such a young age and publicly advised him to sell his shareholding and give it to a more mature management. Wipro dealt in hydrogenated cooking fats and later diversified to bakery fats, ethnic ingredient based toiletries, hair care soaps, baby toiletries, lighting products and hydraulic cylinders. Premji made a focused shift from soaps to software and today, it is the largest independent R&D service provider in the world. In 2000, *AsiaWeek* magazine voted Premji among the 20 most powerful men in the world. He was among the 50 richest persons in the world from 2001 to 2003 listed by Forbes. In April 2004, *Times* magazine rated him among the 100 most influential persons in the world. He has been honoured with a Padma Bhushan.

***Mahindra Satyam*:** Satyam Computer Services Limited was founded in 1987, later taken over by Mahindra. Mahindra Satyam offers consulting and information technology services to several sectors and is listed on the New York Stock Exchange, National Stock Exchange and Bombay Stock Exchange. In June 2009, the company unveiled its new brand identity Mahindra Satyam, subsequent to its takeover by Mahindra's IT arm, Tech Mahindra. Mahindra Satyam has offices in 32 countries and is ranked 17 in the list of IT service providers in India according to a study by Cyber Media's Dataquest Research in 2011. Ramalinga Raju was one of the pioneers of the Information Technology industry in India. He was the founder and chairman of Satyam Computer Services Ltd. Ramalinga Raju moved away from the traditional agriculture business and set up a spinning and weaving mill named Sri Satyam. Thereafter, he shifted to the real-estate business and started a construction company called Satyam Constructions. In 1987, he founded Satyam Computer Services along with his brother-in-law, DVS Raju.

With the launch of Satyam Infoway, Satyam became one of the first to enter Indian internet service market. Ramalinga Raju has won Ernst and Young Entrepreneur of the Year for Services award in 1999 and 2007, Dataquest IT Man of the Year in 2000, CNBC's Asian Business Leader and Corporate Citizen of the Year award in 2002. However, the ever-soaring share prices of Satyam witnessed a sharp decline in December 2008, following a failed acquisition attempt involving Maytas, a company owned by Raju's family. In January 2009, Raju resigned as the chairman of Satyam after he admitted to major financial wrong-doings and confessed of his involvement in inflating the profits of the company.

***Hindustan Computers Limited*:** HCL focuses on the global and domestic market and provides product engineering and R&D enterprise and custom applications, enterprise transformation services, infrastructure management and BPO services and has operations in 31 countries. HCL Infosystems, a listed subsidiary of HCL has a presence in 170 locations and 300 service centres throughout India. HCL Peripherals, founded in 1983, is a manufacturer of computer peripherals. Its enterprise response centre was started to give support to its customers in 2007. Shiv Nadar is the chief executive officer of HCL, India's largest infotech conglomerate. He figures in the Forbes list of Indian billionaires. Originally hailing from Tamil Nadu, Shiv Nadar moved to Delhi in 1968. He worked as an engineer with DCM Ltd. Along with six of his colleagues he launched a firm making office products like copiers. In late 1970s, when IBM quit India, Shiv Nadar's HCL stepped in to fill the vacuum. In 1982, HCL came out with its first computer. Today, HCL derives 80 per cent of its revenue from computers and office equipments. HCL has also been spreading its global reach. Its Singapore subsidiary, Far East Computers, achieved a breakthrough in imaging technology, which, among other applications, enables computers to read handwritten tax returns. HCL has adopted innovative practices to achieve growth. In the US, HCL America has reaped dividends by taking advantage of global time zones. Every morning, the company's Chennai office receives software assignments from the US, just after work stops there for the night. A team of Indian engineers complete the jobs and send them back in the evening.

4.8 Conclusion

India's achievement in the IT industry has been phenomenal and there are many reasons for the success of the Indian software industry. India has a good supply of scientists and engineers and many can be trained and encouraged to become entrepreneurs. This assumption is usually substantiated by invoking the gross enrolment the undergraduate degree programmes in engineering and architecture: the enrolment has increased from 7.08 lakh in 2002-03 to 16.68 lakh in 2005-06 (Ministry of Higher Education, 2008). Most of the successful entrepreneurs have either studied in Tier-1 institutes such as the IITs or NITs or they have secured degrees from foreign universities. Further, Indian IT Industry has grown due to offshoring especially after 1991 liberalisation policy and credit has to be given to growth of domestic companies in auto, retail, banking, telecommunication and manufacturing. Partial privatisation of the telecommunication sector also contributed to the IT revolution. The rapid growth in IT parks and SEZs (specialized economic zones), where opening of software services companies got tax subsidies attracted many companies to set up software shops. The tax breaks and sops offered by the government for upcoming software firms made India one of the most attractive markets for setting up software companies. The existing software service exporters face two major challenges, the first being the difficulty in attracting and retaining talented software professionals and the challenge of developing beyond competing on low costs alone in an environment with rising labour costs. Firms are moving up the value chain by accumulating knowledge about the industry segments for which they currently develop software. Indian firms provide services for the lower portion of the waterfall model and moving up the value chain involves providing conceptualisation, requirement analysis and design services as well. Such a strategy, which ultimately involves getting involved in business process reengineering for overseas clients may be difficult, since accumulating domain knowledge and business expertise are not easy. Firms will have to invest in hiring, training and retaining their employees, in expanding overseas and establishing subsidiaries in many countries and in acquiring the technological and business expertise needed. These firms will also be able to execute large, complex projects on their own with little or no supervision from foreign clients. Also, they may be able to anticipate the business needs of their clients and offer them solutions. These firms can acquire other Indian software firms or their assets or employ the latter as subcontractors. With these prospects, the Indian software companies have to establish their global business leadership. There is the growing 'techie entrepreneur' cult with the emergence of apps and technology tools in code-writing. IT has affected the entertainment industry to such an extent that the sector has generated many '*enterpreneurs*' who have made significant contributions to the film and television sectors by their mega serials and other programmes.

5

Biotechnology Enterprising in India

5.1 Introduction

Apart from IT, it is in the field of biotechnology that India has made significant strides in entrepreneurial development and becoming another lead goose. Biotechnology involves technologies that capitalise on the characteristics of biological systems, processes and organisms along with their contributions to manufacturing industries by utilising molecules such as DNA and proteins to work for human benefit (Singh et al, 2009). The foundations of modern biotechnology were laid in the first half of 20th century. The bioproducts of the innovative efforts need to be protected including the financial investments by strong intellectual property laws. With the sequencing of the human genome and advances made in plant and animal genetics and other aspects of the life sciences, these technological breakthroughs provide the building blocks for major industries with implications for agriculture and human health. Not only mankind benefits from new innovative technologies but also has the opportunity to contribute to the advancement of scientific knowledge and development of the global biotechnology industry. Commercialised biotechnology concentrates in biotechnology clusters surrounded by universities and life sciences research institutes (Friedman, 2006).

Nikkei (2012) reports that Indian pharmaceutical companies, known world-wide as generic medicine producers, have started their global marketing strategies in Japan, the USA and the European Union. The companies already experienced in producing heart disease and steroid medicines will now expand their production capacity both at home and Japan to exploit ever-increasing demand for such medicines. India enjoys its comparative advantage in many generic medicines at prices one-tenth lower than the world market. According to Nikkei (2012), Times Medicare will explore both India and Japanese markets and the company will be a potential partner in Japan. The Ipoca Laboratories will find a possibility of having a partner on a long-term basis to supply raw materials to produce high blood pressure medicines for the foreign companies operating in Japan. Ajanta Farma will explore marketing of heart disease and anti-malaria generics in the USA and will start a new factory in Gujarat, half of productive capacity being specialised for export. Abic Pharmaceuticals will expedite application for new approval (raw materials) from current two tontine medicines within two years timeframe. Further, JB Chemicals and Pharmaceuticals will increase the number of approvals for more medicines every year from the current level of six medicines. These developments have enabled India to enjoy about twenty per cent of world market in end-user consumption of generics (Nikkei, 2012).

India has emerged as a major biotech and pharmaceutical R&D centre and Bangalore has become the capital of both information technology and biotech industry, having the largest number of companies in both the sectors. This chapter discusses the major trends in the biotechnology sector in India in recent times. Section 5.2 describes the development of biotech sector in India, while section 5.3 explains the recent initiatives undertaken for its development in the areas of biopharma, bioagri and bioenergy. The section also touches upon international collaboration in this respect. Section 5.4 showcases the major barriers in biotech innovations, entrepreneurship development being the major focus for growth of the sector. Section 5.5 describes the achievements of major biotech companies like Dr Reddy's, Wockhardt, Nicholas Piramal, Ranbaxy, Biocon and others. Section 5.6 profiles some of the bioentrepreneurs, while section 5.7 concludes.

5.2 Biotechnology Development in India

Biotechnology constitutes one of the essential technologies of the knowledge economy, with its industrial revenue reaching $60 billion in 2006, ten times of its 1996 level (Huggett et al, 2011). It is one of the most R&D intensive industries, as global leaders of the biotech industry spend an average of 20 per cent of their revenue on R&D, whereas other hi-tech sectors like computer hardware and software fields spend less than 10 and 20 per cent respectively (Huggett et al, 2011). While China focuses on ICT hardware, India has been concentrating on ICT software; these countries have also made significant progress as world players in the biotech industry within a short period. For instance, China's biopharmaceutical industry has witnessed 20-30 per cent revenue growth annually since 2001 (Zhou, 2007), while India achieved a growth rate of 36 per cent during 2005-06 (Suresh, 2009). In 2005, China and India were ranked ninth and the eleventh in biotech revenue (Buckley et al, 2005). Although India has currently outperformed China in terms of quantity, scale of manufacturing and globalisation (Buckley et al, 2005), innovative domestic firms have become essential for the expansion of the biotech industry in both countries. In India, 14 of top 20 biotech firms are home-grown and all top six firms are domestic (Suresh, 2009).

The global biotechnology industry is forecast to exceed $320 billion by 2015 (Global Industry Analysts, 2012). The recent economic crisis negatively impacted the biotechnology market and brought about revenue declines in the US and the EU as a result of limited capital inflows and the delay or cancellation of projects. The biotechnology industry was further segmented in 2011, moving away from its traditional drug focus into other fields, including clean technology and chemical manufacturing. The global genetic testing industry has reported a high growth, caused by an increase of genetic disorders, better awareness and an aging population, the market totalling $1.5 billion in 2010 (Global Industry Analysts, 2012). The world genetic testing market is expected to reach $4 billion by 2015. Global enzyme demand is expected to grow, with the market expected to exceed $7.5 billion in 2010. The growth prospects would be lower in advanced economies such as the US and the EU. Enzyme demand in North America will be negatively impacted by a slow switch over to biomass-based biofuel production and the EU enzyme demand will be negatively impacted by the EU debt crisis (Global Industry Analysts, 2012). The US dominates the global biotechnology industry, followed by Germany, Spain, France and the UK. China and India may record strong growth in agricultural and industrial biotechnology industries due to rising income levels and demand. Emerging economies play an increasingly significant role in the biotech drugs market due to relatively low-cost investment and a high level of expertise. The US-based life sciences companies generate over $500 billion in revenues, followed by Japan. The life sciences industry in the Asia Pacific (not including Japan) registered $103.6 billion in 2007, growing at 13 per cent per annum. The rate of adoption of genetic manufacturing and biotech crops is remarkable when we note that their cultivated area was a mere 1.7 million hectare in 1996, but increased to 125 m/ ha in 2008 (Global Industry Analysts, 2012).

In the global biotech market, India's share is two per cent and the sector is fast emerging, according to a McKinsey & Co. study (Kumra et al, 2011). The consumption of biotech products in India was $1.8 billion during 1999, which grew up to $4.3 billion by 2010. It is estimated that ten per cent of researchers and 15 per cent of scientists in pharmaceutical and biotech R&D in USA are of Indian origin. In the human and animal products segment of the industry, the vaccines market is valued at $230 million and is growing at 20 per cent per annum. According to Kumra et al (2011), Indian pharma industry is poised to grow to an innovation-led $25 billion by 2010 with a market capitalisation of $150 billion from the generic-based drug industry. Traditionally, India has been a very strong player in conventional generics due to established track record of process engineering skills and capability to set up comparable manufacturing units at a fraction of the capital cost utilised overseas. Companies such as Shantha Biotech, which started with just one product, are now effectively using this experience to launch other products like plasminogen activators, interferons, sophisticated vaccines etc. Shanta Biotech's Shanvac against Hepatitis B, costs $4, less than half the price of similar vaccines marketed by multinational companies. Eli Lilly- Ranbaxy 50:50 joint venture in India has been marketing a range of biotech products such as Humalog and Huminsulin for diabetes, whereas Hoechst Roussel Vet has developed a cow abortion vaccine (Kumra et al, 2011).

In the agri-biotech segment (hybrid seeds and transgenic crops, biopesticides and biofertilizers) India is the second largest food producer after China. Transgenics of rice, brassica, moon bean, pigeon pea, cotton, tomato and vegetables like cabbage and cauliflower would be ready for large scale dissemination. Hicks Muse will bring forth foreign investment worth $35 million for production and marketing of hybrid and improved variety of seeds (Kumra et al, 2011). The Indian partner in this venture is Mahindra Hybrid Seeds and Bayer functions in India through acquiring New Delhi-based ProAgro group of companies. Marine resource development and aquaculture also hold a great potential with India having more than 8000 kms of coastline. In the agricultural and allied areas India has achieved the cloning and sequencing of at least six genes, developed regeneration protocols for citrus, coffee, mangrove species and new types of biofertilizers and biopesticide formulations, including mycorrhizal fertilizers. An impetus has been given to the plant tissue culture industry after the successful tissue culture pilot plants and micro-propagation of the technology has been started.

Bioindustrial sector deals with enzyme manufacturing and marketing companies and these enzymes are used in detergent, textiles, food, leather, paper and pharmaceutical industries. Industrial biotech segment is expected to show significant growth and products for development include enzymes, bio-instrumentation and bioprocess equipments. Contract research services are focused on molecular biology, bioinformatics, genomics and stem cell research. Clinical research and trials are expected to grow exponentially in the future. Scores of large IT companies have already established bioinformatics units in Bangalore and there are opportunities for data-mining, gene annotation and the development of software interfaces. Major research has been carried out at government funded research institutes like Indian Council of Agricultural Research, Indian Council of Medical Research, Council of Scientific and Industrial Research and Department of Biotechnology.

The Indian biotech industry grew threefold in just five years to report revenues of $3 billion in 2009-10, a rise of 17 per cent over the previous year, according to the eighth annual survey conducted by the Association of Biotechnology Led Enterprises and Biospectrum (2009), based on inputs from over 150 biotech companies. The biopharma sector contributed nearly three-fifth to the industry's revenues at $1.9 billion, a rise of 12 per cent, followed by bioservices at $573 million and bioagri at $420.4 million. The remaining revenue came from bioindustrials ($122.5 million) and bioinformatics ($50.2 million). Biopharma and bioservices sectors contributed 63 per cent and 33 per cent respectively in biotech exports (Kumra et al, 2011). Bioservices market deals with clinical trial, contract research and manufacturing activities. Bioagriculture, bioindustrials and bioinformatics sectors remain focused on domestic operations. India is also gaining importance as a clinical trial destination. According to a joint study by Ernst and Young, the industry-sponsored clinical trial sites in India have grown by 116 per cent during June 2008 and August 2009, with the country moving from 18th to 12th rank across the 60 most active countries. India participates in seven per cent of the global Phase-III trials and 3.2 per cent in Phase-II trials with industry-sponsored trials having grown by 39 per cent during 2004-08 (Kumra et al, 2011). Biopharma focuses on production of vaccines, therapeutics and diagnostics, while bioinformatics concerns with creation and maintenance of extensive electronic databases on various biological systems.

India's biotech activities are not confined to just therapeutic products. In 2002, after a long regulatory process, the first genetically modified product, a *Bacillus thuringensis* (Bt) cotton variety was introduced in the country. The Bt cotton seed variety, developed for the Indian market by a joint venture company of Monsanto was termed as success despite several controversies. Within six years, Bt cotton seeds cover more than 90 per cent of the fields growing hybrid cotton. The total cotton growing area remained unchanged but there was an increase in productivity. India has become the second largest cotton producer after the USA, overtaking China as a net exporter of cotton. The Bt cotton seeds became a $250 million segment within the biotech industry. India's seed companies were highly innovative in adapting the transgenic technologies. Home-grown seed companies like Nuziveedu Seeds, Hyderabad and Rasi Seeds, Tamil Nadu, were stiff competitors to Monsanto in turning out quality Bt cotton hybrids. Other seed companies like JK Agrigenetics, Krishidan Seeds, Ankur Seeds and Indo-American Hybrid Seeds have entered into the bioagri market. Regulators allowed limited field trials of a genetically modified Bt variety of eggplant (aubergine) in 2007. India is second largest global producer with 26 per cent share and its consumption exceeds $2 billion. Over 1.4 million farmers cultivate eggplant in over half a million hectare (Kumar et al, 2011).

Located in Hyderabad, the bio-valley of India, two of the three firms, Shantha Biotech and Bharat Biotech International are innovative biopharmaceutical firms that have managed to gain significant success and recognition (Frew et al, 2007). The Indian firms demonstrate their innovation capability by a large number of their own brands of recombinant products. For instance, Shantha was the first to develop the r-DNA hepatitis-B vaccine, followed by Bharat and others, while Jupiter is the leading world producer in drug intermediates (Fan and Watanabe, 2008). Innovation capability has become increasingly vital for the success of biotech firms as well as the survival of traditional pharmaceutical companies which are struggling with declining profits. Indian biotech firms invest heavily in R&D for biotech products and as a result, seven of 14 recombinant biotech products approved by government have been developed and are currently being manufactured by them (DBT, 2006). Biocon and Dr Reddy's have entered the bio-drug field and traditional pharmaceutical firms are looking for options to overcome their present predicament through the purchase of small innovative biotech firms. Institutional factors like involvement of the government have prompted the firms to conduct indigenous R&D or to import foreign technology.

The change in the intellectual property regime and memberships in World Trade Organisation and Trade Related Intellectual Property regime has provided a push for domestic firms to move towards indigenous R&D. Conventional manufacturing procedures based on reverse engineering are challenged and they are effectively barred from replicating innovations patented in the western world due to the implementation of WTO Agreement in 2005 (Mani, 2009). However, Indian firms may file patents to protect IP rights as India has become a signatory to the Patent Cooperation Treaty administered by the World Intellectual Property Organisation. TRIPS introduced changes in the Indian patent system by banning production and sales of re-engineered pharmaceutical products. It extended product patent protection period applied to all branches of manufacturing, including drugs to 20 years. Also, it forbids discrimination between imported and domestic products. Further, the government has provided stimulus to the innovative firms and encouraged domestic firms to innovate through direct funding, creating new biotech governance and establishing innovation policies particularly for biotech (Fan and Watanabe, 2008).

The Department of Biotechnology was established in 1986 to provide a better environment for biotech development, particularly technology transfer between research institutes and private firms. Similar to the Chinese Guideline on Pharmaceutical Industry Development for the 11th Five Year Period (2006-10), both public and private money earmarked for pharmaceutical R&D has more than doubled from the current one percent of revenue from pharmaceutical sales (Jia, 2007). This also involves greater pricing leeway to producers of innovative drugs to encourage investment in biotech research, whereas the pharmaceutical firms were forced to slash their prices (Frew et al, 2008).

Domestic biotech firms are confronted with financial and human resource constraints. The country has set up technology policies to facilitate funding for R&D activities due to the underdeveloped mechanism in funding hi-tech ventures. As a result, currently government support has been the main avenue for financing domestic biotech firms, especially for start-up firms, although Indian firms are able to channel a quite significant portion of the revenue back to R&D due to their outstanding performance in manufacturing. To deal with limited domestic resources, Indian firms started actively seeking international funding sources, ranging from venture capital and support from World Bank, International Monetary Fund and Bill and Melinda Gates Foundation. Although the country has a good education infrastructure and a large pool of low-cost scientists, their university education cannot meet the standards of the industry. To rectify this problem, the human resource plan of DBT has proposed various approaches for a quick fix of qualified biotech graduates, postgraduate, doctors and scientists (DBT, 2006).

The world's largest biotech company Amgen set up Indian operations in 2007 and has set up research and development facilities. Astra Zeneca established its development centre in Bangalore and its process development division is part of its key global network. Astra Zeneca is concentrating on developing cures against neglected diseases like tuberculosis. The global biotech DuPont set up a biotech research facility at its DuPont Knowledge Centre in Hyderabad and Eli Lilly, GSK and Pfizer, Roche, Novartis and Merck have also started their biological manufacturing and research facilities. India's pharmaceutical majors, Wockhardt, Panacea Biotec, Ranbaxy, Dr. Reddy's Laboratories, Cipla, Intas Pharma, Glenmark Pharma, and Piramal Life Sciences have invested in biopharma product development. Dr. Reddy's has come out with many major biosimilars products. The government launched a three-year $70 million Biotechnology Industry Partnership Programme to fund all innovative biotech research ideas by private companies. Under the National Biotech Policy announced in November 2007, an integrated National Biotechnology Regulatory Authority has been set up to provide a single-window clearance system for biotech products.

To reduce the burden of oil imports, the 2008 national biofuel policy seeks to promote the growing of non-edible fuel crops such as *jatropha* and *pongamia* in 30 million ha of wastelands available in the country. A five per cent blend of biodiesel with conventional diesel has been permitted and the percentage is expected to go up to 20 per cent by 2017. Further, many companies are conducting research with stem cells. Diagnostic kits based on molecular biology are new trends and personal genomics and proteomics will follow. The comparative advantage of Indian companies is in reverse engineering and process improvements that lower the price of generics. The other strategy includes the development of new technological capabilities in new product and process. The launch of a new drug has to go through the stages of basic research, identifying the appropriate active pharmaceutical ingredients, combining these ingredients into a product, performing preclinical and clinical trials to test impact, identifying the right dosage and drug delivery system, seeking regulatory approval through completing a number of procedures and finally marketing the new drug. From start to finish, the commercialisation of a new drug can take 15 to 20 years. With the Patent Law of 1970 Indian firms have developed skills in marketing but not in new drug discovery research techniques, preclinical or clinical trial methods. For western firms, which are proficient in all the above but need to speed up and cheapen the drug discovery process. The new firms have to develop absorptive capacity and technological capability in creating drugs, performing preclinical and clinical trials and seeking regulatory approval. Finally, they also have to build new capabilities to market new products through doctors in western hospitals.

5.3 Recent Biotech Development

There are over 280 companies which are involved in the biotech value chain, located in six bio-clusters of Mumbai-Pune, Bangalore, Hyderabad, Ahmedabad-Baroda, Delhi and Chennai. The companies operate in five distinct segments of bio-pharma, bio-agriculture, bio-industrials, bio-services and bio-informatics. The industry has seen three waves of entrepreneurship in the last three decades. The first two waves took place in the past 10 years. More than 100 companies entered into the biotech industry between 1999 and 2001 prompted by the unveiling of the human genome map. The third wave happened in 2006 when over two dozen companies were set up by first-term entrepreneurs who quit their laboratories, encouraged by the success stories of the second wave of entrepreneurs (Natesh and Bhan, 2009). According to them, Biotechnology Information System (BTISnet-BioGrid India), envisaged during 1986-87, has today more than 150 bioinformatics centres located across the country. This acts as a distributed database and network and has become successful as a vehicle for the transfer and exchange of scientific information, knowledge and technology packages. A national facility for *in silico* drug development has been set up at the Indian Institute of Technology, Delhi. Over 150 subject-specific databases and software packages are now available on the BTISnet for open access to the entrepreneurs. The private sector has also contributed to the success of the biotech sector, especially in the manufacturing and service segments. Due to lack of financial resources and stiff competition among domestic manufacturers, the need arises to balance between doing innovative R&D and delivering affordable quality products. The biopharma segment continues to contribute to the extent of 67 per cent, followed by bioservices (15 per cent), agribiotech (12 per cent), bioindustrials (four per cent) and bioinformatics (two per cent). Exports constitute about 56 per cent share of the sector. Industry sources forecast that by 2015 the sector would be worth $13-16 billion in revenue (Natesh and Bhan, 2009).

The National Institute of Food Technology Entrepreneurship and Management (NIFTEM) play a vital role in developing food standards, quality accreditation and certification, keeping a repository of international standards. NIFTEM focuses on providing comprehensive information to exporters in the food sector and providing incubator services to enable entrepreneurs to develop sustainable businesses. Its theme centres benefit through long-term associations with prominent international institutions, through faculty exchange programme and joint research initiatives in various food processing areas. Another critical role of NIFTEM is to provide adequate operational independence to the food standards testing and safety.

5.3.1 Biopharma Segment

The biopharma segment mainly concentrates on vaccines, non-vaccine therapeutics, other novel products and contract services. Its impact has been on promoting low-cost drugs and forcing a price reduction on multinational bioproducts. India's first domestically developed and marketed r-DNA product Shanvac-B, a recombinant hepatitis-B surface antigen from Shanta Biotech, was cost-efficiently produced in the *pichia pastoris* expression system in 1997. Subsequent local competition from other domestic manufacturers such as Biological E. Ltd., Hyderabad and Indian Immunologicals and Serum Institute of India, Pune, resulted in a 30-fold price reduction (from $15 to $0.50) over the imported product. There are about 15 companies involved in the marketing of over 50 brands for 15 different vaccines. Human and animal vaccines together accounted for 51 per cent share of the total biopharma segment. Shanta Biotech now supplies 40 per cent of the global requirement of Hep-B vaccine for UNICEF. The Serum Institute of India is not only the largest supplier of vaccines to the government's Expanded Programme of Immunization (EPI) but also the country's largest exporter of vaccines. Panacea Biotec, New Delhi, supplies oral polio vaccine to EPI and UNICEF. Because of this vaccine development, newer alliances between DBT, Indian companies, public-funded institutions and global philanthropic institutions such as Malaria Vaccine Initiative, Bill and Melinda Gates Foundation, Programme for Appropriate Technologies in Health and the Welcome Trust have emerged (Natesh and Bhan, 2009).

In biogenerics (biosimilars), Biocon's development of a proprietary process for manufacture of recombinant insulin (insugen) forced international competitors to cut back their prices by 40 per cent, even before the product entered the Indian market. Insugen was priced even lower and remains the most affordable human insulin in the domestic market. Biocon is now developing recombinant oral insulin. Shanta Biotech marketed its recombinant interferon alpha (IFN-a) product, Shanferon at Rs.300, substantially lower than the then imported price at Rs.1200 (Natesh and Bhan, 2009). Other Shanta Biotech and Serum Institute innovative products include pentavalent vaccines for protection against five infectious agents, DPT, Hep-B and haemophilus influenza. Panacea Biotec, Biological, Hyderabad and Transgene Biotek introduced single or combination vaccines against locally relevant diseases such as Japanese encephalitis, anthrax, cholera and meningitis. Bharat Biotech introduced a vaccine against rotaviral diarrhoea and lysostaphin, an antiinfective multi drug-resistant staphylococcus aureus, while GangaGen Biotech introduced bacteriophages as antibacterial agents against multi-drug resistant bacteria (Frew et al, 2007).

The biotech companies are carrying out contract services such as R&D, clinical trials or manufacturing as a route to funding operations and building commercial capacities. India is fast becoming one of the largest hubs for conducting global clinical trials. According to a report by RNCOS, in 2007 the country conducted over 220 clinical trials, accounting for two per cent of the global trials. Low cost, large patient pool, easy recruitment, strong government support and strengthening of the intellectual property environment may up this to five per cent by 2012 (Natesh and Bhan, 2009). The increasing number of clinical trials may create enormous opportunities for a number of entrepreneurs and associated industries, including in vitro diagnostics market, education sector and data management. The registration of clinical trials in India would allow implementation of quality assurance measures. International auditing of centres will also be helpful in promoting enforcement of ethical norms and good clinical practices.

5.3.2 Bioagriculture Segment

Indian agriculture faces the challenge of having to produce more farm commodities for human and livestock population from diminishing per capita arable land and water resources. Biotechnology, in combination with classical breeding techniques has the potential to overcome this challenge to ensure livelihood security. Bt cotton approved in March 2002 is the first and until now the only biotech product in India that has been released for commercial cultivation after regulatory approval (Tuli et al, 2009). Most of the area under transgenic cotton features Bt genes sourced from Monsanto, but bred into local hybrids. From about 50,000 ha in the beginning, the area has reached 7.6 million ha in 2008, occupying 82 per cent of cotton area. In 2008, 30 seed companies were engaged in the production of 274 Bt cotton hybrids in nine states. The first indigenous Bt cotton variety, Bikaneri Narma, the genetically modified crop developed by the Central Institute of Cotton Research, Nagpur and the University of Agricultural Sciences, Dharwad, was approved in 2008 for planting in 2009. Since this is a variety and not a hybrid, farmers can save seeds for planting in the following season. The yield of cotton increased from 308 kg/ha in 2001-02 to 560 kg/ha in 2007-08 season. The government of India's Cotton Advisory Board estimates that there has been a positive impact of Bt cotton on cotton-seed oil production and there has been 22 per cent increase to 1.1 million tonnes production in 2008 when compared to the preceding year. According to the Solvent Extractors Association of India, recovery of cotton-seed oil is higher from Bt cotton hybrids, which has contributed towards increasing the production of cotton-seed oil. However, it has also thrown up some criticisms and regulatory issues which need clearer communication with the consumers and the public. Recent emphasis has been on genomics of rice, chickpea, wheat and tomato and on tolerance to biotic (diseases and pests) and abiotic (drought, salinity) stress. A number of public-funded R&D initiatives focus on the identification of quantitative trait loci and genes and their deployment into cultivars (Tuli et al, 2009). Bt rice is under field-testing and other priorities include enhancement of nutritional quality (beta carotene in rice and mustard, micronutrients such as iron and zinc in rice, wheat and maize and protein quality in potato) and improvement of shelf life in fruits and vegetables, especially through delayed ripening.

5.3.3 Bioenergy

India faces challenges in meeting its energy needs and in order to maintain an annual GDP growth of eight per cent over the next 25 years to meet its goals for poverty elimination, the country needs to triple its primary energy supply and quadruple its electricity supply. India now imports about 75 per cent of its petroleum products and with increasing demand, this could surely increase to 90 per cent by 2025. In this scenario, renewable energy sources such as biofuels represent an attractive option. The focus is on producing ethanol from cellulose biomass, including agricultural and forestry waste, biodiesel from varied feed stocks and optimally harness the energy potential of natural resources. The main challenge is to apply biotech tools for improving the biomass production system, promote the bio-refinery concept aiming at the integral use of biomass and maximising the cost-effectiveness of the final products. Biotech interventions are being used to reengineer feed stock for enhanced ethanol recovery and microorganisms for increased productivity. The Department of Biotechnology has established an Energy Biosciences Centre at the University Institute of Chemical Technology, Mumbai to develop economically and ecologically sustainable technology for biofuel from biomass and provide a platform for evaluating bioenergy-related technologies.

5.3.4 International Collaboration

In the knowledge-based economy, no country can afford to isolate itself today. Moreover, a number of problems relate to health, food and agriculture, energy and environment can be solved effectively only through international partnerships. International alliances are necessary with public and private sector partners for joint intellectual property rights generation towards harmonised regulatory processes and smoothened trans-boundary movements of biologicals besides leveraged markets for biotech products and processes. Companies such as Biocon, Serum Institute, Bharat, Shanta, Mahyco and others have entered into collaborative arrangements with overseas companies and agencies. DBT has forged strategic partnerships in specific R&D areas with chosen countries and institutions. Partnerships include the Wellcome Trust, the UK and Stanford University, California for bringing together medical and engineering experts for the biodesign programme. The partnership includes Biotechnology and Biological Sciences Research Council, the UK for the Biotechnology Young Entrepreneurship Scheme and with University of Wisconsin, Madison for exchange of doctoral scholars and PATH, BMGF and MVI for partnership on late-stage development of vaccines.

5.4 Barriers Impeding Innovation and Discovery

India's lead in biological sciences is relatively small and much of the high-end biology research is pursued only in a few universities and research institutes (Biospectrum, 2009). Moreover, the university system has problems of building excellence in life sciences training, coupled with deficiency of research-intensive universities. This is true of medical, agricultural and veterinary institutions, where patient burden or extension activities take a heavy toll on research. Antiquated rules on faculty hiring and promotions and insufficient infrastructure further aggravate the problems. While IITs have been strong in engineering and physical sciences, they lag behind in biological research, although plans are now afoot to rectify this omission. The brightest of students are no longer opting for a career in science and those that do are not skilled enough to be able to take up entrepreneurial positions. Hence, while India has been successful in producing a strong scientific workforce, the system has not been able to generate a critical base of bioentrepreneurs.

Most academic and research institutions in India are not geared to undertake innovative and translational research. Enterprise is a term wholly lacking in discussions about higher education and research intensive universities. In spite of the current economic downturn, the USA remains the guiding spirit of entrepreneurism (Frew et al, 2008). The US universities have traditionally close relations with the industry and act as economic engines rather than ivory towers, with a number of science parks, technology saloons and venture capital funds. Few Indian academics nurse entrepreneurial ambitions. This tendency has its origin in a society that hates failures, given the weak mechanisms for technology transfer between public institutions and private firms.

Students emerging from this environment are least linked to businesses that can make use of their talent. There are not enough mechanisms to expose students to research openings in the private sector, thereby losing an opportunity to stimulate business interest in science and technology.

Most of the public-funded research centres in India are not industry-friendly. Further, industries in general, including life science-associated companies do not actively seek partnerships with research laboratories, preferring instead to go abroad in search of partnerships. There is also a difference in expectations from such partnerships. Both industry and academic institutions have to meet half way in making adjustments. Institutions also lack units or structures that can flexibly handle interactions with the industry, without the barriers of bureaucracy. One outcome of this is a fragile and only incrementally increasing public–private partnership in biotechnology.

Indian bioindustry is generally risk-averse. This is probably a reflection of the reluctance of Indian banks and investors to invest in biotech ventures. Industry-led R&D is still not adequate in scale or quality when it comes to innovation and discovery research. The government has provided fiscal incentives such as relaxed price control for drugs, removal of foreign ownership limits, subsidies on capital expenses and tax holidays for R&D spending, but until recently, direct investment in industry R&D has not been made available. Moreover, funding agencies have to find ways of breaking the sociologic and behavioural barriers of the current competitive grant system that blocks risk taking. A recent survey of Indian biotech and pharmaceutical companies (Fan and Watanabe, 2008) revealed that till the end of 2007 only 15 per cent of the companies held US patents. While there were 425 pharma patents, the study could identify only 19 biotech patents starting from 2001. Among the biotech patents, 11 per cent were categorised as product patents, 47 per cent as process patents and 37 per cent as design patents.

Angel funding for companies that want to pursue pure research with the intention of marketing products is still hard to come by in India. Increasing domestic and international competition requires a continuous capacity for innovation and bringing innovations to the market, not merely catching up with technology. Investment in hi-tech R&D and synergy between public and corporate sector R&D is crucial, but the institutional framework has to be appropriated to ensure access to start-up financing and for sharing the risks and rewards of innovation. In the life sciences sector, information asymmetry between the scientist, entrepreneur and financier is the most challenging and requires a role for public sector institutions in the incubation and nurture of technology start-ups. Further, no agency provides venture capital to young graduates, academics or working professionals to help turn creative ideas into viable inventions and explore the entrepreneurial potential of scientific ideas. A good example is the ignition grant mechanism of the Deshpande Centre at MIT, which enables the faculty members to take risks and explore uncharted concepts, before they have developed proof of concept or gathered any data. DBT is in the process of developing a new scheme of ignition grants to young innovators.

Research and application of biotechnology has to be guided by a process of decision-making that safeguards human, animal and plant health. A science-based, rigorous, transparent, efficient, predictable and consistent regulatory mechanism for biosafety evaluation is vital to the growth of the biotechnology sector. In recent years, Indian biosafety regulation has become streamlined, but it can respond to changing technologies and develop more effective transparent processes.

5.5 The Neo-biotech Firms

With the growth in the customer base and more investments taking place in the biotech sector, the industry is expected to grow to over rupees for trillion by 2020. The high demand for different biotech products has also opened up scope for foreign companies to set up bases here. Since the establishment of the Department of Biotechnology, many innovations have been made in this field to combine knowledge along with skilled and cheap manpower. A number of research laboratories that have been set up have helped in the innovation of various drugs for the production of insulin, blood clotting and human growth. Life saving vaccines and enzymes are also been manufactured.

According to various websites on biotech enterprises, there are around 350 companies in India which produce specialized products and services in various sectors of biotechnology. The leading biotech companies contribute around 27 per cent of the total revenue of the sector. With the liberalisation in the Indian economy, a number of foreign biotech companies have entered the Indian market. Biocon is one of the premier biotech and healthcare companies, which provides specialized services in the biopharmaceutical market. The main objective of the company is to offer healthcare products in the fields of diabetes, cancer and inflammatory ailments. A number of medical therapies are also offered at affordable rates. Piramal has made itself a big brand name and ranks as fourth in the Indian healthcare market, offering a number of services like medicines and therapies. The company has also successfully launched itself in the markets of Europe, North America and Asia ranks among the premier biotech companies. Dr Reddy's is known for offering specialised facilities in the field of healthcare and therapeutic medicines. It also provides research facilities in areas like inflammation, metabolic disorders and infective diseases.

Indian Immunologicals, established in 1983, ranks among the best vaccine producing companies in the world. Bharat Serums and Vaccines was founded in 1971 and is one of the fastest growing biotech companies, having engaged in development and manufacturing of specialised biological and pharmaceutical products. The Pune-based Serum Institute of India is the world's largest producer of MMR and DTP group of vaccines. The Institute produces several recombinant and combination vaccines (like Gene Vac-B), anti-cancer drugs, as well as anti-Sera, Plasma and Hormonal products. It is India's largest exporter of vaccines, supplying to over 140 countries. Through the UNICEF and the Pan American Health Organisation, this company helps in immunisation of over half the world's children against measles and other dangerous diseases. The Institute is engaged in serious research on measles vaccine on human diploid cells and rabies vaccine, industrial column chromatography and affinity chromatography for separation of immuno-globulins and human growth hormone (rDNA-SAIZEN) in pre-pubertal children with growth hormone deficiency. Biocon specializes in biopharmaceuticals, custom research and clinical research in enzymes. The company is a leader in the field of bioprocessing and clinical research and development and provides solutions in both domestic and international markets. Biocon launched the world's first recombinant human insulin, INSUGEN in 2004. It has produced India's first indigenous monocional antibody BIOMA-EGFRTM. The company has recently divested its enzymes business and decided to concentrate on its bio-pharma business verticals that include active pharmaceutical ingredients, biologicals and proprietary molecules. The company is now focusing on several futuristic projects like microbial fermentation (both submerged and solid state), chemicals synthesis, human insulin and mammalian cell culture.

Panacea Biotech is a health management company that specialises in developing innovative prescription medicines, breakthrough vaccines, peptides and monoclonal antibodies and cutting edge new drug delivery technology. Panacea produces its hepatitis B vaccine in collaboration with the Centre for Genetic Engineering and Biotechnology, Cuba. The company has also developed several combination vaccines, the leading ones being Ecovac (DPT+Hepatitis-B), Easy Four (DPT+HIV) and Easy Five (DPT+Hepatitis-B+HIV). Vaccines for anthrax and Japanese encephalitis are under preparation. Some medicines produced by the company include gels, betaglim, glizaid range of medicines, monovalent oral polio type I and type-III vaccines and Ocimix.

The Mumbai-based Monsanto India is credited with many revolutionary products and technological breakthroughs in agricultural sciences. The company is famous for producing the Bt cotton (Bollgard) and genetically modified crops which play an important role in India's agrarian economy. Rasi Seeds, based in Tamil Nadu is known for its efforts in hybrid cotton and other insect resistant technology. The company is in the process of making rapid advances in the field of plant germplasm (collection, conservation and utilisation in crop improvement); breeding for new lines with earliness, erect leaves, orange-flint and orange yellow semi dent grain colours and development of new single cross, modified single cross and three way cross hybrids for evaluation and identification of high yield hybrid combinations. Venkateshwara Hatcheries of Andhra Pradesh is a leader of poultry industry in India. It is a conglomerate dedicated to integrated poultry development and is credited with its ability to indigenise the Babcock (layer) and Cobb (broiler) breeds. The group has made important strides in genetic research of Venco and VRB, joint ventures of the group with Cobb Vantress and ISA Breeder, especially in the field of specific pathogen free eggs in the manufacture of poultry vaccines; production of specific pathogen-free eggs, manufacture of automated poultry equipment, introduction of combined and inactivated (killed) vaccines and setting up of sophisticated disease diagnostic, surveillance and monitoring laboratories.

Novo Nordisk is well known for its accomplishments in the field of diabetes care and the company has come up with revolutionary products and services. It produces the Novomix-30 (premixed insulin analogue) and NovoRapid (rapid acting insulin analogue) that provide that are useful to diabetes patients. Besides diabetes care, the company is also engaged in research in the fields of growth hormone therapy and haemostasis management. Tulip Group of Companies is involved in the manufacture and marketing of in-vitro diagnostic reagents and kits, both for domestic and international markets. The group comprises of eight independent diagnostic companies like Tulip Diagnostics, Microxpress, Orchid Biomedical Systems, Coral Clinical System, Qualpro Diagnostics, Tulip Marketing, Zephyr Biomedicals and Lilac Medicare. These companies are engaged in specific areas of research, development and design systems and platforms within the assigned technological areas. At present, the group is concentrating on immuno-haematology, immunology (fertility, rheumatology and infectious diseases), immuno-turbidimetry, haemostasis, haematology, clinical microbiology, parasitology, virology, cardiac and cancer markers, clinical biochemistry and instrumentation.

Indian Immunologicals Limited, a subsidiary of National Dairy Development Board (NDDB) deals with veterinary science and medicines. The company produces a whole range of cattle vaccines, canine vaccines, sheep vaccines, etc. Transasia Biomedicals produces clinical diagnostic equipments and reagents and has over 1700 installations all over the country, supported by a network of 25 service centres. In collaboration with SYSMEX, WAKO and NITTEC of Japan, BIOHIT of Finland and TRACE of Australia, the company has been manufacturing many types of equipment in respect of biochemistry and haematology. The company also exports to a number of countries like China, Korea, Germany, Australia, Netherlands, Turkey and the USA.

5.5.1 Dr Reddy's Laboratories

In 1987, DRL launched Norilet, its first brand and its major success came with the launching of Omez, the brand name under which the generic Omezaprozole was sold. A superior process technology allowed DRL to launch it at a price 50 per cent lower than that of the other brands selling in Indian market. Within a year of its inception, DRL began to export active pharmaceutical ingredients to Europe. In 1994, it opened a state-of-art manufacturing facility in Hyderabad in order to increase its production capacity in generics. It filed its first ANDA for Ranitidine 75 mg tablets and improving on that, in 1999 submitted an application for Omeprazole and Rantidine. It got approval before patent expiry and without litigation for these products but lost out in subsequent court battles.

In 2001, DRL became the first Indian company to launch Fluoxentine (a generic version of Eli Lilly's Prozac) with six month market exclusivity in the US. This marketing success was followed by the launch of Ibuprofen tablets in the US under its own brand name. Direct marketing under the DRL brand name represented a significant step in building DRL's fully fledged distribution network in the US. Starting a full-fledged R&D laboratory in 1992, DRL invested about Rs.1.12 billion in R&D over an eight-year period and filed 55 US patents of which 19 have been granted. It licensed three molecules to foreign drug firms (two to Novo Nordisk and one to Novartis) for $8 million in 2001. The R&D intensity has been increased from 5.5 to 8 per cent of its sales revenues.

DRL's transition path towards new drug discovery involves targeting specialty generics products in western markets in order to transit to drug discovery capabilities. The reason that development of specialty drugs can be an important link to the development of new chemical entities is that all the elements that are involved in a new chemical entity (NCE) effort, such as innovation in the laboratory, developing the compound sending the sales team to the market are also stages in the development of a specialty drug, except that the scales are smaller and therefore more manageable. DRL has also invested heavily in building R&D labs and remain the only Indian company to have significant R&D being undertaken overseas. Dr. Reddy's Research Foundation (DRF) was established in 1992 and is dedicated to new drug discovery. Initially, DRF's drug discovery research strategy revolved around analogue research but DRF changed its focus to work in rational drug design with a hiring strategy that targeted fresh scientists especially Indian students studying abroad on doctoral and post-doctoral courses. Though DRF wanted to introduce modern skills such as drug discovery based on genomics and proteomics, it could not find scientists in India equipped enough in these areas of research.

In 2000, DRF set up a lab in Atlanta, Reddy US Therapeutics with the aim of conducting drug discovery using molecular genomics and proteomics approaches for next generation drugs. Research thrust at DRL is focused towards large niche areas in western market like anticancer, antidiabetes, cardiovascular and antiinfective drugs. In terms of new drug discovery achievements, DRF currently has many NCEs in various stages of development in clinical development. The clinical development of three molecules is being undertaken by DRL (on its own) while two other molecules are developed in collaboration with Rheoscience, Denmark (Balaglitazone) and Clintech International, Germany (DRF1042). Although DRF's progress in innovative R&D is remarkable, it had a fair share of failures. For example, in 1998, DRF signed the agreement with Novo Nordisk to develop and market pharmaceutical products of its first molecule, Ragaglitazar. However in 2002, adverse effects appeared during clinical trials and Novo Nordisk abandoned research on the molecule and decided to work on another DRL molecule. In 2003, Novo Nordisk terminated development of the molecule due to adverse effects. In 2002, DRL granted exclusive rights for the development and commercialisation of DRF4158 to Novartis Pharma AG. But in 2003, Novartis opted to replace dual acting insulin sensitizer with another follow-up compound. The most important lesson that DRL has learnt from such failures is that new drug discovery is a risky business and it is necessary to formulate and implement a strategy for risk management, both in terms of collaborative ventures and financial support.

Auriegene Discovery Technologies, a contract research company was established as a fully owned subsidiary of DRL in 2002 in Bangalore to gain experience of drug discovery through contract research for other pharma companies. It has acquired Trigenesis, a dermatological company with new molecules in its product portfolio. DRL has entered into a venture investment agreement with the Indian Bank and ICICI, under which ICICI Venture will fund the development, registration and legal costs related to the commercialisation of ANDAs on a pre-determined basis. On commercialisation of these products, Dr. Reddy's will pay ICICI Venture royalty on net sales for a period of five years. Another way of managing the cash flows is from active pharmaceutical ingredients (API) and formulations businesses. DRL has made a private settlement with Novartis to delay its launch of the generic rival to Exelon, its drug for Alzheimer's. In 2007, the new drug discovery units of DRL were de-merged from the rest of the business, a trend that was followed by Ranbaxy and several other firms.

5.5.2 Wockhardt Ltd.

Wockhardt was started by Khorakiwala family in 1959 as a small pharmaceutical distribution and selling entity. From the early 1990s the company has spent over 20 per cent of its total research budget on biotech R&D. Wockhardt's R&D Centre at Aurangabad initiated programmes in the field of new drug discovery research in 1997, a break from the past when the focus had been uniquely on biogenerics. Wockhardt has decided to concentrate its efforts on the anti-infective therapeutic segment as the main thrust area in new drug discovery R&D. It explores the biotechnology route to drug discovery and in order to gain experience in it has concentrated on the biogenerics segment.

The drug discovery programme has yielded a few lead molecules, one of which, WCK 771, a broad spectrum antibacterial has completed Phase I clinical trials. The other chemical entities WCK 1152 and WCK 1457 are under pre-clinical trials. In 2001, Wockhardt indigenously produced a drug called erythropoietin for severe anaemia using genetic engineering methods. However, the most important milestone in biotech R&D came with development of human insulin. In 2003, Wockhardt launched Wosulin. The company is the first outside US and Europe to develop, manufacture and market this life saving drug used in diabetes. In 2004, Wockhardt commissioned a state-of-the-art production facility dedicated to the manufacture of biotech products. The company is also developing a generic version of the biopharmaceutical Interferon Alfa 2b, which is in the third phase of clinical trials.

From 2000 onwards, the company went through a major re-structuring, splitting the pharmaceutical business from the agro-chemical, intra vitreous fluids and hospital business to form two divisions - Wockhardt Life Sciences and Wockhardt Ltd. The aim of this restructuring was to allow Wockhardt to concentrate more on building skills and capabilities in the pharmaceutical business. Wockhardt started targeting international markets only in the late 1990s, when early entrants like Ranbaxy and DRL had already made exports of generic drugs from India credible. Wockhardt's expansion into Europe and the US is based largely on acquisitions of plants that have FDA approval. Thus, it entered the UK market by acquiring Wallis Laboratory in 1998 and CP Pharmaceuticals in 2003. In 2004, Wockhardt acquired the German pharmaceutical company, Esparma GmbH and this acquisition has given Wockhardt increased depth in product portfolio and helped company to strengthen its presence in the European business. In 2007, it acquired Negma Laboratories, a large integrated pharmaceutical company in France. Wockhardt launched its US operations in 2003 by starting Wockhardt Americas Ltd. and now has its own marketing and regulatory teams and in 2003, it had filed 17 ANDA applications with USFDA.

5.5.3 Nicholas Piramal India Ltd.

NPIL is a part of the Piramal Enterprises with interests in retailing, textiles, auto components and engineering. In 2000, the group consisted of 26 companies with aggregate revenues of about $500 million. The company acquired Roche Products (India) in 1993, Sumitra Pharmaceuticals and Chemicals in 1995 and Boehringer Mannheim India Ltd in 1997, followed by two more acquisitions, Rhone Poulenc (India) in 2000 and ICI (India) Pharmaceuticals in 2002. In 2003, NPIL bought the 50 per cent stake in Sarabhai Pharmaceuticals. Since most of the sellers were multinational pharmaceutical firms which wanted to quit the Indian market, NPIL acquired these firms at attractive prices and quickly synergized skills resulting in large benefits through attaining critical mass, leveraging on effective marketing and distribution. These acquisitions also helped NPIL to create strong linkages with Roche, Boehringer, Allergan, Boots, Aventis, and Novartis. NPIL has developed a two-way approach for developing NCE that builds on their good relationships with multinational firms. The first one is inward co-licensing deals with foreign firms, custom synthesis and contract manufacturing for MNC pharmaceutical firms while the second is to undertake contract research for the development of the product patented molecules to make pharmaceutical drugs. One part of the NPIL strategy involves partnering with innovator companies worldwide across different segments of the pharmaceutical value chain. It has developed the ability to provide end-to-end solutions in a range of activities like chemical synthesis of APIs, intermediates and also dosage formulations. However, NPIL does not provide support to early to market generic product development or contract with generics companies for such work. The early to market generics involve challenging the existing patent and instigating litigation with the original innovator, whereas in late-to-market generics, the patent is already expired and therefore patent litigation is avoided.

In 2003, NPIL set up a subsidiary in the US, NPIL Pharmaceutical Inc. for moving the custom manufacturing business development nearer to prospective customers. NPIL signed its first custom manufacturing contract with the US firm Advanced Medical Optics for manufacturing select eye care products for their global markets. The second constituent of its strategy is development of product patented molecules for licensing to MNC pharmaceutical firms. In 1998, NPIL acquired the research centre of Hoechst Marion

Russell located in Mumbai, which since its establishment in 1972, was focused on new drug discovery research and herbal research. In 2002, NPIL also established a Clinical Research Organisation (CRO) to strengthen its clinical trial capabilities. Aligned with NPIL's concept of partnership, the aim of CRO is to serve the generic pharmaceutical industry by conducting clinical pharmaco-kinetic studies and subsequently, leveraging its skills by partnering with Indian as well as MNC pharmaceutical companies.

5.5.4 Ranbaxy

Ranbaxy Laboratories Limited was established in 1961 and listed on the Bombay Stock Exchange in 1973. Ranbaxy started as a manufacturer of active pharmaceutical ingredients and soon began looking at international markets for securing these ingredients. In 1977, Ranbaxy established a subsidiary in Nigeria through a joint venture and in 1984 it expanded operations to Malaysia. R&D activity in Ranbaxy started in the late 1970s and early efforts were focused on formulating bulk drugs into dosage forms and on developing cheap processes to synthesise bulk drugs. Soon after Ranbaxy began to concentrate its R&D efforts towards developing a novel production process that would let it side-step process patents of other companies with a view to entering the profitable generics market.

Ranbaxy found a novel way to manufacture the anti-ulcerant Ranitidine, the generic molecule of an original drug developed by Glaxo and sold under the brand name of Zantac. This marked the start of a strategy based on the manufacture of generic drugs, accompanied with the opening of the Ranbaxy Research Foundation in 1985. One of Ranbaxy's active pharmaceutical ingredients (API) manufacturing plants was approved by the US Federal Drugs Authority (FDA) in 1988. Ranbaxy started work on developing a new seven stage process for the production of Cefaclor in 1988, despite internal doubts about committing R&D resources to a product that was difficult to manufacture and in addition would be too expensive for the Indian market. After three years and spending nearly $2 million, Ranbaxy emerged with a non-infringing process for the manufacture of Cefaclor and also managed to obtain higher yields from its process as compared to Eli Lilly's original production process. From 1995, Ranbaxy stepped up its R&D expenditures from two per cent of sales to five per cent and established state-of-art multi-disciplinary R&D facilities at

Gurgaon. The company's strategy was to establish capabilities in the areas of discovery research, delivery systems and clinical research by adopting a two stage approach, where development of capabilities in drug delivery systems would result in the development of drug discovery capabilities. In 1999, Ranbaxy registered its first major success, when it developed the once-a-day dosage for the Ciprofloxacin molecule.

This improvement in dose administration promised greater patient compliance compared to multiple dosages offered by the patent holder, Bayer. Ranbaxy licensed the once-a-day technology to Bayer of Germany for $10 million for further development. In 2004, Bayer successfully launched the 500 mg and 1 gm once-a-day formulation in the US, based on delivery technology platforms developed by Ranbaxy. Ranbaxy had no prior experience in drug discovery research and therefore, it concentrated on building a strong, well focused inter-disciplinary research team. Thereafter, it initiated an open policy of recruitment including scientists from India as well overseas. The company has also internationalised its R&D efforts mainly to fortify the developmental aspects of R&D. Ranbaxy's US R&D facility Ranbaxy Pharmaceuticals Inc. does not carry out any laboratory work but focuses on clinical research, regulatory affairs and commercial inputs on diseases, targets and compounds. Ranbaxy's new drug discovery R&D focus includes urology, anti-infective, respiratory, anti-inflammatory and metabolic disorders segments. Ranbaxy's first NCE, for Benign Prostrate Hyperplasia (BPH), was licensed to Schwartz Pharma but after Phase-II clinical trials, the molecule was abandoned. Ranbaxy's other promising drug is an anti-asthma molecule, undergoing Phase-II clinical trials. Besides these, the company has other molecules in its NCE pipeline, which are at different stages of clinical development.

Ranbaxy presents an example of staged growth through integration of pharmaceutical production, R&D activities and internationalisation efforts. It has shown great alertness and foresight in grasping the significance of the generics market opportunity long before liberalisation and TRIPs by making entry into western markets for generics. In expanding its R&D capability the company has concentrated on human resource recruitment to build up skills, internationalising its R&D effort in order to stay close to regulatory market needs and managing risk in undertaking new R&D through targeted small outcomes in drug delivery. However, recognising its limitations in the ability to test and market new drugs, Ranbaxy has also preferred to rely on licensing to multinationals for the direct marketing of its new dosages and molecules.

5.6 Conclusion

The Indian pharmaceutical industry has been one of the high performance industries after the 1990s. About one-third of its 2002 production of $5.2 billion was exported to other countries. Among the ten entities based in India with the largest number of US patents during 1996-2001, Indian pharmaceutical companies are seeking to move from imitative research and reverse engineering to the discovery of new molecules and drug delivery systems. Though the average R&D intensity of large Indian pharmaceutical firms is two per cent, the intensity of the innovative companies is substantially higher. Joint R&D initiatives with multinational drug companies, licensing of new discoveries to MNCs, sponsored research projects at national laboratories with government support and the creation of international marketing networks in the hope of future exploitation of such networks to sell newly developed novel drugs are some of the developments that are taking place in this area. One of the most successful pharmaceutical companies has been DRL, followed by Ranbaxy, Cipla, Wockhardt, Sun Pharma and others. In this way, the Indian biotech industry has been able to contribute to the world's health and India is being globally recognised as a manufacturer of economical, high-quality bulk drugs and formulations. With a huge base of talented, skilled and cost-competitive manpower and a well-developed scientific infrastructure, India has great potential to become a leading global player in biotechnology. The role of biofirms and bioentrepreneurs in this regards had been crucial, though the innovative and R&D efforts have to be firmly established in order to make India a leading biotech country similar to that of IT.

6

Indian Business Houses and Development of Indigenous Entrepreneurship

6.1 Introduction

India provides an example of an economy that has traditionally been associated with inefficient markets, but recently the country has pursued rapid development and economic transformation favouring a free-market system. Many business groups have exploited the changing situations and have continued to contribute to economic growth. The groups have flourished due to policy distortions, informational imperfections and entrepreneurial scarcity and in the absence of specialised intermediaries in the capital market, generating capital and managerial talent. They have maintained easy access to funding even when the external markets remained inefficient (Khanna and Palepu, 2004). In the absence of a well-functioning business market, entrepreneurs made use of political nexus to their benefit and engaged in different lines of business. After the First World War, promotion of new industries in India was accomplished mainly by traditional merchant groups who managed to accumulate wealth reaping on wartime speculation. These wealth creators participated in modern industrial and manufacturing activities shortly after the war and the various entrepreneurial groups that formed out of business families like Birla, Tata, Godrej and others transformed into powerful business groups (Singhal and Tagore, 2002).

This chapter discusses about the business groups in India, the information sourced from their websites, characterising their growth and development of entrepreneurship in terms of innovations, market leadership and future development. It introduces the business groups with reference to general business framework and characterises the major Indian business groups like Tatas, Reliance (Reliance Industries and Reliance ADA), Aditya Birla, ITC, Bajaj, Bharti Enterprises, Godrej and Boyce, Adani, Hero, Escorts and M.P. Birla.

6.2 The Family Business Groups

Family-owned businesses operate in every country and may be the oldest form of business organisation. Family businesses have been described as unusual business entities due to their concern for the long-term over generations, their strong commitment to quality and its relation to their own family name and their humanity in the work place where the care and concern for employees is often likened to that of an extended family. More than 90 per cent of the companies in North America and a majority of businesses located around the world are family-owned. Family businesses provide the only setting for an unusual social phenomenon, the overlap of family issues and business. They provide a number of advantages to family members, the most common being freedom, independence and control. In addition, they also offer many lifestyle benefits such as flexibility, prestige, community pride and creativity. However, family businesses are often recognised as a source of difficulty when it comes to succession issues, identity development and sibling relationships.

Family-owned businesses have a set of shared traditions and values that are rooted in the history of the firm. Family businesses typically evolve through three stages and the type of leadership required at each stage is different. In the entrepreneurial stage, the business is designed around the founder or leader. It is driven by personal and family goals and depends on the leader's direction. The business then evolves into the managerial stage, where it is more organised but still is like a family. The firm begins to require outside expertise and financial discipline, structure and accountability being established. Tension can arise as family members begin to lose some of their freedom from structure, but they recognize that a lack of structure may cause frustration. The firm finally enters the professional stage, where it is driven by what is best for the business. More goal-setting and market-driven strategic planning takes place. Often professional non-family managers are recruited to play a role in the future growth of the business. Some families operate with few or no family members in the business and simply retain ownership. The family can retain ownership by serving on the board of directors or setting up a holding company, which may manage several companies and investments.

Business groups have emerged out of entrepreneurial opportunism depending upon initial success and continued entrepreneurial drive. The growth has been facilitated by the favourable attitude of the financial institutions and markets that fund the growth and new initiatives. While individual firms within a group may be publicly subscribed and listed, the group as a whole might retain its closely-held status and thereby wield influence over governance and management, amassing economic power in the process. In the case of family businesses, which account for the bulk of businesses, the economic power implies that their ownership, leadership, management and control structures and changes might have far-reaching implications than being confined to the private domain of family matters, especially when poor corporate governance within them is noticed (Singhal and Tagore, 2002). Family-centred networks support a cultural orientation of relationships such as the Chinese *guanxi,* which entails an obligation to do business with close and extended family, neighbours and former classmates, in that order and only then, reluctantly, with strangers. There, family is instrumental in helping to establish the business and is a significant factor in the growth of the firm (Pistrui, 2006) owing to the culture being centred on Confucian values built around family, social ethics, education, centralised authority and conformity. Indian business families are different from these and in the west and most of them is part of the old joint family system. In the colonial past, only European entrepreneurs flourished and it was after the mid-19th century that family businesses emerged in India under solely individual funding and family-controlled managing agency system.

After independence until 1991, their growth was subject to many government regulations and licence raj *dirigisme*. It may be a reflection of society, wherein the support may come from family and relatives but the families may not keep their flock together for more than three generations. The Birlas and Bajajs had split after three generations and the Ambanis, in the second generation. The Jindals have divided the business empire operationally, though the control of the company is centralised. Indian business families want to avoid a scriptless family drama and plan for the involvement of members in advance. In 2007, the Indian family business billionaires recorded in the Forbes list included Lakshmi Mittal, Mukesh Ambani, Anil Ambani, Azim Premji, Kushal Pal Singh, Sunil Mittal, KM Birla, Shashi and Ravi Ruia. Their net worth was varied from $8 to $32 billion. The family business can be looked as family owned business, family owned and managed or family owned and led business. Family business governance is based on periodic assemblies of the family, family council meetings and constitution of the family.

6.3 Major Business Combines in India

In the post-liberalisation period, some old Indian businesses have failed not able to compete globally, while newly started businesses could flourish owing to their innovativeness and efficacy. At the same time, many big business groups, in spite of second or third generation splits, were able to restructure and revolutionalise their systems so as to be competitive and global business leaders. Below we present the profile of some of the big business groups that have managed to contribute to the growth of Indian and global entrepreneurship.

6.3.1 The Tatas

The Tata group is one of the largest companies in India by market capitalisation and revenue. Unlike most of India's big business houses, the group is not family owned and Ratan Tata is not on the Forbes list of billionaires. Tata Sons holds the bulk of shares in key companies and philanthropic trusts endowed by the Tata family own 66 per cent of Tata Sons. The group has interests in communications and information technology, engineering, materials, services, energy, consumer products and chemicals. The Tata group has operations in more than 80 countries and exports products and services to 80 nations. It comprises 114 companies and subsidiaries in eight business sectors, 27 of which are publicly listed and 65.8 per cent of the ownership of Tata group is held in charitable trusts. The companies which form a major part of the group include Tata Steel (including Tata Steel Europe), Tata Motors (including Jaguar and Land Rover), Tata Consultancy Services, Tata Technologies, Tata Tea (including Tetley), Tata Chemicals, Titan Industries, Tata Power, Tata Communications, Tata Sons, Tata Teleservices and the Taj Hotels. The 2009 annual survey of Reputation Institute ranked Tatas as the 11th most reputable company in the world. The Brand Trust Report 2011 has ranked Tatas as the second most trusted brand of India.

Tata Motors has adapted its offerings and organisation based on institutional voids, particularly with the development of a new vehicle, the Ace. By 2005, Tata Motors had become India's largest commercial truck maker but found itself squeezed amid growing foreign competition in its home market. At the top end of the market, major foreign truck manufacturers, such as Volvo, were challenging its supremacy in large trucks. Producers of pickup trucks from Japan and South Korea compete against commercial vehicles of Tata Motors. The low end of India's commercial vehicle market was dominated by three-wheelers made by domestic and foreign companies. Tata Motors responded to this competitive challenge by exploiting product market knowledge and adapting business processes with the development of the Ace, a four-wheeled mini-truck, to target a niche in the marketplace. The vehicle opened a new segment for Tata Motors, helping the company reduce the risk of dependence on its main commercial truck business, which was highly cyclical. The Ace was designed in response to market conditions in India and an unmet consumer need identified by Tata Motors.

The Ace was positioned as a replacement for three-wheelers and had a comparable payload size and price but offered many of the benefits of larger light commercial vehicles to serve the last mile of distribution (Gopalakrishnan, 2009). The truck was designed to be the only vehicle in India allowed on all roads. Although the initial cost of the Ace ($5,000) was higher than that of three-wheelers, the truck was designed to be more economical after accounting for its larger payload capacity and fuel costs. Tata Motors designed the Ace to meet higher safety standards than existing requirements and norms in India. The move put Tata Motors in a stronger position than competitors if higher standards were adopted by Indian regulators and would also facilitate the vehicle's entry into international markets having higher standards already on the books. The Ace was unique not only in its concept but also in the ways in which Tata Motors adapted the execution of the project to meet the vehicle's target price point and reach its target customers.

Tata Motors conducted extensive market research through interviews with potential customers to identify their needs and constraints, helping the company refine the Ace's design, pricing and features and substituting for absent market research intermediaries.

The company looked at the product through the eyes of its customers, incorporating, for example, realistic expectations about overloading. Meeting the project's tight budget to enable the Ace to be positioned at such a low price point forced Tata Motors to be innovative inproduct development and procurement. The company employed a cross functional team for product development and adopted a Japanese-style production preparation process, which incorporated suppliers and other stakeholders. Aggregate outsourcing, e-sourcing and the use of existing production facilities also helped to lower costs. To ease concerns about the Ace's high initial cost, the company offered financing through consumer finance. This action filled a void, because auto financing was a relatively new practice and almost unknown among customers in the Ace's target market. Tata Motors also adapted its distribution and after-sales service operations for the Ace to meet the needs of the vehicle's target customers. Many of the Ace's cost-conscious potential customers in rural areas might not be willing to travel long distances to see the vehicle, so the company deployed a new dealership format that would bring the Ace closer to these customers without incurring the expense of a new network of full-service dealerships. Similarly, instead of building an expensive new network of service centres, the company trained local mechanics and gave them tools to take care of common problems. Vehicles would be sent to larger urban service centres only in the event of major repairs or accidents. Less than a year after the Ace's introduction in May 2005, Tata Motors had already sold thirty thousand units even though the vehicle was available in only one-quarter of the country (Gopalakrishnan, 2009).

A survey of Ace purchasers found that more than half were buying their first commercial vehicle, suggesting that the product had expanded the existing commercial vehicle market. Because demand surpassed the capacity of the existing plant where the Ace was initially produced, Tata Motors established a new plant in northern India to produce the Ace and related vehicles with a capacity of 250,000 vehicles. The company also introduced the vehicle in Sri Lanka, Nepal and Bangladesh, with an eye to introducing the Ace in still other developing markets. Similarly, Tata Motors exploited local knowledge to target a difficult market segment with the development of the Nano, a $2,500 people's car introduced in 2008. Tata Motors successfully exploited local knowledge in conceptualising the Ace and adapted to institutional voids to deliver the product. However, the company's market opportunity with this product was closely tied to the state of India's infrastructure at the time of its introduction. The company's success with the Ace soon attracted other companies to develop similar vehicles for India. By filling the void of India's underdeveloped market research intermediaries for its own product development, Tata Motors served as a market researcher for its competition. Tata Motors has a head start in the segment and execution was critical to the success of the Ace. The company's innovative procurement process and investments in developing the ecosystem for the vehicle through its distribution and service operations could help Tata Motors sustain competitive advantage.

The Tata group has helped to establish and finance educational, research and cultural institutes in India. The group was awarded the Carnegie Medal for Philanthropy in 2007 in recognition of its long history of philanthropic activities. The group gets more than two-thirds of its revenue from outside India. In June 2011, based on market value, Tatas have become India's wealthiest group with $98.7 billion. The beginning of the Tata group can be traced back to 1868, when Jamsetji Nusserwanji Tata established a trading company dealing in cotton in Bombay. This was followed by the installation of Empress Mills in Nagpur in 1877. Taj Mahal Hotel in Bombay was opened for business in 1903.

Sir Dorab Tata, the eldest son of Jamsetji Tata became the chairman of the group after his father's death in 1904. Under him, the group ventured into steel production in 1905 and hydroelectric power generation in 1910. After the death of Dorab Tata in 1934, Nowroji Saklatwala headed the group till 1938. He was succeeded by Jehangir Ratanji Dadabhoy Tata. The group expanded significantly under him with the establishment of Tata Chemicals (1939), Tata Motors and Tata Industries (1945), Voltas (1954), Tata Tea (1962), TCS (1968) and Titan (1984). Ratan Tata, the incumbent chairman of the group succeeded JRD Tata in 1991. The Tata group has donated a Rs. 220 crore to Harvard Business School to build an academic and a residential building on the Institute's campus.

A Tata project that brought together TCS, Titan Industries and Tata Chemicals was developing a compact, in-home water-purification device was called Tata *swach* which means 'clean' in Hindi and would cost less than Rs. 1000. Its idea was thought of from the 2004 tsunami in the Indian Ocean that left thousands without clean drinking water. This device has filters that last about a year long for a family of five. It is a low-cost product available for people who have no access to safe drinking water in their homes. The advantage of this device is that it does not require the use of electricity. TCS also designed and donated an innovative software package that teaches illiterate adults how to read in 40 hours.

In 1912, the group included community philanthropy in the workplace. An eight-hour workday was instituted before any other company, with a recommendation of medical services policy for its employees. The company was among the first worldwide to organise modern pension systems, worker compensation, maternity benefits and profit-sharing plans. About two thirds of the profits of the group go to charity. Each Tata group company channels more than four per cent of its operating income to the trusts and every generation of Tata family members have left a larger portion of its profit to charities, founding supporting such institutions as the Indian Institute of Science, Tata Institute of Fundamental Research, the National Centre for the Performing Arts and the Tata Memorial Hospital.

Tata BP Solar, a joint venture company makes and markets solar panels, yielding benefits like delivering access to electricity, generating direct employment through installation and maintenance work and the collection of charges and indirect employment through fabrication shops, outlets to sell solar-powered devices, storage and transport. Tata BP Solar estimates that about 700 persons could be employed for every megawatt of solar power produced. Another example comes from the work that the community initiatives cell of Tata Chemicals did in collaboration with the International Centre for Entrepreneurship and Career Development (ICECD), which has been recognised as a centre of excellence by the United Nations. The focus was to promote enterprise, particularly among women. Using the training imparted by ICECD to its staff, the Tata Chemicals cell conducted a type of rural MBA programme in 42 villages around two of its main facilities. Among the lessons learned were that local government officials can become a threat to successful entrepreneurs and that societal traditions determine who can do what (in one place enterprise was perceived positively, in another, caste became a constraining factor).

The Tata group partnered with *Anand Bazar Patrika*, the largest selling Bengali newspaper to get young persons to undertake entrepreneurship projects. Called *nijer paye darao* (stand on your own feet), the campaign, started in December 2007, involves bimonthly publishing of editorial content that encourages emergence of entrepreneurship. The content includes articles about the Tata group's endeavours, success stories of local entrepreneurs, advice on how to get started in business and answers to questions from readers. Future plans include a contest in which prospective entrepreneurs will be asked to submit their business ideas, which will be evaluated by a panel of experts. The best ideas will be supported with funding leads and those generating them will be given the opportunity to attend an entrepreneurship training programmes. If there is one attribute common to every Tata enterprise, it is the time, effort and resources each of them devotes to the wide spectrum of initiatives that come under social development. The Tata culture in this critical segment of the overall corporate social responsibility matrix springs from an ingrained sense of giving back to society. It never was charity for its own sake or as group founder Jamsetji Tata put it, 'patchwork philanthropy.'

Reinforcing the implicit beliefs, the group brings to its mission of sustainable development an explicit set of structures, embodied by the Tata Council for Community Initiatives (TCCI). A centrally administered agency that helps Tata companies through specific processes, TCCI's charter embraces social development, environmental management, biodiversity restoration, and employee volunteering. This organisation coordinates many community development activities of the Tata companies. TCCI has, in collaboration with the United Nations Development Programme (India), crafted the Tata Index for Sustainable Human Development, aimed at directing, measuring and enhancing the community work that the Tata enterprises undertake. Tatas backing of sports has unfolded in the form of academies for a variety of sporting disciplines and the sponsorship of talented individuals.

The bigger entities in the group, such as Tata Steel and Tata Chemicals have in-house organisations dedicated to the task of social upliftment. The Tata Chemicals Society for Rural Development was established in 1980 to promote community welfare in and around its facilities in western and central India. The society works to protect and nurture the rural populations in these areas and helps people achieve self-sufficiency in natural resource management, livelihood support and the building of health and education infrastructures. Through TCSRD, Tata Chemicals works to improve the quality of life of the people and communities around its operations and to support sustainable development. The Tata Steel Rural Development Society

(TSRDS), set up in 1979 is involved in various social development programmes aimed at helping rural communities living around Tata Steel's operational units in eastern India. Tata Tea, Rallis, Voltas, Tata Power, Tata Consultancy Services and Titan devote considerable resources to community initiatives in spheres such as education, health, livelihoods, environment, tribal development and welfare of women and children.

Tata First Dot, an initiative of National Entrepreneurship Network has been involved in mentoring student start-ups. The Universities of Cambridge and California (Berkeley) and London School of Economics are jointly participating in an international student internship programme called Tata International Social Entrepreneurship Scheme, which offers students an opportunity to work on social entrepreneurship and corporate social responsibility projects within the Tata group.

The accumulation of wealth and glory by individuals is not in the Tata DNA (Gopalakrishnan, 2009), showing why Tatas are not in ritual listings of India's richest. This represents a unique business ethos, in which 65.8 per cent of the shares of Tata Sons, the holding company of the group are controlled by trusts. These trusts, established by members of the Tata family, support a wide variety of causes, institutions and individuals. What the Tata trusts do is separate from the community support initiatives of individual Tata companies. Sustainable and socially conscious business practices are not a Tata preserve.

The group chairman Ratan Tata leads through a consultative style of communication and encourages employees to grasp at the opportunities in an innovative way. He will ask questions that will lead to the theme, never telling them what to do. He never imposes nor demands that employees shall fall in line with his beliefs. As regards cultural compatibility, Tata has never diluted the value system. At a time when Tata Finance was a loser, Tata announced that the holding company would pump in the required money to safeguard the interests of the shareholders. Tata encourages aggression amongst line managers to think big. The group went through significant restructuring around 1998 and reduced the number of group affiliated firms and business portfolios by more than 50 per cent. Specifically, the Tatas shifted their focus from commodity businesses (like cement, pharmaceuticals and toiletries) to brand and services (like software) that provided a more sustainable return.

The group ventured into new business areas that were not very diversified as in the case of hotel division which expanded into luxury business hotels overseas. However, the group has many unrelated businesses that prevent it from achieving the required level of improved focus and synergy of resources to compete with relatively newer groups. The group manages to generate value because reform is still taking place and informal institutions are still influential. Banking on the informal institutions, the group is continuing to leverage its already existing market presence, brand image and age-old business experience. The international brand consultancy Brand Finance has ranked the $68-billion Tata conglomerate as 50th most valuable brand in the world. The most recent Global 500 report by Brand Finance shows that the group's brand value has soared to $15.08 billion for the current year compared to $11.2 billion last year in 2010. So far, the Tata group has concluded 35 cross-border acquisitions and international revenues now account for over 50 per cent of revenues.

6.3.2 The Reliance Group

The Reliance group is the largest business house with total revenues being more than $22.6 billion. It is involved in oil exploration and production, gas refining and marketing, petrochemicals, textiles, financial services, insurance, power, telecommunications and information technology. Reliance has the distinction of being the first Indian company to be named among the five hundred listed in Forbes. Dhirubhai Ambani established Reliance and created the equity cult in Indian stock markets. Dhirubhai started off by selling fried snacks to pilgrims in mount Girnar during weekends. After school he became a dispatch clerk at A. Besse & Company. The company became distributors of Shell and Dhirubhai was sent to manage an oil filling station at Aden. He learnt the ways of commodity trading, high seas purchase and sales, marketing and distribution, currency trading, and money management. During lunch break he roamed the *souks* and *bazaars* of Aden where traders from numerous different continents and countries bought and sold goods worth millions of pound sterling, the then global currency, during the day. He met traders from all parts of Europe, Africa, India, Japan and China. Aden was the biggest trading port of the times, a trading port where goods landed from all parts of the world and were dispatched to the farthest corners of different continents. Speculation in manufactured goods and commodities was rife all over the Aden *bazaars*. At the boarding house where he lived with another twenty-five young Gujarati clerks and office boys, he devoted long hours of the night mastering English grammar, essay writing, current affairs and a host of subjects. At that time, the Yemeni rial was made of pure silver and was greatly in demand in the London Bullion Exchange. Dhirubhai bought and melted the rials and sold it to the London bullion traders. Within three months his work came to a halt but by that time he had made few lakh of rupees. In 1958, he returned to India and he set up a textile trading company. Helped by his wife and two sons Dhirubhai diversified his interests to petrochemicals, telecommunications and information technology, energy, power, finance, capital markets and logistics.

With innovative instruments like convertible debentures Reliance became a favourite in the stock markets and it pioneered in raising funds in the international markets. In 1966, the first textile mill was set up at Naroda using polyester fibre. He branded his products Vimal and retail outlets were set up where 'Only Vimal' brands were sold. With the creation of the equity cult, nearly 60,000 investors placed their trust in Reliance in 1977. In 1982, Reliance Industries came up against a rights issue about partly convertible debentures. Dhirubhai himself provided the required cash when the *bulls* demanded a physical delivery of shares. The net result was that Reliance shares shot up from Rs. 152 to Rs. 180 within a few minutes. The *bears* bought Reliance shares from the market at higher price levels and most probably Dhirubhai himself supplied these shares and earned a profit from this manipulation. Keeping its core in petrochemicals Reliance soon diversified its activities to telecommunications, information technology, energy, power, retail, textiles, infrastructure services, capital markets and logistics. Reliance has the distinction of being the only public limited company whose many annual general meetings had to be held in stadiums with more than 3,50,000 shareholders in attendance. Many of the provisions of the MRTP Act were discarded by Dhirubhai Ambani when the size and scale of the Patalganga, Hazira and Jamnagar complexes are considered, which encouraged business families and politicians to go very big. Despite his almost Midas touch, Ambani has been known to have flexible values and an unethical manoeuvring. His biographer has cited some instances of his unethical behaviour when he was just an ordinary employee at a petrol pump in Dubai. He has been accused of having manipulated government policies to suit his own needs and has been known to be a king-maker in government elections. Although most media sources tend to speak out about business-politics nexus, the Ambani house has always enjoyed more protection and shelter from the media. The Federation of Indian Chambers of Commerce and Industry named Dhirubhai as the Indian Entrepreneur of the 20th century. After his death in 2002, the government of India issued a postal stamp in his honour. Reliance split up into two after the death of Dhirubhai. Mukesh got Reliance Industries and IPCL and this group came to be known, as Reliance Industries Ltd. Anil became head of Infocomm, Reliance Energy and Reliance Capital known as the Anil Dhirubhai Ambani group.

6.3.2a Reliance Industries

Mukesh Ambani is the chairman of Reliance Industries, the largest private sector enterprise in India, listed in *Fortune 500* magazine. His personal stake in Reliance Industries is 48 per cent. In August, 2011, Reliance Industries regained its status as the most valued firm in India, after a contest with ONGC and Coal India. In 2010, he was named among the most powerful personalities in the world by Forbes in its list of 68 individuals who matter most. He is the second richest man in Asia and the ninth richest man in the world with a personal wealth of $27 billion. He is a member of the board of directors of Bank of America and a present member of the international advisory board of the Council on Foreign Relations. The company's petrochemicals, refining and oil and gas-related operations form the core of its business, while other segments include textiles, retail business, telecommunications and special economic zone development. Reliance Life Sciences participates in medical, plant and industrial biotechnology opportunities like biopharmaceuticals, pharmaceuticals, clinical research services, regenerative medicine, molecular medicine, novel therapeutics, biofuels, plant biotechnology and industrial biotechnology. Reliance Industrial Infrastructure was incorporated in September 1988 with the objective to build and operate cross-country pipelines for transporting petroleum products. The infrastructure company constructed a 70,000 kilolitre petrochemical product storage and distribution terminal in Maharashtra. The company is also engaged in leasing and providing services connected with computer software and data processing.

Reliance Retail is the retail business wing which includes brands like Reliance Fresh, Reliance Footprint, Reliance Time Out, Reliance Digital, Reliance Wellness, Reliance Trendz, Reliance Autozone,

Reliance Super, Reliance Mart, Reliance iStore, Reliance Home Kitchens and Reliance Jewel. Reliance Industry is the world's largest polyester producer and as a result one of the largest producers of polyester waste. In order to deal with this large amount of waste, they had to create a way to recycle the waste. They operate the largest polyester recycling centre that uses the polyester waste as a filling and stuffing. They developed an innovative recycling process resulting in an award. Reliance owns world's largest refinery in Jamnagar which has zero discharge and effluent treatment based on best available technology processes the waste release and converts waste into usable product. Reliance has also planted more than five million trees around this refinery in order to reduce carbon-dioxide. Reliance has more than three million shareholders, making it one of the world's most widely held stocks. Reliance Industries has continued to grow since its split in January 2006.

6.3.2b Reliance ADA

Anil Ambani is the chairman of Reliance Anil Dhirubhai Ambani group and is the younger brother of Mukesh Ambani. Anil Ambani joined the company founded by his late father in 1983 as co-chief executive officer and has engineered financial innovations in the Indian capital market. He led the company into overseas capital markets with international public offerings of global depository receipts, convertibles and bonds. He directed Reliance in its efforts to raise around $2 billion from overseas financial markets; with a 100-year Yankee bond issue in 1997. He has been embroiled in a dispute with his brother over the supply of gas from the latter's Krishna-Godavari basin. He recently topped Business Sheet's world's biggest loser list of business leaders who lost money worth $32.5 billion in 2008, which brought him out of the top ten list to number 34 in 2009.

Reliance Communication is the second largest telecom company in India in terms of customers. The company has a customer base of 125 million including over 2.5 million individual overseas retail customers. It ranks among the top five telecom companies in the world by number of customers in a single country. Reliance Communications corporate clientele includes 2,100 Indian and multinational corporations and over 800 global, regional and domestic carriers. Reliance Communications owns and operates the next generation internet protocol-enabled connectivity infrastructure comprising of 190,000 kms of fibre optic cable system in India, the USA, Europe, Middle

East and the Asia Pacific region. Reliance Globalcom serves over 2,100 enterprises, 200 carriers and 2.5 million retail customers in 163 countries. Reliance Capital has interests in asset management and mutual funds, life and general insurance, private equity and proprietary investments, stock broking, depository services, distribution of financial products, consumer finance and other activities in financial services. Reliance Mutual Fund is India's largest mutual fund and Reliance General Insurance is among the top private sector insurers. Reliance Money is a brokerage and distributor of financial products with over 2.7 million customers and has the largest distribution network. The brokerage Reliance Securities is planning to invest Rs. 300 crore for upgrading infrastructure, hiring staff and enhancing the capability of its online trading platform.

6.3.3 Aditya Birla Group

The Aditya Birla group operates in 33 countries with more than 133,000 employees worldwide. The group has diversified business interests and is a dominant player in all the sectors in which it operates such as viscose staple fibre, metals, cement, viscose filament yarn, branded apparel, carbon black, chemicals, fertilizers, insulators, financial services, telecom, BPO and IT services. The group is a $35 billion conglomerate which earns 60 per cent of its revenues from outside India. The group has been adjudged the best employer in India and among the top 20 in Asia by the Hewitt-Economic Times and Wall Street Journal Study of 2007.The origins of the group lie in the conglomerate once held by one of India's foremost industrialists Ghanshyam Das Birla. The group is organised into various subsidiaries that operate across different sectors like viscose staple fibre, non-ferrous metals, cement, viscose filament yarn, branded apparel, carbon black, chemicals, retail (under the more brand of supermarkets), fertilizers, insulators, financial services, telecommunication, BPO and information technology services. The group consists of Hindalco, Grasim, Aditya Birla Nuvo, Idea Cellular and UltraTech Cement. The group's non-ferrous metals are under Hindalco. It is a dominant player in aluminium and copper. Its manufacturing locations are primarily in India and it owns mines in Australia. In 2007, the company entered into an agreement to acquire the Canadian company Novelis for $6 billion, making the combined entity the world's largest rolled-aluminium producer. Hindalco makes alumina chemicals, primary aluminum, rolled products, alloy wheels, roofing sheets, wire rods, cast copper rods, copper cathodes and several other products.

UltraTech Cement was originally the cement business of L&T, which was acquired by Aditya Birla group in 2004. The group is the fourth largest manufacturer of Carbon Black in the world. It operates out of facilities in Egypt, Thailand, India and China. The group is the world's largest player in the viscose staple fibre industry. It operates out of India, Laos, Thailand, Malaysia and China and owns the Birla cellulose brand. The group also owns acrylic fibre business in Egypt and Thailand, viscose filament yarn business and spinning mills at several locations all over India and South East Asia. The group has pulp and plantation interests in Canada and has recently invested in plantations in Laos. The group is a major player in the branded garments market in India. Idea Cellular started off as a joint venture with AT&T and Tatas. However, the stakes of the remaining partners was eventually acquired by the group. After an initial public offer, Idea Cellular now accounts for a third of the group's market capitalisation. The group has involved itself in several community development initiatives and supports development activities in areas like healthcare, education, sustainable livelihood, infrastructure and social causes. It works in 3,700 villages, reaching out to seven million people annually through the Aditya Birla Centre for Community Initiatives and Rural Development. It runs 45 schools and 18 hospitals.

6.3.4 ITC Limited

The company started off as Imperial Tobacco Company and shares ancestry with Imperial Tobacco of the United Kingdom. In 1830, the company was renamed WD and HO Wills and the first brand was Bristol, made at the London factory in 1871, followed by Three Castles and Gold in 1878 and Woodbine ten years later. In 1901, Sir William Henry Wills formed the Imperial Tobacco Company from a merger of W.D. and H.O. Wills with seven other British tobacco companies. It is now fully independent, named as Indian Tobacco Company in 1970 and then to I.T.C. Limited in 1974. ITC is engaged in fast moving consumer goods, hotels, cigarettes, paperboards, packaging, information technology, branded apparel, safety matches and agribusiness. Its turnover is $7 billion and has a market capitalisation of over $33 billion. The company is currently headed by Yogesh Chander Deveshwar.

ITC's agribusiness is India's second largest exporter of agricultural products. ITC is one of the India's biggest foreign exchange earners. Its *e-choupal* (choupal means gathering place in Hindi) initiative is enabling Indian agriculture significantly to enhance its competitiveness by empowering Indian farmers through the internet. The company places computers with internet access in rural villages and the *e-choupals* serve as both a social gathering place for exchange of information and an e-commerce hub. The effort which began tore-engineer the procurement process for soy, tobacco, wheat, shrimp and other cropping systems in rural India has generated a profitable distribution and product design channel. The *e-choupal* system has also catalysed rural transformation that is helping to alleviate rural isolation, create more transparency for farmers and improve their productivity. The initiative leverages information technology to set up a meta-market in favour of India's small and poor farmers, who would otherwise continue to operate and transact in underdeveloped markets. In 2010, services through 6500 *e-choupals* across 10 states, reach more than four million farmers. Its potential is being tested through pilot projects in healthcare, educational services, water management and cattle health management with the help of several service providers including NGOs. Its Classmate Ideas for India plans to reach out to 25 lakh students across 30 cities. ITC is the first from India and among the 10 companies in the world to publish its Sustainability Report at A+ level.

ITC is the first Indian company and the second in the world to win the Development Gateway Award, which recognises ITC's *e-choupal* as the most exemplary contribution in the field of information and communication technologies. ITC also has won the inaugural World Business Award for its efforts to create sustainable livelihood opportunities and enduring wealth in developing countries. ITC is the first company to receive the annual FICCI Outstanding Vision Corporate Triple Impact Award in 2007 for its contribution building economic, social and natural capital. ITC has won the Golden Peacock Awards for Corporate Social Responsibility (Asia) in 2007, the Award for Corporate Social Responsibility (CSR) in Emerging Economies in 2005 and Excellence in Corporate Governance in the same year. ITC Hotel Royal Gardenia, Bangalore is the first Indian hotel and world's largest to get the LEED platinum rating, the highest global green building certification. The Stockholm Challenge award 2006 for the *e-choupal* initiative was for using information technology for rural development. United Nations Industrial Development Organisation Award at the international conference on Sharing Innovative Agribusiness Solutions 2008 at Cairo was given for ITC's initiatives in agribusiness for the *e-choupal* initiative. The Crown Award for Water Practices from UNESCO and Water Digest was given for its work carried out in the water sector and it received the National Award for Excellence in Water Management 2007 for its leadership role in implementing water and watershed management practices. The watershed programme also won the Asian CSR Award 2007 for Environmental Excellence given by the Asian Institute of Management. The group received the Ryutaro Hashimoto Incentive Prize 2007 for Environment and Development from the Asia Pacific Forum. The Corporate Award for Social Responsibility 2008 from the Energy and Resources Institute was given in recognition of its initiatives in implementing integrated watershed development programmes across seven states. The Enterprise Business Transformation Award for Asia Pacific, instituted by Infosys Technologies and Wharton School of the University of Pennsylvania was accorded for its *e-choupal* initiative.

6.3.5 The Bajaj Group

The Bajaj group was founded by Jamanalal Bajaj in 1926 and the group comprises 34 companies. Its flagship company Bajaj Auto is ranked as the world's fourth largest two and three wheeler manufacturer, while other companies include Bajaj Electricals, Mukund and Bajaj Hindustan. The group is involved in automobiles (two and three wheelers), home appliances, lighting, iron and steel, insurance, travel and finance. Jamanalal's foresight in picking the right business at the right time that generated phenomenal growth. However, his business interests were the means to a larger and holistic end. Very active during freedom struggle, Jamanalal was a philanthropist who donated most of his wealth for worthy causes. From the beginning, Jamanalal was always more involved in social and philanthropic activities rather than business. He was a follower of Gandhi and assisted in his activities and was increasingly involved and committed to the Mahatma's programmes and India's freedom struggle.

Kamalnayan Bajaj, the eldest son of Jamanalal Bajaj, started shouldering family responsibilities from an early age. After completing his education from University of Cambridge, Kamalnayan returned to India to assist his father, both in business and in social service. He had earmarked a large portion of the income from his family business for public causes and social service programmes. With foresight and a spirit of zestful enterprise, Kamalnayan acquired ailing industrial units and then miraculously turned them around. He went on to expand the business by branching into manufacture of scooter, three-wheeler, cement, alloy casting and electrical manufacturing.

Ramkrishna Bajaj, the younger son of Jamanalal, took over after the demise of his elder brother Kamalnayan Bajaj in 1972. In addition to shouldering business responsibilities, Ramkrishna's energies were directed towards the social service and social welfare programmes of the group. He was elected as the chairman of World Assembly for Youth (India) in 1961. He also held the office of the managing trustee of the Indian Youth Centres Trust, which conceived and created the Vishwa Yuvak Kendra in 1968. Rahul Bajaj, the current chairman and managing director of the Bajaj group is the grandson of Jamanalal Bajaj. He pursued his studies from St Stephen's College, Delhi and Harvard University. He took over control of the Bajaj Group in 1965 and successfully established one of India's best companies. His net worth is estimated to be at $1.6 billion. He is currently listed 34th on the Forbes list of richest persons in India. His sons Rajiv Bajaj and Sanjiv Bajaj are involved in the management of his companies.

Under Rahul's leadership, the turnover of the Bajaj Auto has risen from Rs.72 million to Rs.46.16 billion. He established factories at Akurdi and Waluj. In 1980s, Bajaj Auto was top scooter producer in India and its Chetak brand had a ten-year waiting period. The slump in the sale of scooters and the downfall of the stock market of 2001 hit the company hard. It was even forecast that Bajaj industries would have to shut down soon. But without losing hope Rahul Bajaj with his business expertise re-established the battered company. He established another factory in Chakan, invested in R&D and came up with Bajaj Pulsar motorcycle. Bajaj Pulsar is presently a leader in its sector. In June 2006, Rahul Bajaj was elected as a Rajya Sabha MP from Maharashtra. The group is involved in a variety of welfare activities, which are carried out with the support of its companies and trusts. Shiksha Mandal, Wardha was established in 1914 for educating the youth of India. Kamalnayan Bajaj School was established in 1976. The group also started management schools in Bombay and upgraded three industrial training institutes. The company enabled education of eligible bright backward students has helped many backward students to achieve academic excellence. A hospital and a HIV centre were established by the group. A village development institute was created to empower women and it has been doing so by training women in using improved technology for storage of foodgrains and initiating goat rearing projects owned and managed by women, emphasising the importance of family planning particularly tubectomy operations and securing loans for women members for both consumption and income generation. An award was instituted for outstanding contribution women entrepreneurs for rural development. The Institute of Gandhian Studies, established in 1987, promotes long-term and short-term study courses on Gandhian thoughts and methodology. The rural development activities are aimed at improving the living conditions of the rural population via income generation, training for self-employment, improved health and sanitation, supply of drinking water, improved agricultural and land maintenance practices such as horticulture, social forestry and reclamation of wasteland. Other activities include distribution of solar-lanterns and solar cookers, installation of bio-gas plants, deepening and widening of wells and drinking water scheme, tree plantation, veterinary services like insemination, vaccination and distribution of cattle feed, watershed development and building of model villages, distribution of agricultural equipment and building a centre of child labour welfare.

6.3.6 Bharti Airtel

Established as a start-up by Sunil Mittal and with more than $5 million in annual sales by 1992, Bharti Airtel grew into one of India's largest telecommunications providers, with a market capitalisation of $31.8 billion by 2008. The company's partnerships with a range of foreign firms over the course of its history were central to its growth into a capital-intensive industry and take on tough competition from state-owned enterprises and well-funded offshoots of powerful business groups. Bharti partnered first with Compagnie Generale des Eaux of France, Mauritian cell operator Emtel and Mobile Systems International of the United Kingdom in a successful joint bid for India's first cellular service licence. Soon after Bharti launched cellular services in Delhi in September 1995, it faced competition from Sterling Cellular, which was controlled by Indian steel giant Essar. The company targeted small business owners and retail customers instead of the corporate market, where larger business groups would have an advantage.

Italian state-owned telecom operator STET invested $58 million in Bharti in 1996 and from 1997 through 1999, British Telecom made $250 million in equity investments and helped Bharti improve its operations by providing assistance in corporate communication, lending technology support by extending procurement benefits to Bharti through its own vendor network. In 1995, a second round of cellular service licences came up for auction, but Bharti did not bid high enough for the desirable locations. Winning bids turned out to be too high and unsustainable for some new entrants. Bharti wanted to expand through acquisitions, but it needed more capital. In 1999, Warburg Pincus purchased a 20 per cent stake in Bharti for $60 million. The following year SingTel invested $400 million, and in 2001, Warburg Pincus and SingTel each invested an additional $200 million. Bharti received smaller investments from New York Life Insurance, Asian Infrastructure Fund Group, and International Finance Corporation. Bharti was still a relatively small operation when it attracted these major investments. Warburg Pincus and SingTel offered other resources and advice that helped Bharti build its business. Bharti and SingTel jointly built an underwater cable network linking Bharti's domestic voice and data network to SingTel's global network. Warburg Pincus offered significant strategic advice on Bharti's geographic expansion, acquisition approach and financing operations. Warburg Pincus helped Bharti to acquire existing operations, even those not fully meeting the company's high standards and to look beyond northern India to craft a pan-India strategy to tap in to opportunities in the wealthier south. Bharti went public in 2002, listing ten per cent of its shares on the National Stock Exchange and subsequently has raised capital through loans. By 2005, Warburg Pincus had earned $1.1 billion by selling two-thirds of its stake in Bharti. Bharti's partnerships were particularly valuable because of the institutional voids in its home market and the deeper expertise and richer resources it gained from foreign partners than would be possible to access locally. These capabilities and resources helped Bharti to combat the inherent advantages of state-owned and business group-affiliated rivals and to grow into one of India's largest telecom service providers. Bharti has demonstrated not only a highly promising business model and successful track record but also credibility in its management and corporate governance.

6.3.7 The Godrej Group

The Godrej group is one of the largest family-owned businesses in the country. The group was founded by Ardeshir Godrej and Pirojsha Godrej in 1897. Its seven major companies have interests in real estate, FMCG, industrial engineering, appliances, furniture, security and agricare, its turnover crossing over $2.6 billion. Its products include locks, access control systems, security systems and safes, typewriters and word processors, rocket launchers, refrigerators and furniture, outsourcing services, machine tools and process equipment, cosmetics and detergents, engineering work stations, medical diagnostics and aerospace equipment, edible oils and chemical, mosquito repellents, car perfumes, chicken and agri-products, material handling equipments like forklift trucks, stackers, tyre handlers, sweeping machines and access equipments. The group's Godrej Industries (chemicals, FMCG, agriculture and services) is headed by Adi Godrej and Godrej and Boyce manufacturing company by Jamshyd Godrej. Adi Godrej is the second richest person of *parsi* descent in the world after Pallonji Mistry. After his MBA from MIT, he joined the family business and modernized its management structures and implemented process improvements. In the early 2000s, the group completed a 10-year restructuring process through which each business became a stand-alone company with a chief executive from outside the Godrej family.

In 1897, Godrej introduced the first lock with lever technology in India. In 1902, the group made the first Indian safe. In 1920, it made soap using vegetable oil and in 1955 produced India's first indigenous typewriter. In 1989, Godrej became the first company to introduce polyurethane foam and introduced India's first and only 100 per cent CFC, HCFC, HFC-free refrigerators. The group owns vast land in Vikhroli, Bombay occupying 3500 acres. In 2001, Godrej Consumer Products was formed as a result of the demerger of Godrej Soaps and was renamed Godrej Industries. In 2003, the group entered the BPO solutions and services establishing Godrej Global Solutions. In 2004, Godrej HiCare was set up to provide a safe environment to customers by providing professional pest management services. In 2006, the foods business was merged with Godrej Tea and Godrej Tea was renamed Godrej Beverages and Foods which was later renamed as Godrej Hershey Foods and Beverages. In 2011, Godrej and Boyce shut down its typewriter manufacturing plant, the last in the world.

Godrej is major supporter of the World Wildlife Fund in India. The group has built schools, dispensaries and a residential complex for their employees. Trusts established by Godrej continue to invest in education, healthcare and upliftment of the underprivileged. It was adjudged as the highest ranked Indian FMCG in Asia's Hot Growth

Companies' List by Business Week. Godrej Consumer Products has been ranked 14th in The Best Companies to Work For study. Godrej Consumer Products Ranks sixth in ET-Hewitt Best Employers of India survey. Godrej Consumer Products Limited was adjudged as a Business Super brand by the Super Brands Council. It also features in the top 25 list of Great Places to Work for four years in a row.

6.3.8 The Adani Group

The Adani group is a Gujarat based company, having Gautam Adani as its promoter. The core business of the group includes commodities trading, edible oil manufacturing, Mundra port operations and distribution of natural gas. The Adani group has more than 50 companies and a thermal power project in Mundra, Kutch district. Adani Power is the largest private company having largest power production on coal-based power. Adani Energy is one of the largest natural gas distributors in India. Adani Enterprises bought a coal mine in Australia for about Rs.126 billion in a cash and royalty deal and has invested $6.9 billion in developing its recently acquired Australian coal mines. The group will develop mine, rail and port projects in its Galilee Basin coal mine in Queensland, Australia to produce up to 60 million tonnes of coal a year. Adani Enterprises is the largest trading house of India in importing coal with a market share 60 per cent. The group became India's largest private coal mining company after Adani Enterprises bagged Odisha mine rights. The group manages one management college and a medical college at Ahmedabad. Adani Enterprises was placed among the top 50 Asian Companies by Forbes Asia in 2009.

6.3.9 The Hero Group

In 1956, Munjal brothers founded Hero group with Hero Cycles as the flagship company. The group had focused on manufacturing automobile parts and other related goods and comprises of 19 companies, 300 ancillary suppliers and has market penetration with over 5,000 outlets. However, the group could not transform itself to suit the changed Indian business scenario in reform era when national economy opened up considerably, thereby enhancing business competition. Further, the market for bicycles and related products did not appreciate as compared to other markets like pharmaceuticals and software.

6.3.10 The Escorts Group

The Escorts group has played a pivotal role in the agricultural growth, especially in farm mechanisation. It offers a range of tractors (about 45 variants starting from 25 to 80 HP) and Escort, Farmtrac and Powertrac are some of the popular brands. The group manufactures and markets a wide range of cranes, loaders, vibratory rollers and forklifts. The group is the world's largest pick-n-carry hydraulic mobile crane manufacturer. Escorts has been a major player in the railway equipment business, offering brakes, couplers, shock absorbers, rail fastening systems and composite brake blocks and vulcanized rubber parts. In the auto components segment, Escorts is a leading manufacturer of auto suspension products including shock absorbers and telescopic front forks. Throughout its evolution, technology has contributed to its growth. Over a million tractors and over 16,000 construction and material handling equipments have rolled out from the facilities of Escorts. With technological and business collaboration and with competitive indigenous engineering capabilities and 1600 sales and service outlets and footprints in over 40 countries the group is truly a multinational. At a time when the world is looking at India as an outsourcing destination, Escorts is rightly placed to be the dependable outsourcing partner of world's leading engineering corporations looking at outsourcing manufacture of engines, transmissions, gears, hydraulics, implements and attachments to tractors and shock absorbers for heavy trailers. The group is on the path of an internal transformation, which will help it to be a key driver of manufacturing excellence in the global arena.

6.3.11 The MP Birla Group

It was in 1862 when Shiv Narain Birla moved out from Rajasthan to Mumbai and set up a trading house. The group has operations in over 12 countries and a turnover that exceeds $8 billion. In the initial years, the group was only involved in commodity trading and in exports and imports. In 1918, the group diversified out into manufacturing and set up its first jute mill. The group was involved in the manufacture of a vast range of textiles made from jute, synthetics, cotton, wool and fibres. Each unit is an independent public limited company listed on the stock exchange. It was the Birlas who pioneered the concept of public holdings and professional management.

The group owns over 500 factories in a wide range of industries such as textiles, man-made fibres, cables, woollens, automobiles, industrial and textiles machines, sugar, paper, shipping, cement, jute, aluminium, copper, fertilizers, chemicals, power plants, non-ferrous semis, etc. The group also has over 40 joint ventures and management contracts in several countries such as Nigeria, Kenya, England, Philippines, Indonesia, Thailand, Uganda, Ethiopia and Egypt. The group's Universal Cables manufactures cables and capacitors by the brand name 'unistar'. Vindhya Telelinks manufactures jelly filled telephone cables in technical collaboration with Ericsson Cables AB of Sweden. Birla Ericsson Optical has technical and financial collaboration with the same company and produces optical fibre cables. The company also produces polyurethane jelly filled insulated cables and optic fibre. Hindustan Gum and Chemicals manufactures guar gum and exports to various countries. Birla DLW, a joint venture with DLW Aktiengesellchaft, Germany produces linoleum flooring for exports. Birla Financial Corporation limited is involved in the financial sector.

Birla Corporation Limited is the flagship company of the group, which was incorporated as Birla Jute Manufacturing Company Limited in 1919. Madhav Prasad Birla transformed it from a manufacturer of jute goods to a leading multi-product corporation with widespread activities. Under the chairmanship of Priyamvada Birla, the company crossed the Rs. 1300 crore turnover and the name was changed to Birla Corporation in 1998. The group runs several institutions, including the MP Birla Planetarium, Belle Vue Clinic, South Point School and the MP Birla Foundation Higher Secondary School in Kolkata, Bombay Hospital, Birlapur Hospital, West Bengal and Birla Vikas Hospital in Madhya Pradesh. The MP Birla Eye Clinic was established in 2001.

6.4 Prospects of Indian Business Groups

Entrepreneurship development has enabled the business groups in identifying and using the opportunities that exist in the market and convert the ideas into action and striving for excellence. Entrepreneurship has created many innovative responses. The state also plays the role of the entrepreneur in encouraging the groups and there has been a significant increase in entrepreneurship in the country in the post-liberalisation period. Entrepreneurship has helped the formation of capital, besides providing large-scale employment opportunities, promoting balanced regional development in the country and helping to reducing concentration of economic power.

Entrepreneurs of the major business groups have wide knowledge of the economic and non-economic environment of business and the willingness to assume risk, besides having open mind, optimistic outlook, adaptability, self-confidence and strong leadership qualities.

Before 1991, Indian business success was a function of ambition, licences, government contracts and an understanding of the bureaucratic system. Decisions were based on connections, rather than the market or competition. Business goals reflected a continuation of the swadeshi movement, which promoted import substitution to attain economic freedom from the west. Pre-1991 policies were inward looking and geared towards the attainment of self-reliance. During this period, entrepreneurship was subdued, capital was limited and India had very few success stories. As well, society was risk averse and the individual looked primarily for employment stability. In the post-liberalisation era, family businesses faced competition from multinationals that had superior technology, financial strength and efficient managerial resources.

For the old business houses, success had come from the close-knit joint family structure that fosters family values, teamwork, tenacity and continuity. Under this structure, generations lived and worked together under one roof, reaffirming the Weberian values and trust that have built successful businesses. Wealth from the businesses supported the joint family by providing a social safety net for members. In the structure, businesses and families were intertwined though they were also distinct entities with separate rules. Hence, survival of the family became synonymous with the survival of the business.

Liberalisation changed the very nature of the joint family. If large Indian businesses were to succeed, the family would have to re-orient itself to compete in a global, competitive environment. Post-liberalisation, businesses succeeded because they were customer focused and professionally managed. The old, family-managed businesses, which formed the backbone of the economy, needed to evolve and become more institutional, if they were to extend their life cycle. The businesses had to move from an entrepreneurial-driven, unstructured culture to one dominated by professional managers. Sunil Mittal of Bharti, a first generation entrepreneur, identified an opportunity in mobile telecom. In 1994, Mittal successfully bid for a telecom licence and services were launched under the brand name Airtel. The business model was innovative and IT management services and hardware (telecom towers) were outsourced to vendors. Fixed costs were converted to variable costs. Mittal was able to professionalise the organisation early, something that helped him build a larger institution. As a result, India now has one of the lowest-priced telecom services in the world. As Indian businesses became professional, opportunities to acquire global businesses increased. In 2006, Corus, an Anglo-Dutch steel maker accepted $7.6 billion bid by Tata Steel, to enable it to become a global leader in the steel business instead of continuing to remain a large domestic steel manufacturer. Once an acquisition target, Tata Steel has itself grown into an acquirer.

In India, the prevalence of joint family system and traditional caste system, wherein *vaishyas (banias)* are engaged in trade and business, has led to strengthening of family businesses. The family business sector was small in 1946, but currently dominates the private corporate sector, constituting 80 per cent of the 500 biggest companies. Many new business groups have emerged after 1991 liberalisation due to foreign collaborations, cross border acquisitions or business restructures as a result of family split. There is some variation in the number of family firms in the biggest companies (Dutta, 1997), wherein the top 17 private business groups by market capitalisation (Tatas, Mukesh Ambani, Aditya Birla, Bajaj group and Vijay Mallya) have increased or maintained their stakes in at least 55 companies out of the total of 91. Changes in the financial system and take-over threat are some of the reasons for the increase in the stake by the promoters, though in the olden days, promoters relied heavily on foreign investors for support. For example, Tata Steel has increased its stake from 30.26 percent in December 2006 to 34 per cent in June 2007 after the takeover of Corus and Tata Tea has increased its stake from 29 per cent in June 2006 to 35 per cent in June 2007.

6.5 The Tata Entrepreneurs

This section profiles some of the leading entrepreneurs of the Tata group like Jamsetji Tata, JRD Tata and Ratan Tata to showcase the emergence of entrepreneurial culture in India. The profiles have been sourced from various Tata and other websites on important entrepreneurs. Jamsetji Tata, the founder, belonging to a trading family, chose to be a businessman very early in his life. Tata was successful in redefining the concept of industries and has rightly been regarded as the father of Indian industry. Jamsetji Tata was the son of Nusserwanji Tata, the only businessman in a *Parsi* family that earned its living as Zoroastrian priests. Along with his wife Jeevanbai Tata, Nusserwanji Tata had moved out of his family to carry on his business in Bombay and did quite well. Jamsetji Tata completed his graduation at Elphinstone College in Bombay, where he was known as a bright student that the principal decided to refund his fees once he completed his degree. Tata took up trading at 14, a time when he was still studying. Jamsetji Tata became actively involved in his father's export business at a time when the business scenario in India was far from prosperous.

Nusserwanji Tata sent his son on a trip to Hong Kong in 1859 to expand his business interests there, which the young Tata completed successfully. Jamsetji Tata remained in Hong Kong for the next four years, trying to fulfill and realise his father's dream of setting up a branch of the Tata and Co office there. The establishment of the new Tata office in Hong Kong was the beginning of the expansion of the Tatas throughout Asia and the first step towards the creation of Tata and Sons. By 1863, there were Tata offices not only in Hong Kong, but also in Japan and China. Jamsetji Tata travelled to Europe, but unlike in Asia, he faced with a hindrance in the initial stages. Part of Jamsetji Tata's aims in visiting England, apart from increasing the number of contacts for his father's export business based in India, was to establish an Indian bank in London. This project, however, proved highly unsuccessful because it was not favourable time for the banking sector, with a financial crisis hitting the markets in several parts of India. The Tata companies in India and all over Asia faced huge monetary loss after the failure of the establishment of the Indian bank. The Empress Mill set up in Nagpur in 1874 brought Jamsetji Tata huge amounts of money. The mills made large amounts of profit, later sold off by Jamsetji Tata for a higher sum of money. Jamsetji Tata's cotton mills produced cloth used in India and also exported to countries of Japan, Korea, China and several parts of the Middle East (Nakra, 1996). The mills were largely established to satisfy Jamsetji Tata's business interests, but the Dharamsi Cotton Mill which was later renamed as Swadeshi Cotton Mill kept the nationalistic sentiment and made use of only Indian products, particularly promoting the non-use of British raw materials.

Jamsetji Tata made it a point to look after the best interests of the workers in Tata and Sons. The Tata companies were then also known to provide the best working atmosphere for its workers. Policies which were unheard of during those times, like medical facilities for the sick and for women with children, provision of pensions, accident compensations and on-the-job training, were a part of Tata companies. It was Jamsetji Tata who appealed to the Japanese Steam Navigation Company to reduce freight charges, a factor which was largely diminishing his profits. Though it was for the benefit for the entire nation, Jamsetji Tata made it a point to spend his own money to get the case solved when his demands led to huge upheavals in Japan. Eventually, Jamsetji Tata did emerge successful in reducing freight charges and thereby increasing profits for Indian traders.

The cotton mills satisfied his business interests, but to remain stuck on the production of cloth was not the aim of Jamsetji Tata. His vision was to establish an iron and steel plant, a world class hotel, a learning institution and a hydro-electric power project. Among his four wishes, only the second was fulfilled during Jamsetji Tata's lifetime when the Taj Mahal Hotel was established in 1903. In 1901, Jamsetji Tata travelled to Europe and America to educate himself on the making of steel. In addition, he made it a point to educate himself on the latest technological progress that had taken place over the years all around the world so that he may use it for the betterment of the industries under Tata and Sons. The Tata group was succeeded by his two sons, Dorabji Tata and Ratanji Tata. A pioneer of his field, the vision and aim of Jamsetji Tata came to life with time as his family gave wings to each of his dream projects. In fact, such was his contribution that the city of Jamshedpur in Jharkhand is today known as Tatanagar, because of the many facilities that the group has endowed the city with. Today, the group has been the founder of projects like Tata Steel, the Indian Institute of Science, the Tata Power Company, the Taj Mahal Palace and Tower, the Tata Institute of Fundamental Research and others. JRD's father Ratanji Dadabhoy Tata and Jamsetji Tata shared their philosophy from the same great-great-grandfather, Ervad Jamsheed Tata, a priest of Navsari.

JRD Tata was the second of four children. He was educated in France, Japan and England before being drafted into the French army for a mandatory one-year period. JRD wanted to extend his service in the forces but destiny had something else in store for him. By leaving the French life was saved because shortly thereafter, the regiment in which he served was totally wiped out during an expedition in Morocco. JRD Tata had the honour of being India's first pilot, was chairman of Tata and Sons for 50 years. JRD Tata was one of the most enterprising Indian entrepreneurs. He was a pioneer aviator and built one of the largest industrial houses of India. On February 10, 1929, JRD became the first Indian to pass the pilot's examination. With this honour of being India's first pilot, he was instrumental in building Tata Airlines, which ultimately became Air India. His passion for flying was fulfilled with the formation of the Tata Aviation Service in 1932. In 1938, JRD was elected chairman of Tata and Sons making him the head of the largest industrial group in India. He started with 14 enterprises under his leadership and half a century later, it was a conglomerate of 95 enterprises. Under his guidance, Sir Dorabji Dadabhoy Trust established Asia's first cancer hospital and the Tata Memorial Centre for Cancer, Research and Treatment. It also founded the Tata Institute of Social Sciences, the Tata Institute of Fundamental Research and the National Centre for Performing Arts. In 1948, JRD Tata launched Air India International as India's first international airline. In 1953, the Indian Government appointed JRD as chairman of Air-India and a director on the Board of Indian Airlines, a position JRD retained for 25 years. For his achievements in Aviation, JRD was bestowed with the title of Honorary Air Commodore of India.

In 1956, JRD Tata initiated a programme of closer employee association with management to give workers a stronger voice in the affairs of the company. He believed in employee welfare and espoused the principles of an eight-hour working day, free medical aid, workers' provident scheme and workmen's accident compensation scheme, which were later adopted as statutory requirements in India. In 1979, Tata Steel instituted a new practice, wherein a worker would be deemed to be at work from the moment he leaves home for work till he returns home from work. The company is financially liable to the worker if any mishap takes place on the way to and from work. Tata Steel Township was selected as a UN Global Compact City because of the quality of life, conditions of sanitation, roads and welfare that were offered by Tata Steel. JRD Tata was awarded India's highest civilian honour, the Bharat Ratna and was also bestowed with the United Nations Population Award for his action towards initiating and successfully implementing the family planning movement in India, much before it became an official government policy.

Ratan Naval Tata is presently the chairman of Tata Sons, the holding company of the Tata group. Ratan Tata is also the chairman of Tata companies such as Tata Steel, Tata Motors, Tata Power, Tata Consultancy Services, Tata Tea, Tata Chemicals, Indian Hotels and Tata Teleservices. He has taken Tata group to new heights and under his leadership group's revenues have grown manifold. Ratan Tata had a short stint with Jones and Emmons in Los Angeles, California, before returning to India in late1962. He joined the Tata group and was assigned to various companies before being appointed director-in-charge of The National Radio and Electronics Company in 1971. Ratan Tata was appointed chairman of Tata Industries in 1981. He was assigned the task of transforming the company into a group strategy think-tank, and a promoter of new ventures in hi-tech businesses. In 1991, Ratan Tata took over the chairmanship from JRD Tata. Under him Tata Consultancy Services went public and Tata Motors was listed in the New York Stock Exchange. In 1998, Tata Motors came up with Tata Indica, the first truly Indian car. The car was the brainchild of Ratan Tata. Ratan Tata was honoured with Padma Bhushan. Cyrus Mistry is the present chairman of Tata Sons.

6.6 The Bioentrepreneurs

This section presents brief profiles of some noted entrepreneurs in the field of biotechnology. Anji Reddy is a pioneer in the pharmaceutical research in India and is founder-chairman of Dr Reddy's. Kallam Anji Reddy did his BSc in Pharmaceuticals and Fine Chemicals and subsequently completed his PhD in Chemical Engineering from National Chemical Laboratory, Pune. Anji Reddy served in Indian Drugs and Pharmaceuticals Limited from 1969 to 1975. Reddy was the founder-managing director of Uniloids from 1976 to 1980 and Standard Organics Limited from 1980 to 1984. In 1984, he founded Dr. Reddy's Laboratories and soon the company established new benchmarks in the Indian pharmaceutical industry. Dr. Reddy's Laboratories transformed Indian bulk drug industry from import-dependent in mid-1980s to self-reliant in mid-1990s and finally into the export-oriented industry that it is presently. In 1993, DRL became the first company to take up drug discovery research in India and in April 2001 it became the first non-Japanese Asian pharmaceutical company to list on New York Stock Exchange. By the end of 2005, DRL was India's second largest pharmaceutical company and the youngest among its peer group. Presently, Dr. Reddy is a serving member of the Prime Minister's Council on Trade and Industry and has been nominated to the Board of National Institute of Pharmaceutical Education and Research (NIPER). He is the founder-chairman of Dr. Reddy's Foundation for Human and Social Development, which acts as a catalyst of change to achieve sustainable development. The awards and honours received by him include Sir PC Ray award (1984, 1992) and Federation of Asian Pharmaceutical Associations Ishidate Award for Pharmaceutical Research in 1998. Business India voted him Businessman of the Year in 2001 and CHEMTECH Foundation bestowed on him the Achiever of the Year award in 2000 and the Hall of Fame award in 2005 for his entrepreneurship, leadership and thrust on Innovation and in 2001, he was awarded the Padma Shri.

Habil Khorakiwala, the chairman of Wockhardt, founded that company in the early 1960s. Under his leadership, Wockhardt has emerged as a leading biotechnology and pharmaceutical company, driven by research and global strategies. Today, Wockhardt has an annual turnover of $650 million and a market capitalisation of over $1 billion. Khorakiwala leads a team of 7000 employees based in India, the UK, Ireland, the US and France. Khorakiwala advocates a customer-centric approach that has filtered down to every decision and action in Wockhardt's. The management process at Wockhardt is an open culture, participative management practice aimed at innovative and continuous improvement for speedy response, empowerment of individuals and enjoyment of one's job and contribution to the community. He has been the past president of FICCI and president of Indian Pharmaceutical Association. He has been awarded the Ernst & Young Entrepreneur award of 2004 in Healthcare and Life sciences.

Bhai Mohan Singh, the founder of Ranbaxy, began his business career in the construction business during the Second World War. His firm bagged a contract to build roads in the North East. After partition, he left Rawalpindi and settled down in New Delhi. He started business as a moneylender. Ranbaxy was started by his cousins Ranjit Singh and Gurbax Singh. They were distributors for A Shionogi, a Japanese pharmaceutical company manufacturing vitamins and anti-TB drugs. When Ranbaxy defaulted on a loan, Mohan Singh bought the company in 1952 for Rs. 2,50,000. He collaborated with Italian pharma company Lapetit Spa and later on bought it. He made his mark in the pharmaceuticals industry in the late 1960s when he launched his first super brand, Calmpose. Calmpose was an imitation of Roche's Velum. But Roche had not patented it in India. He established an R&D facility at Mohali and launched many pills such as Roscillin and Cifran. Ranbaxy went public in 1973. At this time Mohan Singh introduced his eldest son Parvinder Singh in the company, who later on became the company's managing director in 1982. Mohan Singh also co-founded Max India with his youngest son, Analjit Singh. With liberalisation differences arose between Mohan Singh and Parvinder Singh over the expansion and professionalisation strategy of Ranbaxy. Subsequently, in 1999 in a boardroom coup, Bhai Mohan Singh was forced to bow down and Parvinder took over the company. This broke Mohan Singh's spirit and he retired from active company affairs. Bhai Mohan Singh was a former vice president of the New Delhi Municipal Corporation and was awarded the Padma Shri for his contribution in civic matters. For his contribution to the industrial development of Punjab, the Punjab government had named an industrial township near Ropar after Bhai Mohan Singh.

Kiran Mazumdar Shaw is the chairman and managing director of Biocon, India's biggest biotechnology company. After completing her B.Sc. in Zoology from Bangalore University in 1973, she went to Ballarat University in Melbourne, Australia and qualified as a master brewer. Kiran Mazumdar Shaw started her professional career as trainee brewer in Carlton and United Beverages in 1974. In 1978, she joined as trainee manager with Biocon Biochemicals in Ireland. In the same year, Kiran founded Biocon India in collaboration with Biocon Biochemicals with a capital of Rs.10,000. She initially faced many problems regarding funds and banks were hesitant to give loan to her as biotechnology was a totally a new field and she was a woman entrepreneur. Biocon's initial operation was to extract an enzyme from papaya. In 2004, Biocon came up with an initial public offer and the issue was over-subscribed by over 30 times. Post-IPO, she held close to 40 per cent of the stock of the company and was regarded as India's richest woman with an estimated worth of Rs. 2,100 crore.

The New Yorker cites her company's work on diseases prevalent in countries like India and also her philanthropic work in bringing healthcare to the poor. Since 1996, Biocon has been developing its own drugs, in addition to generics and produces drugs for cancer, diabetes and auto-immune diseases. It is in stage-three clinical trials for both a cancer treatment drug and a variety of insulin that can be taken orally. Biocon Park has a 90-acre campus in Bangalore and houses 5,000 molecular biologists, technicians and other employees. At the entrance is an enormous sculpture of a double helix with the words 'Recombinant Revolution' on the base. Mazumdar Shaw works a few doors down from her husband, John Shaw, who became Biocon's vice chairman in 2001, three years after the couple married. John

Shaw, who grew up in Scotland, came to Bangalore in 1991 as chairman of Madura Coats.

In 2004, Biocon held an initial public offering, which brought Shaw's net worth to half a billion dollars. It is now almost double that. She started the Biocon Foundation to carry out her philanthropic work. She has spent $15 million on her cancer hospital and the Arogya Raksha. Her 1,400-bed Mazumdar-Shaw Cancer Centre in Bangalore treats poor patients for free or at steep discounts, similar to the Madurai-based Aravind Eye Hospital. Aravind's founders use a tiered pricing structure that charges wealthier patients more, letting the firm cross-subsidise free care for the poorest. Aravind rotates its staff at its five hospitals to deal with both paying and non-paying patients so there is no difference in quality. In addition, to starting the Huskur clinic and nine others in Karnataka, Arogya Raksha has started a micro-insurance programme and hired local women to go door-to-door offering screening services for oral cancer. Every year, Shaw donates $2 million to support health insurance coverage for 100,000 villagers. She is the recipient of several prestigious awards, including ET Businesswoman of the Year, Best Woman Entrepreneur, Model Employer and Ernst & Young's Entrepreneur of the Year Award for Life Sciences and Healthcare, Leading Exporter, Outstanding Citizen and Technology Pioneer. The Government of India also felicitated her with Padma Shri (1989) and Padma Bhushan (2005).

Dr. Pratap Reddy is the founder of the Apollo Hospitals, India's first corporate hospital group. He revolutionised the whole health care scenario of India and inspired others to follow the suit. Today, India has over 750 corporate hospitals all over the country. Dr. Pratap Reddy came to India after serving as the chief resident of the Worcenter City Hospital in the US to start his practice in Madras with a modest earning of Rs.100 per day. The idea to establish Apollo Group of Hospitals came when Dr. Reddy lost a patient who could not make it to Texas for an open heart surgery. This inspired Dr. Pratap Reddy to create a world class medical infrastructure in India and make it more accessible and affordable to common people and the first centre of the Apollo Hospitals was established in Chennai in 1983. Since its inception, Apollo has demonstrated that Indian skills are equivalent to the best centres in the world and has produced world class results in the most complicated Cadaver Transplant. The Apollo Hospitals group has over 22 centres in major cities in India and a combined turnover of over $100 million. The group opened its first clinic in

Dubai in 1999 and has come up with projects in Sri Lanka, Africa, Bangladesh and Oman. Dr. Reddy is currently looking at secondary health centres in semi-urban and smaller cities and has already identified 23 sites for the purpose. The latest initiatives include Med Varsity, a virtual medical university providing total access to experts in the field of medicine anywhere in the world and Mednet Hospital Systems Management package.

6.7 Conclusion

Family business has different characteristics in different economies and differs in outlook and has been influenced by sociological and economic and political factors. A study by Ward (2004) of 200 successful manufacturers in Illinois between 1924 and 1984 shows that less than 20 per cent had survived over 60 years, with 65 per cent of these remaining with the same family. Only 25 per cent had grown significantly and 80 of the 200 companies closed within 30 years and the same number within 60 years. In Indonesia and the Philippines, family businesses control more than half of each country's corporate sector in terms of market capitalisation (Dutta, 1997). Less than ten per cent of Japanese companies are controlled by families, while nearly 80 per cent are widely held. In Korea and Taiwan, families control 48 per cent of corporations. In Thailand, family control is 62 per cent and in Malaysia 67 per cent.

According to the 1972 Dun and Brad Street study, 70 per cent of family firms either close or are sold after the founder retires or dies (Lansberg, 1988). In India, the survival rate has been 54 per cent. Of the 200 big companies, 16 are more than 75 years old and about 80 per cent continue to be with the same ownership. The comparable figure in the US was 65 per cent (Ward, 2004). In Korea, only 30 per cent of the *chaebols* are listed on the stock exchange and the biggest four *chaebols* contribute bulk of country's GNP. Indian businesses are subject threats of splits, succession-planning, takeovers, transnational competition and lack of focus (Piramal et al, 2000). Of these, the transnational competition poses the biggest danger followed by splits in the family. The three major problems faced by family businesses include how to find and hire the best managers a group can afford; how to ensure that the next generation is able and capable of taking over the baton and how to encourage each business unit within the group to become focused and to maximise its core competencies to best advantage.

The groups founded by Tata, Godrej and others have promoted and maintained a typical kind of culture over the decades. There are other icons, which have evolved from being culturally embedded through being market driven. The groups belonging to this category are Wipro, Ranbaxy and Sundaram Fasteners, which have used organisational culture for business growth, market capitalisation and market leadership. Following these examples, many small and medium enterprises have drawn on organisational culture of the above business groups to achieve competitive advantage in niche markets.

7

Entrepreneurship Development in Small and Medium Enterprises

7.1 Introduction

Entrepreneurship in India was traditionally less organised, based on the unique caste and economic systems. The enterprise activities were in mainly in respect of textiles, handicrafts and woollens and manufacturing activity was based on traditional methods, the mercantile communities being involved in marketing and financing. Entrepreneurship in the modern sense began with the entry of the East India Company during the 18th century, but the colonial rulers never encouraged local entrepreneurship, they being interested only in the export of raw materials to Britain and the import of finished goods from there. Trading operations were greatly influenced by traditional business communities like *parsis* and *banias*. During and after World War I, owing to increasing demand for several commodities, self-made entrepreneurs started setting up enterprises in spite of the unfavourable climate of the colonial rule. After independence, a systematic approach for developing entrepreneurs was adopted through five-year plans and various other interventions.

The dynamics of business is undergoing a major transformation in the wake of globalisation and the liberalisation policy of India, which has opened up new avenues of opportunity and also posing new challenges in respect of knowledge-based economic development (APO, 2007). Therefore, knowledge assessment must include not only economic parameters, but also other important aspects like education, health, emancipation of women and an improvement in overall standard of living to sustain the spirit of entrepreneurship. Emerging markets and technologies present both challenges and opportunities for businesses and individual entrepreneurs in focusing on competitive.

This chapter enumerates the achievement of small and medium enterprises to the growth of entrepreneurship in India and how the sector has been able to sustain the pace of development in the economy. Section 7.2 briefs about the SMEs, while section 7.3 discusses the prospects of SMEs in the auto industry. The growth of entrepreneurship as evidenced by establishment of various entrepreneurial institutions is discussed in 7.4, while section 7.5 characterises the growth through technology and information-based institutions. Section 7.6 briefs about the diffusion of entrepreneurship in SMEs and section 7.7 presents five SME case studies, three in Hyderabad, two in Bangalore and one in Tamil Nadu. Section 7.8 concludes.

While many countries place entrepreneurial firms in the category of small and medium-sized enterprises (SMEs), in India they are termed as micro, small and medium enterprises (MSMEs). The Micro, Small and Medium Enterprises Development Act, 2006 provides for the definition of these enterprises besides paving way for a statutory national board exclusively for them. SMEs have an important role to play in integrating their operations with other small businesses and ultimately with global firms to justify their own existence and realise their growth. A strategy of vertical integration and horizontal cooperation would enable the local SMEs to work with global transnational corporations for the production of intermediate goods and also for networking linked up with global firms for the production and marketing of consumer goods (Balasubrahmanya, 2007). Economic size of an entrepreneurial unit may be measured by employment, output, fixed capital investment and export variables and its economic performance may be indicated by capital-output ratio, output to labour ratio and labour to capital ratio. Small enterprises are the engine of growth in countries like India in generating employment, fostering entrepreneurship, utilising local skills and resources and strengthening the industrial base The small scale industry (SSI) sector accounts for 90 per cent of all industrial enterprises, 40 per cent of total industrial output, 34 per cent of exports and 8 per cent of GDP (Balasubrahmanya, 2007). The sector accounts for nearly 35 per cent of gross value of output in the manufacturing sector and over 34 per cent of total exports.

Most of the owners are first-generation entrepreneurs who act as owners, managers and also as employees. The result is that the enterprises suffer from excessive engagement (both positive and negative) by these entrepreneurs. Most of them suffer from lack of experience, seasoning and entrepreneurial maturity and vision. In analysing the proliferation of small scale family farms in India, Das contends that widespread involuntary unemployment in the rural economy is the cause for the problem of failure to coordinate. This can be overcome by breeding in capitalist farmers (Das, 2009). The US has served as a model for other countries to emulate in applying technology to the economy and of directing finance to smaller and innovative companies. Many technology companies are becoming rapidly globalised by transferring or outsourcing part of their activities to emerging markets (OECD, 2008). In this, SMEs have improved their performance and presence through industrial cluster approaches and suitable cluster interventions are necessary for enhancing their competitiveness and sustainability.

7.2 SMEs in Indian Automobile Industry

The Indian automotive component industry is highly fragmented and there are nearly 6,400 players in the sector, of which only about six per cent are organised. In terms of value-added, the organised sector accounts for nearly 77 per cent of output in the sector. During the colonial era, the country had no automotive industry and all automobiles were imported from the global manufacturers such as General Motors and Ford Motors. In the 1940s, Hindustan Motors and Premier Motors were established by Indian entrepreneurs, by importing know-how from General Motors and Fiat. In the 1950s, Mahindra and Mahindra, Ashok Leyland and Bajaj Auto entered the market for manufacture of commercial vehicles and two-wheelers. Most of these companies either imported auto components or produced them domestically under import substitution programme. This development, followed by the LK Jha Committee's recommendations in 1960 to develop an indigenous ancillaries sector, resulted in the evolution of a separate auto component sector. From a highly-protected pre-1980s regime, the auto component industry has gradually emerged as an important industrial sector. Until 1991, the phased manufacturing programme, under which domestic original equipment manufacturers had to increase their proportion of domestic inputs over a specific period, had laid the foundation of the sector. The policy initiatives have ranged from excise duty, concessions and tax incentives for investment, to incentives for promoting R&D, measures for export promotion and the reduction of import duties on components. Apart from the central government, several state governments also have focused on attracting investments in the auto sector.

While in the advanced countries, the typology of SMEs tends to be homogeneous mainly in term of firm size and technology, the developing countries are characterised by low industrialisation, with co-existence of both very small enterprises in the informal and SMEs in the organised sectors. With the establishment of WTO and its conditionality, many of the existing support structures had vanished and SMEs have to struggle on their own. SMEs are not able to compete with MNCs due to their inherent weaknesses such as obsolete technology, uncompetitive prices and poor quality of goods, costly credit, weak infrastructural facilities, cumbersome labour legislation and lack of cohesion among SME units, ineffective associations and lack of up-to-date information, lack of international exposure and lack of standards conforming to international standards. With the removal of quantitative restrictions (QRs), SMEs are subjected to global competition. However, the removal of QRs would imply that raw material is available at cheaper rates which will in turn, reduce cost of a product thereby making it more competitive in terms of pricing. There is a vast market potential for the products of small sector in developing countries, as removal of QRs is also applicable to these countries. Therefore, SMEs should adopt an export policy aimed at optimum utilisation of the opportunities available by removal of QRs. There are certain areas where MNCs would not be able to supply goods and SMEs have the opportunity to provide such products at cheaper rates. In this case, the government has established sub-contracting exchanges which maintain data about the SMEs to match the requirements of large scale industries which will become increasingly knowledge intensive.

In the auto industry foreign companies are present through joint ventures, equity participation or with technology tie-ups. India ranks eleventh in car production and thirteenth in commercial vehicle production. In the pre-1983 period, the development was characterised by closed market, market growth limited by supply and outdated models. The 1983-93 decade was characterised by a joint venture between Suzuki Motors and Maruti Udyog and other joint ventures for manufacture of commercial vehicles and auto components. The sector was delicensed in 1991 and imports were allowed from 2001 onwards. Domestic sales and exports of the auto industry had grown from 5.5 million units in 2001-02 to 15 million units in 2010-11 at a compound annual growth rate of 17 per cent. This growth had been driven by a buoyant economy, increasing purchasing power of the middle class, new product launches and attractive finance schemes from automobile manufacturers and financial institutions. The auto parts industry has emerged as one of fastest growing manufacturing sector. The industry has adopted a strategy of product portfolio enhancement, market expansion and efficiency improvements to achieve this stature, wherein higher capacity utilisations has contributed significantly to this growth.

In regard to automotive components, 55 per cent is the share of vehicle industry for the original equipment, while replacement demand constitutes 35 per cent and exports account for the remaining 10 per cent. Exports mostly serve the replacement market abroad. The Indian automotive component industry is low-volumed and fragmented, having 400 firms in the organised sector and more than 5000 firms in the unorganised sector. The growth of auto industry depends on increasing demand for vehicles, stable economic policies of the government, availability of low cost skilled manpower and high quality standards. The financial demands arise due to working capital requirements and demand for new investment. Investment demand can be for replacement of obsolete machinery or technological upgradation and modernisation, expansion, quality improvement, new ventures and diversification, introduction of labour saving devices and R&D towards innovations. Part of investment demand will come from the factory sector, because of technology upgradation and modernisation, expansion and quality improvement and also from transformation demand of the unorganised sector like workshops and household industries and their subsequent entry into the factory sector. Though R&D is not yet significant, the competitive pressure and the urge to grow will prompt many small enterprises to setup their own R & D facilities. The major problems faced by them, not only in the auto but in general relate to availability of loan without collateral, delay in getting loan, high cost of funds, delayed payments, marketing problems, WTO related issues and sickness (Kamesam, 2003).

Over 10 per cent of the SSIs have been identified as sick and when the sickness prolongs, it leads to the closure of the units. This trend has wider implications, including funding assistance from the lending institutions reporting non-performing assets. It also leads to loss of scarce material resources and loss of existing employment. Continued diversification of export market, improvement of export quality and productivity, increased technology intensity in production, enhanced R&D activity, reduction of cumbersome regulatory environment, adding flexibility to the existing labour laws and removal of infrastructural bottlenecks can make the SSIs more innovative and participating (Trivedi et al, 2011).

7.3 Growth of Entrepreneurship in SMEs through Interventions

During the 1970s various strategies and models were developed and tested for developing entrepreneurship in various parts of the country. Many institutions adopted the entrepreneurship development programme (EDP) strategy for creating MSMEs during the 1970s and 1980s. The EDP model has been sourced from empretec, the UN-funded entrepreneurial training programme (UNCTAD, 2004). In 1969, Gujarat state established the first Centre of Entrepreneurship Development (CED) in Ahmedabad, which conducted a number of EDPs to attract first-generation entrepreneurs within that state. Entrepreneurship Development Institute of India (EDI) developed a general EDP model for developing first-generation entrepreneurs nationally. The success story of CED, Gujarat led to the establishment of EDI in Ahmedabad in 1983 with support from many financial institutions. The establishment of EDI has facilitated the growth of entrepreneurship through its activities of entrepreneurship education, training, and research (Awasthi, 2011). Prior to the 1960s, entrepreneurship in India was a topic of academic and philosophical discussion by economists and other social scientists. McClelland (1965) conducted a pioneering study on entrepreneurship along with NISIET, Hyderabad in the early 1960s, disproving the popular belief that 'entrepreneurs are born'. But entrepreneurs are not necessarily born and can be groomed and developed with systematic training and pro-business interventions. Any person, irrespective of caste, religion and region of origin, can learn to be a successful entrepreneur.

Based on these findings, the National Institute of Small Industry Extension Training (NISIET) has developed the first Entrepreneurship Development Programme model to develop first-generation entrepreneurs. This integrated model indicates that a support mechanism beyond training intervention is necessary to develop entrepreneurs. Promotion of entrepreneurship can be viewed as a cyclic process associated with stimulatory, supportive and sustaining activities. Stimulatory activities are those that stimulate entrepreneurs in any community, while supportive activities help entrepreneurs in establishing and running their enterprises and sustaining activities ensure continued, efficient and profitable functioning of the enterprises. NISIET, set up in 1960 with the support of Ford Foundation, has been the forerunner of entrepreneurship development in India. It was the first Indian institute to provide training to officers dealing with small industries and other entrepreneurs. The institute undertook entrepreneurial research in the1960s through experiments on achievement motivation, which led to the first entrepreneurship development model. Later, other models and approaches were developed, heralding the concept of growth centres. At present, NISIET is involved with promotion and development of SSIs through a cluster approach.

Indian Institute of Entrepreneurship (IIE), Guwahati began as a branch institute of NISIET to promote entrepreneurship in the north-eastern states. IIE activities include identification of training needs, designing and organising training programmes for entrepreneurs and concerned agencies, evolving effective strategies and methodologies, organising seminars and workshops, undertaking research in entrepreneurship and documentation and dissemination of information on self-employment. National Institute of Entrepreneurship and Small Business Development (NIESBUD) was established in 1983 in Delhi to promote, support and sustain entrepreneurship and small business through training, education, research, consultancy and other interventions in India and other developing countries. Its main activities include evolving effective training strategies, standardising model syllabi for entrepreneurship training, organising trainers' training programmes and undertaking research in entrepreneurship development. In addition to the national institutes, there are 14 state-level Centres of Entrepreneurship Development (CEDs) and Institutes of Entrepreneurship Development (IEDs), established under the scheme for strengthening the training infrastructure of existing and new entrepreneurship development institutions.

A few institutions with women as their focus have been established through private initiatives to develop women entrepreneurs in various parts of the country. Association of Women Entrepreneurs of Karnataka (AWAKE) was established in 1993 in Bangalore with the mission of empowering women through entrepreneurship development. AWAKE develops, guides and extends assistance to potential women entrepreneurs in Karnataka through counselling, training and peer group support. Association of Lady Entrepreneurs of Andhra Pradesh (ALEAP) was established in 1993 at Hyderabad by several women entrepreneurs with the aim of empowering women to establish small and medium enterprises. Its major activities are identification of projects, guidance for finance, training, organising exhibitions and creating industrial infrastructure for developing women entrepreneurs. In 1997, ALEAP set up a centre for entrepreneurship development, with financial support from central and state governments to promote women entrepreneurs. Consortium of Women Entrepreneurs of India (CWEI) works for the economic empowerment of women through entrepreneurship strategy. Its main activities are participating in trade exhibitions, organising training programmes, providing escort services and export marketing for the benefit of first-generation women entrepreneurs. CWEI uses e-governance, e-commerce and other services. Rural and tribal women with traditional skills have been greatly motivated towards entrepreneurship by CWEI, which has recently started networking with women entrepreneurs of other countries to market the products manufactured by Indian women entrepreneurs.

National Entrepreneurship Development Board (NEDB) is the apex body for entrepreneurship development. It devises and recommends government schemes for the promotion of entrepreneurship through self-employment or setting up of SSIs. Grants are provided to organisations engaged in entrepreneurship development for organising workshops and seminars and conducting research in entrepreneurship development. Programmes under Entrepreneurship and Business Development Centres (EBDCs) are being implemented through selected organisations and educational institutions. It is initially in operation for two years with an extension of two more years in deserving cases. After four years, the host institution assumes the responsibility of continuing the scheme and arranging the funds for it. Training institutes, universities and colleges, NGOs and other industry associations conduct surveys and studies on various issues of entrepreneurship development and problems of first-generation entrepreneurs that are published for wider dissemination.

Small Industries Development Organisation (SIDO) advises, coordinates and formulates policies and programmes for the development and promotion of the small-scale sector. It also maintains liaison with central ministries and other government agencies and organisations, including financial institutions. Under the Ministry of Agro and Rural Industries, Khadi and Village Industries Commission (KVIC) and Coir Board implement their respective schemes to develop rural entrepreneurship. The Prime Minister's Rozgar Yojana was launched in 1993 to assist educated unemployed youth in setting up small enterprises and is implemented by state industries departments through district industries centres and other government organisations. KVIC launched the rural employment guarantee scheme in 1995 to generate employment in rural areas under the KVI sector. This scheme promotes entrepreneurial culture particularly in rural areas and entrepreneurial development training is important for the selected entrepreneurs. KVIC also extends fund assistance to public and private institutions for organising EDPs in the KVI sector. The Coir Board facilitates EDPs through public and private institutions to develop entrepreneurs in the coir sector. Their programmes focus primarily on skill development with entrepreneurship input.

The Department of Science and Technology (DST) under the Ministry of Science and Technology has made efforts to tap the talents of the country's science and technology students through entrepreneurship strategy. National Science and Technology Entrepreneurship Development Board (NSTEDB) promote knowledge-based and technology-driven entrepreneurship. The Board aims to convert job seekers into job generators through science and technology interventions. The main objectives of the Board are to generate an entrepreneurial culture among science and technology individuals and to facilitate and launch promotional services for developing entrepreneurship with a network of various supporters, including academic and R&D institutions. With a view to educating students and faculty at S&T institutions, Entrepreneurship Awareness Camps are conducted by specialised institutions. The DST organises EDPs based on the NISIET model with the aim of training S&T graduates and diploma holders in the essentials of successfully conceiving, planning, initiating and launching an enterprise. Through faculty development programmes, S&T faculty are trained in entrepreneurship development to motivate S&T students towards entrepreneurial career. The Open Learning Programme in Entrepreneurship has been initiated with the help of EDI for S&T personnel to speed up the process of entrepreneurship promotion by training a large number of beneficiaries in a short time. This 11-month distance education programme provides potential entrepreneurs in different parts of the country not only with study material, but also with guidance from resource experts during the contact sessions.

7.4 Technology and Information-based Initiatives in Entrepreneurship

Technology-based entrepreneurship development programme is designed to develop and motivate entrepreneurs in specific products, technologies and processes developed by CSIR labs and other R&D institutions (Awasthi, 2011). This is based on the EDP concept, with a more technical focus. In addition to training programmes, Entrepreneurship Development Cells (EDCs) have been established to generate entrepreneurial culture in S&T institutions and to foster techno-entrepreneurship. Science and Technology Entrepreneurship Development (STED) aims to bring about socioeconomic development in the selected areas through S&T intervention. The project envisages matching the material and human resources of the district to create enterprises based on select S&T processes. Science and Technology Entrepreneurship Parks (STEPs) help to create an atmosphere for innovation and entrepreneurship through interaction between academia and industries in sharing ideas, knowledge, experience and facilities for the development of new technologies and their rapid transfer to the end-users. They also promote innovative enterprises by technopreneurs.

Technology Business Incubators (TBIs) provide services to new and existing entrepreneurs and offer a congenial atmosphere for their survival and growth. For example, recently food processing and agro-industries have been accorded high priority. The Ministry of Food Processing Industry is facilitating EDPs through nodal agencies to attract potential entrepreneurs for the creation of food processing enterprises. The nodal agencies function at the national level, implementing agencies at the field level. Through this project, enterprise development inputs are shared by the agencies in a comprehensive way to promote enterprises in the food processing sector. Besides the public sector organisations, private institutions like Confederation of Indian Industries, Federation of Indian Micro and Small and Medium Enterprises, Associated Chamber of Commerce and Industry, All India Manufacturers' Organisation and World Association for Small and Medium Enterprises actively are involved in the development of SMEs and the entrepreneurial culture in them.

The Department of Scientific and Industrial Research promotes R&D among industries and support small and medium industrial units to develop state-of-art competitive technologies towards faster commercialisation of R&D and enhancement of share of technology-intensive exports. It provides a link between scientific laboratories and industrial establishments for transfer of technologies through the National Research Development Corporation (NRDC) and facilitates investment in R&D through Central Electronics Limited. The National Research Development Corporation has the objective of developing, promoting and transferring the technologies emanating from various national R&D institutions. It provides services to improve the manufacturing base with innovative technologies and acts as an effective catalyst translating innovative research into marketable industrial products. NRDC's repository of indigenously developed technologies includes drugs and pharmaceuticals, biotechnology, metallurgy, electrical and electronic technologies instrumentation, building materials, mechanics and food processing. It also exports proven technologies to both developed and developing countries.

The Techno-Entrepreneur Promotion Programme (TEPP) promotes, supports and assists individual innovators in becoming technology-based entrepreneurs. TEPP also assists technopreneurs in networking and forging linkages with other constituents of the innovation chain for commercialisation of their developments. It provides financial support to selected and screened individual innovators to convert original ideas into working models and prototypes. Central Electronics Limited emphasises on indigenous technology, inducted both from its in-house developments and from national laboratories, for its production programme in diverse hi-tech areas. The Council of Scientific and Industrial Research (CSIR) provides scientific industrial research and has a country-wide network of many laboratories and field centres, converting fundamental and applied R&D science and technology (except atomic research). It develops and nurtures S&T human resources through extramural support and promotes scientific talent through awards and fellowships.

Information and communication technology plays a crucial role in enhancing the export competitiveness of SSIs. The Kakinada experiment, under the guidance of David McClelland was an important effort in the area of entrepreneurship research and training in the early 1960s. McClelland (1965) opined that the need for high achievement (n-Ach) was an essential ingredient for the emergence of entrepreneurs and that it could be taught in order to stimulate economic growth. He speculated that external resources (materials, markets, trade and trade routes) were as important as the entrepreneurial spirit in exploiting the resources. He believed that economic activity could be increased through training of prospective entrepreneurs. McClelland's theory of achievement motivation moulded entrepreneurship training and education in India and many other developing countries. The theory was put to use to motivate poor, illiterate, disadvantaged and other non-business communities to empower themselves through creation of new enterprises. NISIET developed an integrated model with appropriate training modules to develop entrepreneurs through pre-training, training and creating a favourable climate in the selected areas like Assam, Jammu and Kashmir, Karnataka, Maharashtra, Nagaland and Orissa in 1970. NISIET has also pioneered trainers' training programmes to develop potential trainers in local areas.

7.5 Diffusion of Entrepreneurship

The EDP mainly focused on entrepreneurial stimulation through a training-cum-counselling package that includes motivation, project guidance, managerial orientation and information, preparation of a project plan and implementation of projects (Awasthi, 2011). The duration of the EDP varied from a few days to three months. The EDI combined NISIET's entrepreneurship model and its own academic resources for active participation in entrepreneurship development activities. Its programmes are aimed at special target groups, such as rural entrepreneurs and women. NIESBUD offers accelerated programmes for developing model syllabi for various target groups, besides manuals and tools for spreading the entrepreneurship movement. NIESBUD organises EDPs and related activities to create an entrepreneurship culture in the north-eastern states of India. In the 1990s, entrepreneurship development became a national movement.

Small Industries Service Institutes organise EDPs to benefit technical graduates, educated unemployed youth, women and other rural entrepreneurs at the state level. The National Productivity Council is engaged in organising EDPs, seeking sponsorship from national and state-level support institutions. The Rural Development and Self-Employment Training Institute with support from Syndicate and Canara banks, organises training programmes to develop skills and assist in entrepreneurial activity. Their training modules are focused mainly on rural youth and function in many locations in the country. It provides technical know-how and familiarises potential entrepreneurs with the steps required for establishing and managing enterprises. District Industries Centres support the organisation of EDPs at the district level in collaboration with regional resource institutions. In addition to these public efforts, non-government organisations are also participating in organising programmes to inculcate entrepreneurship. They are mainly participating in organising Prime Minister Rojgar Yojana scheme and state-level programmes for developing entrepreneurs and supporting them. The National Small Industries Corporation sponsors EDPs through various training institutes. The Industrial Technical Consultancy Organisation, jointly sponsored by financial institutions organises EDPs and creates a satisfactory climate. CEDs/IEDs also strive to promote entrepreneurship through training, research and consultancy and by providing information in respective regions. The success rate of EDPs is influenced by target groups, training organisations and enterprise climate, including access to finance, infrastructure and other facilities. However, many entrepreneurship development programmes sponsored by certain organisations lack quality and do not create an entrepreneurial culture. Entrepreneurship is now introduced as a subject in postgraduate courses at engineering, management and technical institutions, with the aim of creating awareness on self-employment avocations among the students. A few institutions arrange interaction with local entrepreneurs and visits to enterprises run by them.

The potential of clusters as a vehicle for economic growth is recognised world over. The National Resource Centre for Cluster Development was established at NISIET with fund assistance from SIDO and has been working on manufacturing, service and traditional clusters. Achievement motivation is essential for entrepreneurial success and it can be imparted through training to stimulate economic growth. EDPs are developed as packaged solutions consisting of helping entrepreneurs to learn business by actually doing it in incubation facilities. Empirical studies on the growth of entrepreneurial activity in India (as evidenced by Global Entrepreneurship Monitor research) shows that the level of entrepreneurial activity increased from nine per cent in 2000 to 12 per cent in 2001 and 18 per cent in 2002, doubling in the following years. The study states that in 2002, entrepreneurial activity in India stood second among 37 countries studied, next only to Thailand (19 per cent). The analysis affirms that awareness creation, counselling, guidance and other services have been on the rise in recent years, thus accelerating entrepreneurial activity.

7.6 Case Studies

Case studies 7.6.1 to 7.6.3 refer to Andhra Pradesh-based entrepreneurs and are sourced from Kondaiah (2007). 7.6.4 and 7.6.5 refer to Karnataka entrepreneurs and are sourced from D'Costa (2011), while 7.6.6 referring to Tamil Nadu is sourced from FAO (2006).

7.6.1 Anuja Electronics

B. Vijayalakshmi is the first-born of six children in a middle-class family without a business background in Andhra Pradesh. Her father, who was the inspiration behind starting her venture, has been an employment officer. Her husband, a mechanical engineer and industrialist, supported and encouraged her to start up and run the enterprise. Vijayalakshmi is a graduate in electronics and communication engineering from Kakinada Engineering College and joined a polytechnic college as assistant lecturer. From her childhood she had a strong desire to do something on her own and never liked working under someone in controlled conditions. Thus, the dominant entrepreneurial trait of independence was evident in her behaviour. She got an opportunity to start an ancillary industry with Andhra Pradesh State Road Transport Corporation. She experienced a dilemma in trying to choose between her job and the enterprise and subsequently decided to quit the job. She started supplying solder sticks to all the depots in Andhra Pradesh as a rate contractor. She was in this business for 16 years and in 1989 when there were power cuts during the summer, she realised that there was a demand for electronic generators. She decided to develop inverters for the open market, starting Anuja Electronics and began marketing under the brand name Anu generators. Anu generators grew in size and in 1996 the company started manufacturing power-saving electronic ballasts and lighting fixtures with electronic ballasts.

Anticipating a slump in the industrial market and heavy competition from other parts of the country, Vijayalakshmi decided to reduce the production of solder sticks and started looking for other products. She looked at soft plastic products, such as insulation sleeves and dust-proof covers, produced with a new process called dip moulding, which was not very popular in India and dip moulding to manufacture soft plastic PVC products, which are import substitutes and supplied them to automobile and electrical industries. After many hurdles, the company has achieved a lead position in the dip moulding and also services multinational companies.

Vijayalakshmi is inquisitive, creative and innovative and enjoys solving problems and driven by a need for achievement, prefers an independent career. Though she is an introvert and has only a few close friends, she admits that she is a consistent goal setter and results-oriented individual. She does not make decisions in haste and once a decision is made she will follow through on it. She can totally handle the mental load but experiences some physical constraints. Despite coming from a non-business family, she appears to be totally committed and dedicated and believes in her own ability to reach her goals. She is vice-president of ALEAP, always ready to help other aspiring women entrepreneurs. She believes in giving employees complete freedom provided they also take responsibility.

Vijayalakshmi, with 28 years of experience has acquired sufficient knowledge to enter into franchises, joint ventures, technical collaborations and strategic alliances. She is well-informed about different government and non-government programmes supporting the SSIs and uses her knowledge to guide the new generation of women entrepreneurs. Her company keeps in touch with buyer preferences and modifies its products accordingly through continuous R&D efforts. Products are manufactured against advance orders and sold directly to auto part vendors. The primary buyers of the products are Hero Honda, Bajaj and Maruti Suzuki. With an annual turnover of Rs. 50 million, the inherent strengths of the company are a large installed capacity, a spacious shop floor, an in-house tooling facility, experienced and vibrant staff, vision and commitment and the ISO 9002 quality system. The firm uses total quality management, quality circles and just-in-time techniques for productivity improvement. Whenever there is an opportunity the employees are sent to relevant training, seminars or workshops. Employee performance is reviewed monthly and annually and rewards, incentives and rewards are based on performance appraisal. She attributes her success to her hard work, commitment and self-confidence and also to the cooperation and support of family and friends. Her advice to upcoming entrepreneurs is that 50 percent of profits should be reinvested for upgrading the enterprise. She was named best woman entrepreneur of 2000 by CII. When she started her venture, she had absolutely no business knowledge. She started with a small loan from Andhra Pradesh State Finance Corporation plus her personal investment. In 1977, through NISIET's three-month entrepreneurial development programme, she acquired the knowledge and skills necessary for starting up an enterprise. Today, she is confident of her proficiency and can handle all functions of management, from planning to implementation and evaluation.

7.6.2 ELICO

Electronics and Industrial Instruments Co (ELICO), the first electronics company in the state of Andhra Pradesh was incorporated in 1960 at Hyderabad and started with the manufacturing of pH meters for the first time in India and kept on adding several firsts in the areas of spectrophotometry, electrochemistry, flame photometry, water quality and gas analysis. In 1970, the name of the company was changed to ELICO Pvt Ltd and in 1995, was converted into a public limited company. In 1976, ELICO diversified into manufacturing professional-grade switches and introduced a wide range of toggle and push-button switches for use in the consumer electronics and telecommunication industries. Ramesh Datla was hired as senior test development engineer by Cirrus Logic Inc, USA, a semiconductor company, where he was responsible for design evaluation, prototype debugging and device characterisation of advanced graphics and datacomm products used for notebook and desktop PCs. For a brief period, he worked as research assistant in Indian Institute of Science, Bangalore. He then joined his father's company as works manager and held various positions before becoming Elico's managing director. He personally takes care of the design, development and manufacture of electronic analytical instruments and software development and services.

A second-generation entrepreneur, Ramesh comes from a middle-class family with a business background. He is inquisitive, creative, innovative, energetic, enthusiastic, imaginative and also aggressive at the same time. He enjoys solving problems, makes very quick decisions on his own and does not depend on external influences. Always taking up challenging tasks and making things happen, he believes in taking moderate risks, whether personal or financial. He believes that failure is a stepping-stone to success. He knows that networking is a must for the success of an enterprise and enjoys moving around. He has a flair for exploring new technologies, markets and business opportunities and in recognition of this, he was honoured with the industry award for best new product brought into commercial production for the first time in the state by a small scale industry during 1996-97. ELICO is an ISO 9001 company, manufacturing electronic analytical instruments and professional-grade switches and software development and services. In 1988, ELICO expanded into software, providing microprocessor-based embedded solutions to its customers. Since 1992 graphical user interface based instrumentation software has been offered as a bundled solution. In 1999, ELICO established a 100 per cent export-oriented software division for software development and services and IT-enabled services in healthcare for its US and European clients. The company has established its own R&D division and has won a number of awards for its R&D efforts like the award for excellence in electronics from the Department of Electronics, Government of India. The firm exports to more than 25 countries and aims to progress in the areas of chromatography, spectroscopy, electrochemistry and life sciences. In 1996, the company obtained ISO 9001 certification for design, development, manufacturing and servicing of analytical instruments and also obtained ISO 14001 certification. In 1999, the company received a national award for quality in small scale products. To improve productivity, the company uses Kaizen and 5S TQM and 6 Sigma and a department-based quantification matrix is used to quantify performance levels. In order to control production costs, the company has devised its own methodologies for in-time delivery, inventory management, reduction of re-works and rejects and improvement in communication and customer satisfaction.

The company plans its manpower on the basis of periodic business demands and market trends. Employee performance is rated annually and salaries, rewards, incentives and promotions are based on performance. The company gives top priority to employee training and development and plans an annual training calendar for all areas and a separate budget allocation is made for training. The technical education Ramesh acquired in India and the US has helped him to keep pace with the latest developments in electronics. His dedication, commitment, determination, self-confidence, inquisitiveness, creativeness, interpersonal strengths, concern for his staff, quality consciousness and ability to keep abreast of trends in the market have all contributed to the success of his enterprise.

7.6.3 Cheminnova Remedies

M. Seshagiri Rao was the resident director of the Hyderabad unit of American Remedies Ltd. After its merger with Dr. Reddy's Laboratories, the unit was taken over by Cheminnova Remedies by Rao. Its initial investment was Rs. 3,00,000 and the entire project cost was financed by the State Bank of Hyderabad under its scheme for technocrats. It is the largest manufacturer of oral liquids and solid dosage form of pharmaceuticals. The company has ventured into backward integration and started a Clinical Research Organisation (CRO) with state-of-art facilities and equipment, offering services such as product development, process development, formulation development and analytical process development. Rao as the managing director has been in the field for the past 40 years and is well recognised in the pharmaceutical industry. Before starting the enterprise he worked for 15 years at Biological Evans, Bio-chemical Enterprise and Nath Laboratories and American Remedies. He was instrumental in the smooth functioning of American Remedies while it was in existence.

The company's mission is to keep the life line vibrant and believes in team work and management by objectives and all the department heads are involved in setting goals. Each employee is made responsible and the reward to good performers takes the form of pay increases. The company also believes in human resource development and organises induction training for new recruits. A few officers are also sent to other reputable institutions for seminars and training programmes. The company is ISO-9001-2000 certified by AQA USA and also WHO-GMP certified. Quality aspects of the products are looked after by a manager for quality, assisted by quality executives and analytical chemists. The firm believes in innovation and creation of new ideas and is in the process of establishing a separate R&D department. It has developed a multivitamin tablet for Novartis. The company is in the business of contract manufacturing for firms like American Remedies, Dr. Reddy's Laboratories and Ajanta Pharma. The company has two granulation areas for manufacturing products of various batch sizes with separate AHUs and all the other requirements as per GMP. It has the capacity to manufacture 2.5

million tablets per day and also manufactures several liquid products and syrups. Cheminnova treats employees as its valued assets and their welfare is of paramount importance. It makes efforts to retain talent by maintaining a good management–employee relationship. Equipped with sophisticated state-of-art machinery, Cheminnova has joined global efforts for preservation of the environment. No harmful chemicals are released that could damage land, water and air. Every precaution is taken and executed in pursuit of environment protection. The company has its own effluent treatment plant situated on a 60-acre site where the water is treated and used for irrigation, setting an example to other pharmaceutical units with regard to environmental concerns.

The theory that entrepreneurs could be made was shown to be valid in the case of Rao. With no business background, he is the managing director of three companies. Over time, he has developed and enjoys the skill of solving the most critical problems. He has a strong belief in what he does and does not seek advice from external sources. He does not depend on luck and destiny and he enjoys taking personal and financial risks. He strongly believes that hard work pays off and finds time for socialising and networking. He is the deputy district governor and zone chairman of Lions Club International and chairman of Navya Nataka Samithi, which promotes cultural activities. Rao has thorough business knowledge and can enter into a franchise, joint venture, technical collaboration or strategic alliance for business growth. Even though the company has a competent person to handle current business, tax laws, regulations and policies, Rao has a thorough knowledge of all aspects and can handle them with ease. He was vice-president of the Indian Pharmaceutical Association and has many more laurels to his credit.

7.6.4 Ducom

Ducom is a first generation enterprise and is engaged in the production of custom-designed laboratory equipment, specific electronic instruments for defence and academic institutes like Indian Institute of Science, Indian Institutes of Technology and other engineering institutions. When completing his masters in mechanical engineering at IISc, the Ducom entrepreneur responded to an advertisement of Karnataka Small Scale Industries Development Corporation inviting applications for industrial sheds. When he obtained an allotment, he had virtually no finance to start an enterprise. His father was a school teacher from whom he could not seek the needed financial support. Much support was given by one of his professors in IISc who paid him on the basis of invoice to supply products on a later date. Thus, he started his enterprise with Rs. 8,000 and three employees. The first product manufactured by Ducom was an X-ray defractometer, the product line expanding gradually and steadily. Ducom supplies wear and friction meters, journal bearing test rigs, photo-resistance spinners, dry abrasion testers, metallurgical sample saws, spin-on-discs, four-balltesters and reciprocating friction meters. The technological innovations sprang from initiative to manufacture and supply customer-specific products. To acquire sufficient product development capability, the entrepreneur visits IISc frequently to discuss with professors in the departments of physics and metallurgy and to conduct research at the IISc library. In addition, Ducom has established its own exclusive technical library for the acquisition of technical journals and books.

The major factor responsible for the company to acquire technological capability was the government's protective industrial policy, which was pursued until 1991. During this period, in the absence of threatening competition, Ducom could develop product development capability gradually and engage itself in import substitution. While the entrepreneur is the prime factor responsible for technological product innovations, he develops an organisational set up at Ducom to facilitate innovation processes. The design department consists of mechanical, design, computing and final design sections. This department has been made part of the marketing department and it is also well integrated with the fabrication shop. Some of the early new product development efforts made by Ducom have been spin-on-disks developed in the mid-1980s to eliminate noise using an exclusive software, a major product related to fusion reaction for the Institute of Plasma Research in 1986, a highly automated four-ball tester in 1991 and a scratch tester in 1995.

During 1977 and 1996, Ducom focused on the domestic market only. The turning point came in 1995 when the entrepreneur attended an International Exhibition on Tribology in Boston, USA. Product advertisements in the Tribo-testing journal, along with a stall set-up in the international exhibition attracted many visitors. Inquiries about his products arrived. However, there were no orders because of the poor credibility of Indian high-technology products. In 1996, Koelher Instruments of New York exhibited Ducom products under the Koelher brand name. Such entry into the international market helped Ducom learn about attending to minute details in terms of quality, finishing, certifications and environmental requirements. Its initial entry into the international market through Koelher in the US has enabled it to secure a foothold in many other countries, including Austria, France, Greece, Italy, Poland, South Africa, Malaysia, Malta, Saudi Arabia, Taiwan and Vietnam. The major products exported are four-ball testers, air jet erosion testers, abrasion testing machines, multi-specimen testers, scratch testers, wear and friction monitors and reciprocatory friction and wear monitors.

Ducom's design department is an organisational component of its marketing department. The marketing group has the major role of projecting its technical capability to potential customers, including mostly scientific and technical educational institutions and R&D organisations and manufacturing industries. When a customer requirement is communicated to Ducom, the entrepreneur interacts initially with the design and marketing departments to clarify the product idea. He interacts with IISc and browses the internet for relevant product information. Through in-house brainstorming sessions, the product idea is developed and a prototype is then developed based on several interactions with concerned customers. After customer evaluation, the design is finalised and the newly fabricated instrument is then subjected to trial runs before it is finally standardised. This involves close interaction with customers before embarking on the design, manufacture and installation of customised equipments to ensure customer satisfaction. At the course of the interaction, considerable technical knowledge is obtained by Ducom from its customers. Along with the products, comprehensive product details, instruction manuals and calibration kits are provided by the enterprise. Comprehensive post-warranty services are provided with several combinations, tailored to the needs of individual customers.

7.6.5 Micro FX

Micro FX represents a case of entrepreneurial emergence from an engineering institute. The entrepreneur of Micro FX has always been fascinated with electronic merchandise since his childhood days. Soon after obtaining a degree in electronics in Bangalore, he joined a small-scale instrumentation enterprise as a design engineer. After a year, he shifted to another enterprise involved in the manufacture of uninterrupted power supply equipment where he worked as head of the design section. Although the work did not provide him opportunities for learning, he was able to develop an electronic alarm system for cars. The absence of job satisfaction led him to plan his own enterprise and to widen his technological initiative and abilities. Hence, he started Micro FX as a partnership enterprise to produce uninterruptible power supply systems. Micro FX manufactures handheld electronic ticketing machines for public transport bus corporations. With only a million rupees, along with just two partners as employees, Micro FX started its operations. The partners were able to forge a contract with Industrial Process Automation (IPA) at the Peenya industrial estate of Bangalore and began making electronic weighing instruments. In 1995, the entrepreneur's partner decided to venture into textile trading instead, because a technology-oriented industry was not to his liking. Thus, Micro FX became a proprietary firm and until 1999, focused only on IPA orders by designing, developing and supplying electronic weighing machines. In the beginning, Micro FX was engaged in customer-focused product development. However, this monotonous line of work, with the same product being developed led the entrepreneur to seek newer challenges.

A friend from Dubai returned to Bangalore and joined Micro FX as a partner without any investment. His only responsibility was product marketing, an area from which the entrepreneur distanced himself. With this, he gained more time to concentrate on new product development. In response to one of his customer's casual inquiries, he designed a cash register (billing machine). In 1998, his partner won a deal with their first customer, a beverage corporation for this new product. The corporation ordered 13 cash register machines, with each having two components of keyboard and a printer. In 1999, they set up another unit in Kottayam, Kerala with just one employee. In the following year, they had orders from the Consumer Federation of Kerala. In 2002, one of the employees of Bangalore Water Supply and Sewerage Board approached the entrepreneur to know whether he could produce handheld billing machines. This urged the entrepreneur to design and develop such a device, which was immediately accepted by BWSSB, by placing an order for 60 machines. The Karnataka Electricity Board placed orders for two districts but the company lost this market very soon due to the copying of their design and the production of similar machines by a larger company based in Hyderabad. Nevertheless, the company got orders for electronic handheld ticketing machines from Kerala Road Transport Corporation for its buses.

In 2003, the Karnataka State Road Transport Corporation placed an order for 2,000 ticketing machines and another request for 600 ticketing machines came in 2004. In the following year, Micro FX supplied 5,000 more machines to that corporation. In 2006, 6,000 machines were supplied to North East Karnataka Road Transport Corporation and North West Karnataka Road Transport Corporation. This position was achieved despite two major competitors in Hyderabad and another in Bangalore. The reputation that Micro FX has built over the period has helped it through the competition. An important achievement of Micro FX in the process of developing handheld ticketing is its entry into the international market. In 2004, it exported a few machines to Sri Lanka, which resulted in exporting another 500 machines in 2007. In 2009, the entrepreneur got an order for 1,000 machines from Sri Lanka and Dubai. Recently, they have sent some samples to Malaysia and businessmen from Nigeria and Dubai have visited Micro FX to know more about its products and to forge business deals. The entrepreneur anticipates a huge potential in the Indian market itself. Currently, the company is in the process of developing point of sale machines. Shops, canteens and restaurants will be targeted for the potential application of these machines in different forms because they are usable in multiple situations. Even filling stations have made use of their billing machines. The entrepreneur is working on adding a biometric sensor to the handheld ticketing machine. He is developing a new version of this machine for the specific use of traffic policemen. The company has made e-ticketing machines viable and is ready to develop spot billing machines for mobile banking.

The Micro FX case represents an entrepreneur who is highly motivated technologically and his dynamic and ambitious nature proved instrumental to the enterprise's continued success. His childhood fascination with electronic goods and his subsequent technical education have transformed him into a technopreneur who targets and creates technological innovations. The process began when he became an employee in an instrumentation enterprise where he developed an electronic alarm system for cars. However, to widen his perspective on technological product innovation, he established his own enterprise. His attention to technological concerns, rather than to managerial ones, is reflected in his company's current organisational setup, in which marketing is looked after by his partner. His approach to innovation involves initial interaction with customers. After this, he himself carries out innovative/developmental tasks with the help of a designer and two design assistants. He again interacts with customers at the stage of product acceptance through ongoing experiments and trials. The company does not emphasise repeated interactions and this could explain its failure in the electronic weighing machine. Most of the innovations are characterised by new technology being incorporated into a product without altering much of the product's features. Most of these could be considered novel innovations because they have been introduced for the first time in the country.

7.6.6 Safety Match Industry

Food and Agriculture Organisation has been sponsoring many Indian agriculture and agro industries projects since 1970s. One such project relates to safety match production in Tamil Nadu. Wooden match production is split into three sectoral categories, the mechanised large-scale sector, the handmade small-scale sector and the cottage sector. About 82 per cent of total match production is in the handmade small-scale (67 per cent) and cottage (15 per cent) sectors, where technology has remained relatively simple. These two non-mechanised sectors of the match industry are distinguished primarily by output size. The industry directly employs an estimated 250,000 workers, with only 6,000 of these in the mechanized sector. The cottage sector, which involves totally manual operations and produces less than 75 million match sticks per year and is often household-based, accounts for about 50,000 workers. Thus, small-scale, factory-based match production units employ a large number of workers involved in the match sector. Manufacture of wooden matches is best suited to handmade and household-based production. For every worker employed in the mechanised sector, four workers may be employed in the non-mechanised sector. Men, women, children, the elderly and partially handicapped persons are employed. Match making by hand is labour-intensive and requires low levels of technology and relatively small capital investments. A number of operations in the production process can be easily undertaken at home. Future expansion of the match industry is reserved for small sector, with particular emphasis on the cottage sector. The veneering and splint industry in the adjoining state of Kerala is an important ancillary industry, providing nearly 90 per cent of the wood used in Tamil Nadu.

The origin of the safety match industry in India goes back to the beginning of this century. Around 1910 immigrant Japanese families who settled in Calcutta began making matches with simple hand and power-operated machines. Local workers soon learned the necessary skills and a number of small match factories sprang up in and around Calcutta. These small match factories could not meet the total requirements of the country however, and India began to import matches from Sweden and Japan. During the First World War, when Swedish matches could not be imported, the Indian market was fed mainly by imported matches from Japan and by the locally made ones which followed the Japanese pattern introduced in Calcutta. After the war, factories in Calcutta were unable to compete with imports and handmade match production shifted to southern India, especially in the Ramanathapuram and Tirunelveli districts of Tamil Nadu. This shift was due to the pioneering efforts of P. Iya Nadar and A. Shanmuga Nadar who went to Calcutta to learn the process from Purna Chandra Roy, a local businessman, who had learned the trade in Germany. The Nadars set up a number of manual match production units in extremely poor regions of Tamil Nadu, where a combination of the dry climate, cheap labour and availability of raw materials from nearby Kerala created ideal conditions for match production. The first sulphur match that would burn when brought into contact with a rough surface was produced in South India in 1923 and the first safety match in 1932.

Mechanisation came to the Indian match industry in 1924 when Wimco started operations in 1924 as a unit of the multinational Swedish match company. Wimco is still the only representative of the large scale sector in wooden match manufacturing and is the only fully mechanised match factory in the country. Government policies protected Indian matches by placing protective tariffs on imported products and specifically favoured the expansion of the handmade, small-scale sector through the use of differential excise taxes. There are now 12,000 units in the small-scale, non-mechanised sector, of which 75 per cent is situated in Tamil Nadu. In 1943, a major change in policy was introduced with the differential excise levy. The rate remained unchanged at Rs. 3.00 per gross for units producing over 100 gross per day while it was lowered to Rs. 2.87 per gross for units producing less than 100 gross per day. Over the next ten years, further classification resulted in five levels of production with progressive concessions to smaller units. In 1967, the basis for differentiation was expanded to include the mode of production as well as the volume produced. This decision further strengthened the small-scale enterprises and remains as a main plank of government policies in the present. In 1979, an even more dramatic spread in excise duties was mandated, raising the duties of the mechanised sector and lowering those in the handmade sector. Most recently, production limits on the middle and cottage sectors have been removed with an excise duty of Rs. 3.50 per gross established on both. Additional incentives to hand-made match production units have been given by state governments in the form of sales tax exemptions. To further insure that the hand-made sector continues to expand the central government has frozen the capacity of Wimco, the only large-scale mechanised match producer, at 695,000 cases (one case 7,200 boxes) per annum.

Between 1926-28 and 1949 the number of factories increased from 27 to 192. Since that time there has been a continuous expansion of the hand-made sector whose share of the market has shot up from 22 per cent in 1949-50 to 50 per cent in 1969-70 and now constitutes 82 per cent. With Wimco's production level frozen and growing population fuelling an increase in demand estimated at six per cent per annum, the handmade sector will clearly increase even further in the future. The cottage sector under the coordination of the Khadi and Village Industries Commission (KVIC) has been selected to be the major growth sector in the future. There are a number of match producers who have fragmented their units to get the benefit of concessions, but at the same time there is a growing trend towards centralised ownership of many smaller units. In Sivakasi and Kovilpatti, 18 families (so-called match kings) control almost two-thirds of the total match production in the country.

Safety matches manufactured in the country are of the standard type with wooden veneer or cardboard boxes and wooden splints, each box containing 50 splints. Other types of matches produced include book matches containing 10 to 20 sticks and fancy or advertisement matches made to the buyer's specifications. Most of the raw materials are the same regardless of the level of production, but the process is slightly different in the mechanised and hand-made sectors. The major raw materials used in the production of safety matches are soft woods used to make the match sticks (splints) and boxes and chemicals for the match heads and the friction surface of the boxes. With the exception of sulphur, all the basic raw materials are produced within India. Both the quantity and quality of matchwood are determinants for quality products. The Indian match industry depended on imported wood including aspen from Sweden, Canada, America, and Russia, cotton wood from Canada, balsam poplar from Manchuria and linden from Japan. But the government quickly moved to encourage the use of indigenous woods by restricting the import of foreign poplars. One result of the early use of poplar wood has been that the consumer continues to associate good quality matches with light coloured wood, placing further limitations on the selection of indigenous species. Wood supplies have drastically declined in the last 25 years and the demand for matches continues to grow. Further, prices of other materials such as match wax, potassium chlorate, potassium bichromate and blue match paper have risen dramatically.

In mechanised match manufacture the entire process of match making takes place under one roof from log to match. In the hand-made sector veneer for match boxes and splints are produced separately. The remaining stages are all done manually, often as piecework at home and then assembled or boxed at small factory units. The technology of match making is relatively simple and involves a number of stages, whether they are mechanised or not. Processing timber logs into outer and inner box veneers and splints is the first stage. This process requires power operated machines but these can be simple, locally made, slow speed log peelers or the high speed Swedish made peeling lathes, splint choppers, and splint dryers used by Wimco. In the mechanised sector the cut splints and box veneer are fed directly into box making machines and match dipping machines. In the small-scale and cottage sectors the cut splints and box size veneer are transported from producers in Kerala, across the border to factories in Tamil Nadu.

Box making is done both by machine as well as manually. In the hand-made sector outer veneers are issued to workers either at the factory or at their homes along with blue match paper cut to size. Tapioca flour-paste is used to assemble the outer boxes by hand. Although rates are currently under revision an average worker can make 40 to 50 gross boxes per day, at little more than Re 0.10 per gross. Inner boxes are prepared the same way, usually by women, at home, with 35 gross a day at Re 0.15 per gross being an average worker's production. Dipping and filling in the handmade sector begins with the distribution of the cut and cleaned splints to workers along with wooden frames consisting of 50 *laths*, each with 50 grooves. These frames must be filled by hand; each splint fitted into a separate little groove and is the most labour-intensive of handmade match operations. The filled frames are first dipped in wax and then into the head chemical composition which includes potassium chlorate. The dipped matches are now dried atmospherically in racks. This is where the dry climate of match districts is so essential. Once dry the splints are filled in boxes at the rate of 50 per box and put into side-painting frames and levelled. Thereafter, a mixture of red amorphous phosphorous, glue and bichromate of potash is manually painted with a brush on one side. This side painting is usually done by monthly paid adult workers, mostly men. Labelling and packing come next, once the side painting dries. Workers take the painted boxes from the frames and affix labels and excise stamps on them. The labelled boxes are then packed into dozen packets and 12 dozen packets are packed into a one gross box. Five gross boxes are made into a bundle containing 60 dozen match boxes, and finally shipped to the market.

Handmade match production technology has a definite edge over mechanised manufacture in being able to accept more kinds of tree species for splints as well as boxes. Also, being made by hand, losses are negligible in this sector compared to those in highly automated mechanised units. The handmade sector, with its low wages, is far more flexible in accepting a wider variety of low girth logs. Handmade box making and filling operations are slow and the conditions enable the handmade sector greater freedom to absorb non-standard wood species in match manufacture. The handmade sector is supported by an ancillary veneer and splint industry where the selection of logs is primarily guided by the consideration of the end product. The quality of the matches produced out of these splints is good and can be consistently maintained. However, the rapidly declining availability and quality of wood has now also affected the handmade sector which has been called upon to take over the leading role in the industry. The production of box veneer and splints is relatively simple and very labour-intensive. All of the machinery used in the process is produced locally within Kerala. A typical unit produces both splints as well as box veneers and runs from September to May, for about 200 days during the dry months. Veneer and splint enterprises are recognised as small-scale industries by the government and once they are registered, are entitled to receive a special share of match wood annually from government forests. Log peelers and saws used in small-scale veneer and splint making are small, work at slow speeds and accept logs as small as eight centimeter circumference. After peeling, the splints and veneers are dried for 8 to 10 hours in the open on cement platforms. The drying, packing and storage of the products is done manually. Work is normally suspended during the monsoon, although a few units have improvised semi-automatic drying chambers for splints, which can be fired during the monsoon with wood waste.

The above rigorous standards of quality and safety require a great acumen of entrepreneurship action. Splints used must be of good quality so that they do not break while striking. Match heads should ignite without spurting and match head particles should not fly when the head is struck against the friction surface of the box. Matches should not catch fire under impact. Because of the rigid nature of the standards, neither Wimco nor most of the match kings carry the ISI markings on their matches. The handmade, middle sector is confident that the entire requirement of safety matches for the nation can be met by them in the near future. They lobby vigorously for the total exclusion of Wimco from match production and complain about lower excises levied on cottage level units. Since the development of a major fireworks industry in the Sivakasi region, labour is presently not as easily available as it once was. Moreover, thirty per cent of these middle level factories now use card board boxes, so these are actually semi-mechanised relying on power driven machinery to form these boxes. Finally, operating in an extremely poor region, the match kings are frequently accused of exploiting women and child labourers, paying extremely low wages under poor working conditions. Nonetheless, the middle-level hand-made sector has helped the growth of ancillary industries for the manufacture of splints and veneers, potassium chlorate and factories producing glue and paper. The small-scale sector also produces non-glowing deluxe matches, book or strip matches and wax matches.

KVIC as an entrepreneur, entered the picture in 1977 to create opportunities for new entrepreneurs to set up small-scale match units in rural areas of India. The intent of this effort was to increase employment, reduce exploitation by traders, stabilise the market price at a reasonable profit level and raise the wage levels of workers in both cottage and small-scale sectors of the non-mechanised units. Small-scale units have several distinct advantages. They may be household-based, are often more efficient in their use of a wide variety of materials, produce less wastage and distribute benefits to a deeper labour pool. The KVIC cottage match industry programme emphasises technical, financial and marketing assistance. It endeavours to offer a total assistance package from the opening of the unit to the marketing of the completed matches. However, the substitution of wooden match boxes by cardboard, pioneered by Wimco, has introduced a definite technological and material improvement in the industry. But along with this change, a degree of semi-mechanisation of operations has also been introduced. Cardboard skillets used mainly for manufacturing outer box match manufacture are printed in central, automated printing machines and are purchased by small match manufacturers. This innovation has naturally resulted in lowering the employment rate, much against the planned concept of promoting employment-oriented technologies. Another approach to the raw material problem is substituting wax instead.

7.7 Conclusion

Companies in the electronics industry are able to aim, plan, strategize and implement technological innovations successfully in terms of new product developments. Entrepreneurial motivation is the primary factor responsible for the emergence and implementation of innovations. Small entrepreneurs play an instrumental role in recognising market opportunities, building crucial in-house technological capability, supplementing it with appropriate external assistance, putting in place technological innovation processes, including their modifications to suit customer requirements and finally delivering innovations to the market. The innovation process is marked by a built-in mechanism for continuous customer interactions. The outcome of innovations is reflected in the overall growth experienced by the companies not only in terms of factor inputs, but more importantly in terms of sales turnover. The SME sector has been performing under stressed institutional framework. However, efforts have to be made in order to assist the sector in many more respects so that it contributes to the core of entrepreneurial growth in the country. Project profiles and feasibility on behalf of entrepreneurs have to be effectively. Undertaking of industrial potential surveys has to be with a view to provide first hand information regarding raw material, required labour and other critical inputs to the entrepreneurs. This has to be followed by proper identification of potential entrepreneurs and providing them with adequate technical and managerial assistance. Market researches and surveys for specific products have to be done so that in future the units may not take any difficulties in marketing products, besides providing them with consultancy for export oriented projects. Many entrepreneurship development programmes have to be conducted with a view to make aware, create and groom new entrepreneurs. Procurement and distribution of scare raw materials as and when required and supply of machinery on hire purchase system, besides rendering marketing assistance to SMEs to effectively sell their products have to be properly ensured so that there are no leakages in the system with provision of consultancy and trading services to strengthen their competitive ability and gain advance. They are also required to undertake construction of industrial estates with basic facilities and provide infrastructure and accommodative facilities to the entrepreneurs.

8

Development of Social, Ecological, Public, Institutional and Women Entrepreneurship

8.1 Introduction

Entrepreneurship may have supply-side or demand-side perspective, wherein the former focuses on the availability of suitable individuals to occupy entrepreneurial roles and the latter on the number and nature of the entrepreneurial roles that have to be met (Thornton, 1999). The demand-side perspective suggests a number of ways to examine the context of organisational founding, such as the generation of new ventures by organisational hierarchies. Individuals and organisations affect and are affected by their social context and as Weber (1930) has shown, religious doctrines provide the cultural justification needed to shape the economic behaviour of individuals. We can characterise the supply-side perspective to expose the non-profit objectives and how culture and personality can empower individual entrepreneurship, wherein their chances of success are determined by the structure of their networks.

This chapter presents the various aspects of entrepreneurship in its social, public, ecological, institutional and gender perspectives to showcase some of the recent deliberations on the subject. Section 8.2 deliberates on social entrepreneurship, while section 8.3 briefs about ecological entrepreneurship. Section 8.4 discusses public entrepreneurship in its various dimensions, while section 8.5 touches on institutional aspects. Section 8.6 characterises women entrepreneurship from its developmental aspect. Section 8.7 concludes the discussion leading to the emergence of innovativeness that is the bedrock of entrepreneurial development.

8.2 Social Entrepreneurship

Entrepreneurs with a social mission are called social entrepreneurs and they participate as change agents in the social sector by adopting a mission to create and sustain social value (not just private value). They recognise and pursue new opportunities to serve that mission, engaging in a process of continuous innovation, adaptation and learning, acting boldly without being limited by resources currently in hand and exhibit a sense of accountability to the constituencies served for the outcomes created (Dees, 1983). When entrepreneurs exhibit goal-setting and problem-solving qualities, social change takes place. Entrepreneurial quality does not mean the just the ability to lead, to administer or to get things done but also to someone who has a very special trait and causes a vibrant change. Social entrepreneurship extends the definition of entrepreneurship by its emphasis on ethical integrity and maximising social value rather than private value or profit. Grameen Bank of Bangladesh and the Self Employed Women's Association of Gujarat banking institutions, owned and governed by the poor themselves and their innovation figure out as viable ways to substitute traditional collateral requirements. While they organise people in groups, their loans and other financial products and services are provided to individuals. In this way, social entrepreneurs attempt to create alternative financial services and models of funding social ventures.

Bill Drayton, the founder of the world's first organisation in promoting social entrepreneurship, Ashoka Innovators for the Public, (founded in 1980 and global headquartered in Arlington, VA, USA) describes social entrepreneurs as practical visionaries who possess qualities associated with vision, innovation, determination and long-term commitment, but are committed to systemic social change in their field (Ashoka Innovators for the Public, 2000). This need makes the entrepreneur persist for years and decades through all these steps, despite the resistance of many forces that would frustrate others. They instinctively reject solutions that depend on local circumstances that would not work universally. Ashoka's central hypothesis is that the most powerful force in the world is a pattern changing big idea in the hands of an entrepreneur. Apart from individuals, institutions and firms can also be social entrepreneurs. Each such major pattern shift results in follow-on innovations, adaptations and local applications.

A social entrepreneur is someone who recognises a social problem and uses entrepreneurial principles to organise, create and manage a venture to make social change. Whereas a business entrepreneur typically measures performance in profit and return, a social entrepreneur assesses success in terms of the impact on society as well as in profit and return. While social entrepreneurs often work through nonprofits and citizen groups, many are working in the private and governmental sectors and making important impacts on society. Social entrepreneurs may be individuals with innovative solutions to society's most pressing social problems. They are ambitious and persistent, tackling major social issues and offering new ideas for wide-scale change. Rather than leaving societal needs to the government or business sectors, social entrepreneurs find what is not working and solve the problem by changing the system, spreading the solution and persuading entire society to take new steps. The main aim of social entrepreneurship and social enterprise is to further social and environmental goals for a good cause. Although social entrepreneurs often are associated with nonprofits, this need not be incompatible with making a profit. Social enterprises are for 'more-than-profit,' using business models that combine a revenue-generating business with a social-value-generating structure.

According to Raman (2010), the first phase of social entrepreneurship was around 1980, represented by the founding of Ashoka by Bill Drayton to develop and legitimise the field. The second phase occurred soon after and the two were part of the same wave of the early 1980s with the response to the increasingly growing gap between the haves and the have-nots. Social entrepreneurs, like many others who came together to address public sector shortcomings, responded to these gaps. But the difference between social entrepreneurs and others wanting to do good to society is the way they go about it. Unlike the latter, social entrepreneurs rather than just offering simple responses to basic needs in addition, provide practical, transformational solutions to change the systems and patterns that keep people poor. They also offer solutions instead of merely joining the protesters advocating change. Social entrepreneurs become the new social architects drawing up and testing the blueprint for a different way of creating a new world and proving that it can be done.

The third phase of evolution of social entrepreneurship is related to Corporate Social Responsibility (CSR) in the early 1990s that holds that the business of business is not just increasing shareholder value; rather, companies must embody transparency and ethical behaviour, respect for stakeholder groups and a commitment to add economic, social and environmental value. CSR was much less the result of an internal decision on the part of companies as it was a response to the popular movement led by the organised citizen sector and consumer groups and empowered by internet technology that forced business to acknowledge that its shareholder value was tied to its ability to measure and reduce negative environmental and social impacts and to maximise positive impact. Another related to some social entrepreneurs turning the concept of CSR and rather than setting up a business to generate profit first and then trying to make it socially and environmentally responsible, they felt it would be a great idea to start out with the premise that the bottom line is social and environmental transformation and then build for-profit activities around making that happen. Many social entrepreneurs have done that paving the way for the social corporation.

The fourth phase began in the early 1990s (Raman, 2010). The search to prove that one non-profit was a more effective investment than another was best accomplished by the establishment of clear measurable goals, benchmarks and outcomes so that such comparisons could be made. This occurred among foundations, philanthropists and not-for-profit ventures influenced by business approaches drawn primarily from the world of venture capital, which the social entrepreneurs embraced this challenge.

By the end of the 20th century, the term social entrepreneurship had started to become synonymous with socio-economic and sustainable development. The earliest example of social entrepreneurship in India is that of Vinoba Bhave, founder of the Bhoodan movement, which caused the redistribution of more than 70,00,000 acres of land to aid India's landless. Other notable entrepreneurs are JRD Tata, GD Birla, the Godrej family and Dhirubhai Ambani. Some examples of entrepreneurial ventures include Barcamp, an international network of user generated conferences and DARE, a media platform for the Indian entrepreneurs. The latter is an interactive platform for enabling entrepreneurs to start and run their own business. It analyses what businesses need to do, rather than report on what businesses are doing. The George Foundation's Women's Empowerment programme empowers women by providing education, cooperative farming, vocational training, savings planning and business development. In 2006, the cooperative farming programme, Baldev Farms, was the second largest banana grower in South India with 250 acres under cultivation (Raman, 2010). Profits from the farm are used for improving the economic status of the workers and for running the other charitable activities of the foundation. 'By Stupid Common Man' is a volunteer online association of business professionals for revival of declining industries in Andhra Pradesh. This is an open forum with free membership and seeks the participation of a broader intellectual population. South East Asia Pacific based Global Indian Foundation which is headquartered in Singapore runs schools for tribal students in Gujarat, India. The public private partnership project aims to lift the education standards of the tribal students and make them employable in public or private sector.

While business entrepreneurship deals with application of entrepreneurial energy primarily for generating wealth for a commercial business group and its shareholders by producing and supplying products and services, social entrepreneurship deals with application of entrepreneurship for addressing social and environmental and causing social and environmental change through non-violent, non-coercive methods by generating significant impacts in the target. The social entrepreneurial strategies and activity plans usually include elements of positive, life building and socially and ecologically enriching values, attitudes and behaviours. Entrepreneurial energy is the capacity of certain individuals for spotting high-potential opportunities for intervention, generating innovative products, services and approaches for solving problems and resource mobilisation, risk taking and sustained striving for achieving their goals in an ethical manner. The profit earned by these ventures is used mainly for social development activities and for reinvestment in the business itself.

Many of the public sector enterprises (Housing Development Corporation, Agro-Industries Corporation, Irrigation Development Corporation and so on) were established with primarily social goals in view. However, most of them have turned bureaucratic, ineffective and loss-making units over the years. There is considerable scope for injecting entrepreneurial energy and passion for social development in many of these enterprises through collaborative arrangements or through outsourcing of works to NGOs. In order to be successful in developing such collaborations, the support from policy-makers is often required. In recent years, micro-credit, micro-enterprises and self-help groups have emerged as major tools for development of poor people. The NGO sector has been playing a major role in these fields. In many areas, mutually aided cooperative societies and linkages with banking institutions have been formed to provide sustainable structure for these initiatives. Such initiatives have also infused some degree of business discipline, leadership and entrepreneurship among a section of poor and NGOs.

In 2008, Rajnish Sinha and Siva Cotipalli started Bangalore-based Dhana-X with the idea of clubbing it with person to person (P2P) lending. Dhana-X is a platform where people contribute small amounts online as loans and the NGOs take up the task of disbursing these loans to needy communities in their areas of operation. Richa Pandey was a media professional in New Delhi for eight years, but her calling was rural India. The retail and BPO sectors were creating job opportunities and she focused on vocational training for rural youth in these areas. In 2007, she approached the Rural Technology Business Incubator at IIT Madras with a business plan outline, resulting in the emergence of *e-jeevika*, a programme, connected with designing course content and online training in the areas of retail sales, data entry and security services and subjects candidates to psychometric tests to determine where they would fit in best and trains them accordingly. One of the best examples of social entrepreneurship will always be Amul, a cooperative milk federation. Amul was created by government initiative and by the passionate entrepreneurs like Verghese Kurien. They wanted to bring out change in the way milk was produced and distributed on a massive scale as to result in a white revolution.

Other examples include Scojo Foundation Vision-Spring, founded in 1999 by Jordan Kassalow as a spinoff from Scojo, a distributor of high-end glasses in the US which seeks to provide through an effective supply chain and economies of scale, high-quality reading glasses, previously unavailable to the communities where they worked, at an affordable price. Scojo Foundation, because of its relationship to Scojo Vision is able to source glasses at low cost and that low cost is passed on to the Scojo Vision Entrepreneurs, which in turn, sell the glasses to customers in their communities thereby enabling the women to earn a sustainable source of income (Raman, 2010). The Schwabb Foundation does not help anybody with money, instead helps social entrepreneurs with their resources, connecting interested investors and social entrepreneurs through technology. They are connected with schools all over the world, which train social entrepreneurs for them. Muhammad Yunus of Bangladesh is the founder of microcredit and the Grameen Bank. Maria Montessori developed the Montessori approach to early childhood education and Margaret Sanger founded the Planned Parenthood Federation of America and led the movement for family planning efforts around the world. Florence Nightingale founded modern nursing and established the first school for nurses and fought to improve hospital conditions. John Muir, the naturalist and conservationist established the National Park System and helped in the founding of The Sierra Club. Jean Monnet was responsible for the reconstruction of the French economy following World War II, including the establishment of the European Coal and Steel Community.

Social enterprises are traditionally non-profit business models and their social mission is an explicit and central objective, which affects their perception and assessments of opportunities. They focus on the social impact of their business activities and not on wealth creation. Though commercial businesses may be fulfilling various social needs along with their business motive to earn maximum profits, social entrepreneurs are completely different from them. The performance of social entrepreneurs is measured on the basis of social value delivered along with financial returns, while that of a non-profit organisation is evaluated merely on the basis of social value they have delivered. Social enterprises are run in an entrepreneurial domain, using marketing tools of commercial and social sales promotion for marketing their products and services in a sustainable manner.

Women's cooperatives, microfinance institutions, Arvind Eye Care are recent examples of social entrepreneurs in India, whereas Helpage India, CRY and AID are recent examples of non-profit organisations. Devi Shetty founded Narayana Hrudayalaya, where upto twenty five heart surgeries are performed in a single day at a cost as low as Rs. 50,000 compared to Rs.15 lakh in other hospitals. It is one of the largest healthcare centres in Asia. Water Health International (WHI) financed by the Acumen fund provides sanitation solutions. A particular ultra violet water work (UVW) has been adopted which is three times more powerful than other UVW technologies. WHI started its operations in 2006 by setting up water purification plants at under-serviced locations. WHI has 300 community water plants in Andhra Pradesh, Tamil Nadu, Gujarat and Maharashtra where each plant costs Rs. 50 to Rs.115 lakh. WHI runs its business by using the resources of their local community such as the land, water and electricity. WHI uses the land for setting up the plant with an agreement to hand it back to the local community after 10-15 years without any cost to the community. The business strategy of WHI is totally society-oriented as it sells the purified water to the local community at an affordable price by reducing the cost of purification, packaging, distribution and logistics. After providing purified water at a low cost the very next challenge, WHI faced was the public awareness. To overcome this challenge WHI used various marketing tools including door to door marketing, water health awareness programmes and oath taking ceremonies in schools. With the help of its marketing team, women self-help groups and school children, it raised the awareness about various water diseases and the usefulness of the purified water.

Gupta (2002) describes Drishtee, a for-profit social enterprise that came into being in 2000 to solve the problem by implementing a sustainable development of rural economy and society with the use of information and communication technology. Through a franchise and partnership model, Drishtee provides access to information and local services to the rural community at a nominal price. The business model is driven by village entrepreneurs, who own the village node to operate a self-sustaining, profitable kiosk. The kiosk provides access to information like government records, agricultural data, and health insurance. It helps in filing applications for licenses, certificates, compensations and other benefits, besides providing product rates and courses like computer training and spoken English. The mini-entrepreneurs earn by charging the community a nominal fee for the services they provide. Drishtee has a fixed revenue sharing model with kiosk operators and a variable revenue sharing with service providers. Drishtee has successfully implemented this concept with over 1000 kiosks in different states of India. Each kiosk caters to approximately 1200 households, the majority of which have an aggregate income of less than Rs. 100 per day.

We can narrate success stories of some of the social entrepreneurs (both institutions and individual entrepreneurs) highlighted by Schwab Foundation for Social Entrepreneurship. The Foundation, in its 2012 'Outstanding Social Entrepreneurs' has conferred the Social Entrepreneur of the Year 2010 to Aajeevika Bureau of Rajasthan run by Rajiv Khandelwal and Krishnavatar Sharma for the benefit of migrant labourers in issuance of identity cards, insurance, pension and counselling.

Vikram Akula's SKC Microfinance is a commercial model, obtaining investments from venture capitalists and trusts for more than seven million borrowers. Akula has also started a mobile banking ecosystem in village petty shops and has been conferred the Social Entrepreneur of the Year 2006.

Basix, the Hyderabad-based microfinance institution, one of the first to attract international commercial equity, has the objective of promoting business opportunities to rural people and micro enterprises.

Arvind Eye Care System, founded by Dr. G. Venkataswamy in 1976, is the largest eye care facility, providing 55 per cent of its services free or very much subsidised for the poor. It has been involved in the production of high quality, low cost suture blades and intraocular lenses and uses telemedicine and training to access and benefit rural areas in many parts of the country.

The Comprehensive Rural Health Project has impacted on health and social development in Maharashtra villages under through self organization under the leadership of Raj Arole and his wife.

Development Alternatives has been advocating handling of climatic risks in central India towards community mobilisation for environmental assessment and protection. It manufactures eco construction materials, handloom textiles, briquette presses and electricity from biomass, besides providing information services. Ashok Khosla, its entrepreneur is a Schwab Fellow of the World Economic Forum.

Empower Pragati Vocational and Staffing entrepreneured by Rajendra Joshi, is a social enterprise, specialising in skill development of disadvantaged youth, especially in slums. Training in vocational and life skills is undertaken in different cities in India. It provides home management services to urban areas.

Gram Vikas of Odisha, under the leadership of Joe Madiath, pools community participation in the improvement of village infrastructure, road construction, biogas, access to safe drinking water and sanitation. The institution has won UN Habitat Award in 2003.

International Development Enterprises, established in 1991 by Amitabha Sadangi, a Schwab Fellow of World Economic Forum, provides business and management initiatives towards commercial agriculture in low-cost irrigation, enabling farmers on year-round cultivation and also exporting its technologies to Africa and Southeast Asia.

Industree, co-founded by Neelam Chhiber, is involved in artisanal development in Karnataka and Tamil Nadu, through community self-help group model and creating Mother Earth stores.

Nidan, started by Arbind Singh in Bihar, involves the informal sector (waste pickers and others) in collectivising social capital towards organised occupational enterprises.

PlanetRead, started by Brij Kothari, has developed Same Language Subtitling in Doordarshan broadcasting in different programmes. The innovative subtitling programme has won the World Bank Development Marketplace Award in 2002.

RIVER, founded by Padmanabha and Rama Rao of Andhra Pradesh, has innovated School-in-a-box, an activity learning programme, aimed at training the teachers through information exchanges and distance learning. It is replicating the model in many countries.

SELCO, under the leadership of Harish Hande, has spearheaded a movement linking renewable energy, technical services, financing and improved quality of life, in organising energy service centres through business centres in the southern states.

SEWA, started by Ela Bhatt, a Schwab Fellow of World Economic Forum, is the largest union of women in India, offering financial, health and childcare, legal, insurance, cooperation and vocational education services.

SPARC, in association with National Slum Dwellers Federation and Mahila Milan, mobilises urban poor in managing community resources for housing and infrastructure and has shown that cooperation amongst non-government organisations, communities and government would bring in grassroots innovations for a better change. Sheela Patel and Jockin Arputham manage the activities of this social enterprise.

Ahmedabad-based National Innovation Foundation's Technology Acquisition Fund, under which the rights of technologies from innovators will be obtained after compensating them. The first set of purchases was with reference to many improved varieties of crops like paddy, wheat, mustard, bean, pigeon pea, cardamom and pepper.

8.3 Ecological Entrepreneurship

Sustainability-driven activities of business are driven by innovative market-based mechanisms that might make these firms profitable apart from achieving the objective of sustainable development. Such mechanisms offer vast scope for various players including small enterprises (Trivedi, 2012). For example, the recently established perform-achieve-trade of the government of India through the Bureau of Energy Efficiency may strengthen energy efficiency practices, besides providing a market-based trading mechanism for high achievers in the forms of energy saving certificates. The renewable energy certificates is also an attempt to involve industry at providing market-based incentives to project developers in renewable energy to develop clean technologies and increasing the overall share of renewable energy in the energy mix. These organisations include mining, manufacturing, farming, utilities and communication.

Several of NGOs have made major contributions and innovations in implementing natural resource management projects such as watershed management, wasteland development and participatory irrigation management. Implementation of these projects has included strategies for empowerment of poor people in rural areas and in encouraging them to set up micro-enterprises. The quality of people's participation in development programmes has improved significantly during the last two decades and the credit for this goes to ecological entrepreneurs in the NGO sector. Another field where NGOs like MSSRF and BAIF have made significant impact is promotion of rural eco-entrepreneurship. Many international organisations (Ford and Ashoka foundations) have made important contributions by supporting innovative endeavours. The Centre for Environment Education (CEE) has been working on model programmes in villages around Rajkot district of Gujarat to demonstrate approaches to sustainable development in environmentally fragile rural areas (Krishna et al, 2007). Village level institutions have been established to mobilise savings and credit. Having been exposed to aspects of education for sustainability, communication and managerial skills through CEE, these micro institutions espouse thrift system backed by ecological initiatives. This has resulted in the creation of an eco-entrepreneurship initiative called *gram nidhi* with the help of Eco-Enterprise Fund (EEF) which generates the means to working capital investments for the eco-enterprises. The funds are channelled through Narmada Trust, a local NGO and the eco-enterprises produce goods and services that are economically efficient and viable, ecologically sustainable and socially acceptable using local resources and appropriate technology from substantially modified market mechanisms that account for full-cost pricing and social benevolence. Eco-enterprise options spring from indigenous creativity in response to local needs and possibilities aiming directly to improve the quality of their lives (Ashby et al, 2009). They derive maximum leverage from local cultural and natural environments by drawing upon existing managerial and technical skills and developing a cadre with social sensitivity and environmental concern.

The fund is a one-time grant managed by an Eco-Enterprises Investment Committee (EIC) that oversees its operations. The break-up of the fund comprises of EEF and Technical Assistance Fund for Capacity Building and Information Servicing. The EEF will generate the means to working capital investments for eco-enterprises channelled through the EIC. Preference is given to eco-enterprises that are unable to secure financing from conventional sources due to their small size, innovative nature of business and financial risks involved. The EIC will then grant approval to eco enterprises after rigorous screening employing sound environmental practices, provide financial benefits to community and strict standards for biodiversity conservation, sustainable use and community involvement. The areas studied for venture capital initiatives include sustainable and alternative agriculture, horticulture, agro-forestry and herbal farming, agro-processing, sustainable forestry and non-timber forest products and eco-friendly cottage industry.

The portfolio of ventures that work in partnership with EIC, use market principles to achieve conservation goals and venture specific training modules give clear cut implementation project cycle guidelines to entrepreneurs. The EIC committee will administer venture capital and monitor activities with continuous technical assistance and capacity building. A formal mid-term monitoring and evaluation workshop provides interim support and checks and balances for fund flow. Effective documentation disseminates the learning and experience and reports are distributed to a wider audience. *Gram nidhi* has an orientation to replication in similar socio-ecological conditions, where the scheme has an inbuilt process of organisational and financial sustainability. The repayments to the capital and interest earned by the Trust continue to be a revolving fund for future operations. The success of the programme helps to leverage funds from other sources.

In this way, sustainable development of a region is inherently linked to the ability of its communities to generate livelihoods on a sustainable basis. Ecological niches are better able to achieve stability if their human populations and communities achieve sustainability in their livelihoods. This is particularly true for those ecological areas that are fragile and are witnessing degradation or transformation due to human pressure. Since rural communities traditionally have no access to micro-credit, with greater needs for training and technical assistance, in order to meet the credit needs of eco-enterprises with reduced operating costs, increased revenue, reduced risks and organizational adaptation. While credit is a necessary for promoting SMEs, it is not a sufficient condition and other inputs and services are required to complete the package, including systematic identification of livelihood possibilities, motivating and training potential rural entrepreneurs to take up those livelihoods, ensuring the supply of raw materials and other inputs, equipment, infrastructure and technology, establishing linkages with marketing channels and seeking changes in regulations and policy. Environmental and ecological sustainability is an approach which utilises already existing pool of groomed village institutions and developing a cadre of environmental professionals at the rural level.

8.4 Public Entrepreneurship

Schneider and Teske (1992) define public entrepreneurs as individuals whose policy proposals and political positions represent a dynamic change from existing procedures. They maintain that a theory of political entrepreneurship depends on some concept of economic profit, which cannot be easily employed in the study of political entrepreneurs. As political actors do not produce goods and services that are bought and sold in markets, political gains cannot be measured in monetary terms, in the same way as economic profit (Mises, 1944). Therefore, political entrepreneurship requires subjective measures of benefits and costs from the actor's point of view (Penrose, 1959). Examples include perceptions by the electorate of fairness and subjective valuations by special-interest group members affected by political actors.

Political entrepreneurship may be defined as the identification and exploitation of political profit opportunities, which are identified as gains from trade analogous to those resulting from market exchange and the theory takes a Schumpeterian perspective focusing on creative political innovations that modify the way public entities operate (Kuhnert, 2001). They may be characterised as helping to start dynamic policy changes in the communities. However, public entrepreneurship may be driven not by the pursuit of profit, but the fear of loss imposed by existing political institutions (Ostrom, 1990), wherein a negative externality problem like over-exploitation of ground water basins in California was successfully solved through public entrepreneurship by the decentralised water companies themselves, but only after a judge issued a credible threat to enforce a solution that would have disadvantaged all decision-makers involved. In this instance, public entrepreneurship by the judge involved the shaping of incentives in a way unanticipated by Schumpeter's (1934) approach, which treats entrepreneurship as *sui generis*, not as a response to market or institutional incentives. Yet, despite some of these differences, the relationship between the entrepreneur and the institutional environment may be similar across the private and public sectors (Ostrom, 1990) and unlocking the human potential of individuals requires an opening of both public and private institutions to mobilise collective action and to attenuate opportunism. Effective public entrepreneurship requires the co-evolution of an active public enterprise system together with a vigorous private enterprise system (Ostrom, 2005). Public entrepreneurship can bring together unique combinations of public and private resources to take advantage of social opportunities. Political entrepreneurship can also be conceived as the creation or definition of property rights in ways that make political action more effective (Barzel, 1989), subject to the perception by the political actors that this will confer to them personal gain.

As noted by Teske and Schneider (1994), political entrepreneurship theory can benefit from more precise conceptualisations of objectives, benefits and costs and efficiency. Holcombe (1992) opines that if political goals are not implemented in the least-cost way, there is a profit opportunity from restructuring the nature of the government activity so that the goals are achieved at least cost and the cost savings are a political profit that the entrepreneur can then apply towards the satisfaction of other goals. Such goals relate to re-election (promotion or expanded authority) and even to private appropriation of pecuniary benefits. If the political actor is a private entrepreneur or group of entrepreneurs seeking to use the political system to achieve economic goals like an industry association lobbying for an import tariff or a firm seeking regulation that raises rivals' costs, then the goals may be strictly pecuniary. Therefore, one opportunity for the development of the theory of public entrepreneurship is in integrating a conception of value-capture seeking private and public entrepreneurs with a framework that accepts the complexity of these institutions to frame and pursue public interest (Kaplan and Murray, 2009).

Besides the issue of measuring gains from trade in politics, there is another important distinction between market and political behaviour, where allocation of resources through politics is based on forced transfers rather than through voluntary consent. Political actors can benefit from forcibly transferring resources from one individual or group to another. In Baumol's (1990) terminology, political entrepreneurship can be productive, unproductive or destructive. Destructive political entrepreneurship includes not only forced wealth transfers resulting from regulatory capture or other forms of rent seeking but also the discovery or creation of new forms of moral hazard, the creation of holdups, increasing transaction and information costs and similar activities and problems that can arise in private organisations (Foss et al, 2007). Thus, political actors whether elected officials, government bureaucrats or civil servants or individuals and organisations seeking to use the political process to accomplish private objectives, can be using entrepreneurship theory, though not always perfectly. Like Kirznerian (1973) entrepreneurs, political actors seek to create or discover opportunities for gain, whether private or social. Like Knightian (1921) entrepreneurs, they invest resources, tangible and intangible (time, effort, reputation), in anticipation of uncertain future rewards. Like Schumpeterian (1934) entrepreneurs, they can introduce new products and processes. Unlike the entrepreneurial firms, they cannot use privately appropriated benefits as a criterion for success and the selection mechanism for allocating resources over time towards more successful political entrepreneurs is complex. Political entrepreneurs are likely to undertake actions that foster economic value if they personally benefit from these actions in ways other than the mere private appropriation of value created. An important challenge facing political systems is finding ways to encourage productive political entrepreneurship while discouraging its non-productive and destructive characteristics.

Political entrepreneurship has to consider the institutional environment or the rules of the game (constitutions, laws, norms, property rights and regulatory systems), while commercial entrepreneurship aims at creating economic value for the purpose of private appropriation within a given set of (shifting and non-immutable) rules (Lee et al, 2007). Such arrangements are included in a particular institutional environment and any change in the institutional environment brought about by public-sector entrepreneurship changes the setting in which private-sector entrepreneurship takes place. As Baumol (1990) emphasises, the legal, political and institutional system establishes the general constraints concerning political entrepreneurial behaviour. Public and commercial entrepreneurial processes evolve in ways that are mutually reinforcing, challenging and legitimising.

Kaplan and Murray (2009) maintain that private entrepreneurship in biotechnology was influenced by the co-evolution of public institutions, private corporations and scientific discovery. Analysis of major phases of the biotechnology industry's development since the 1970s shows that the commercial viability of the biotechnology industry rested on the resolution of questions about public safety, the legitimacy of private ownership of the human genome and rules for private use of findings from public funding. Entrepreneurship in the public domain to resolve these questions is essential for the effectiveness of successful commercial entrepreneurs. In established industries, private-sector entrepreneurship involves communication of shared visions, alignment of interests, monitoring, and governance. Private-sector entrepreneurial firms have to work within and sometimes shape the design of public institutions such as regulatory bodies, though this process can involve not only cost-saving innovation but also rent-seeking and other forms of wealth transfer.

In industries like automobiles, banking and healthcare, the mal-alignment of public and private interests has created failures in both private and public institutions. Yet entrepreneurship occurs frequently in the pursuit of public interests and many public servants have worked to improve the efficiency and effectiveness of public institutions. Individuals and groups also work continually to reshape public institutions to create and extract economic rents and it can be difficult to distinguish the former set of activities from the latter, when the pursuit of private gain is in public interest (Yandle, 1983). The growth of private military companies such as Blackwater since the end of World War is an example of public-sector organisational innovation (Avant, 2005). The growth of these industries depends on the interplay between the resolution of public institutions and relative effectiveness of private organisations over public agencies in fulfilling public interests.

As a successful serial entrepreneur, Howard Jarvis gained fame and was featured on the cover of the June 19, 1978 *Time* magazine for advocating Proposition 13 in California, which cut property taxes by 57 per cent and inspired a national debate over taxation. Entrepreneurs such as Jarvis often arrive into public life with agendas, accumulated skills, relationships and capabilities that become the cornerstones of their impact. Private organisations also have an impact on public debate through hybrid structures in which their agenda are temporarily or partially aligned with public interests. Examples include multinationals that provide goods and services to public agencies and in the public interest for private gain (IBM, General Electric and General Motors). Other firms, including Nestle and Coca-Cola have sold products both to the government and private purchasers concurrently but with controversy, wherein Nestle's baby milk products have been promoted as a healthy alternative to breast milk, contrary to the advice of many physicians (Sethi, 1994). Coca-Cola has been cited as an inappropriate consumer of precious clean water in India (Kaye, 2004). Dominance of multinationals in private and public life has become so great that global firms operate across national boundaries with sovereign authority. Hertz (2002) opines that the culture of commerce has become so dominant and prevalent that private life has taken over public interests in a way that while often benign, is sometimes pernicious. The interplay between public and private interests is important and political mechanisms seem to be increasingly constrained by private organisations.

8.5 Institutional Entrepreneurship

Both the institutional theory and institutional economics perspectives conceptualise institutional entrepreneurs as innovators or agents of change who promote new institutional arrangements (Pacheco et al, 2010). The institutional theory perspective does not require economic self-interest and institutional entrepreneur becomes an institutional innovator, whereas, institutional economics restricts the entrepreneur to one of self-interest with economic purpose in the pursuit of institutional change. The institutional economics approach is more consistent with entrepreneurship theory that focuses on economic opportunity as a fundamental determinant of entrepreneurial action (Shane and Venkataraman, 2000). Within the institutional theory perspective, institutional entrepreneurs recognise the obsolescence of institutions, design new institutional arrangements and engage in a variety of strategies (e.g., garner resources, mobilise constituents, frame issues to their advantage) to implement institutional change (DiMaggio, 1988). Hence, institutional entrepreneurs reflect on the institutional status quo and are able to challenge existing rules and practices and institutionalise the alternative rules and practices they are championing.

Institutional entrepreneurship characterises the entrepreneur as an institutional innovator or agent of institutional change, driven by a wide range of motivations (Oliver, 1992) and operating in a variety of contexts. These entrepreneurs may be motivated by functional or economic pressures but also by political or social forces that may deem existing institutions obsolete. In pursuing their motives, these entrepreneurs find opportunities for institutional restructuring within their organisations or macro settings. Endogenous institutional change occurs wherein the bounded rationality acts in pursuit of economic self-interest to change the rules that determine economic behaviour and rewards (Coase, 1974). The entrepreneur is more than an institutional innovator and is an individual who is alert to the potential for capturing economic value from new institutional arrangements. Hence, differences in institutional entrepreneurship activity are determined by differences in the alertness of individuals towards profit opportunities that may arise from institutional change.

Studies of institutional entrepreneurship centre on private arrangements and conventions, changes in professionalised practices and sponsorship of technological standards (Garud et al, 2007). As institutional forms move from individual-firm or industry-level practices to state-level policy, they evolve from micro-variations to macro-regulations. Because practices can vary within firms and even within work groups, they can be conceptualised as the most approachable level for institutional change. In the area of practices, scholars have looked at how variations in standard practices have led to changes in accounting, mutual funds and corporate social responsibility (Dejean et al, 2004). Standards represent the organization of practices into voluntary sets of rules that can determine the evolution of industries. The creation and adoption of standards has been shown to influence the development of the hi-tech industry (Garud et al, 2007). Standards can be affected through industry-level trade associations or through the actions of outside stakeholders such as activists or industry watchdog groups (Rao, 1998).

Recent work has focused on institutional entrepreneurs at the corporate firm or trade association level, where they may seek to influence state-level policies. Ingram and Rao (2004) detail the efforts of chain store owners to influence the legal environment and legitimize the chain store model. Regulatory prohibitions brought about largely through the efforts of anti-alcohol activists not only increased the failure of breweries but also increased the founding of soft drink producers. Through the efforts of dispersed individuals collaborating, institutional entrepreneurship has been foundational to influencing country-level and global environmental policy (Weik, 2011). While institutions comprise both formal written rules (such as constitutions, laws, and property rights) and informal constraints such as conventions and codes of conduct (North, 1990), there is no common structure utilised to categorise these institutions. Williamson (2000) categorises them into four types based on level of social analysis and ranges from underlying norms, traditions and customs at the highest level to organisational governance structures at the lowest level, including social embeddedness and institutional environment. Social embeddedness consists of informal institutions such as norms, cultural factors, customs and codes of conduct and traditions. These institutions are highly inertial and tend to change only over long time frames (DiMaggio and Powell, 1983).

Institutional economics is studying the role of institutions such as ideology, culture, cooperation and the emergence of group norms (Ogilvie, 2007) and there is a growing interest in game theory on the emergence of group or social norms, such as collusion (Greif, 1998). At the intermediate level, the institutional environment consists of formal rules such as property rights and government policy (Williamson, 2000). Formal property rights define the privileges, obligations and duties of individuals with respect to an asset and generate expectations in society that are necessary for the existence and functioning of markets (Barzel, 1997). For instance, the market for land is subject to the expectation that owners are able to exclude others from the land, use the land and transfer its ownership. In this, the emergence of government policies focuses on the determinants, the process of change and the outcomes derived from government legislation (Binswanger and Deininger, 1997).

Institutional entrepreneurs may act in response to functional, political or social pressures that challenge existing institutional structures (Oliver, 1992). Functional pressures arise when individuals perceive issues associated with the performance or utility derived from existing institutions. These pressures may be related to environmental changes, such as competition and demand characteristics. On the other hand, political pressures originating from changes in power and interests may also prompt individuals to question the legitimacy of the institutional status quo (Oliver, 1992). In this case, the source of change may be political in nature. For example, entrepreneurs may force change in a direction that portrays them (or their organisations) as more competent or better aligned with public preferences. In contrast to functional purposes, these political forces do not seek change towards greater efficiency (Beckert, 1999). Also, institutional change can be induced from social pressures arising from changes in social norms and expectations and social conflicts. For instance, when individuals interact in a group with diverse beliefs, experiences and assumptions, they are more likely to question the validity of institutional arrangements (Oliver, 1992). This divergence in social expectations creates an atmosphere of discussion and debate, which may diminish inter-group agreement (Zilber, 2002).

The concept of organisational legitimacy is based on the manipulation of symbols or particular frames to obtain societal support (Downing, 2005). Legitimacy is depicted as an organisational resource that organisations acquire from their environments and that is subsequently used to meet established norms. Entrepreneurial success may depend upon the legitimacy that the institutional entrepreneur enjoys and his or her efforts in portraying the new institutional form as legitimate (Suchman, 1995). Garud et al (2007) show how legitimacy tensions arise between interdependent organisations in a technological field as alternative technological trajectories compete to become dominant design. Those agents in possession of superior resources, knowledge or strategic social network positions are better able to use their political power to shape institutions in their favour (Beckert, 1999). In this way, power is both a stabilising force for institutionalisation and a driver of institutional change, as powerful actors can shape the institutional environment in either direction depending on their particular interests (Lawrence, 1999). Further, the extent to which institutions within an organisational field can be proactively transformed depends on the structure of that field (maturity, concentration) and the position of the entrepreneurial organisations within the field (Greenwood and Suddaby, 2006). An organisational field evolves through recurring social interactions across members, which produces mutual understandings and common practices that characterise the institutional environment of that field. Thus, mature fields represent relatively stable structures under which behaviour patterns (conflict or cooperation) are well defined. Institutional entrepreneurs are more likely to succeed at promoting radical change in premature fields, where institutional order is not completely developed and resistance to change is not as concerning as in established fields (Greenwood and Suddaby, 2006). The position of players in an organisational field determines when they will alter their institutional environment. Kraatz and Moore (2002) show that when a leader migrates from an organisation at the periphery of the field, he or she is more likely to introduce institutional change in the new environment. A leader who migrates from an organisation that has implemented a particular practice is more likely to implement that practice in his or her new organisation because that individual possesses the appropriate expertise and the cognitive reasoning to deem that practice as appropriate.

Institutional entrepreneurs tend to be those actors whose position provides them with legitimacy and allows them to bridge stakeholders to gain access to resources from a variety of sources. Institutional economics is concerned with the economic motivation behind institutional entrepreneurship, wherein they are depicted as calculative agents who alter institutions when it is economically desirable to do so. Thus, profit-seeking behaviour provides the engine for institutional change and new institutions arise when the benefits that entrepreneurs can accrue from these arrangements exceed the costs of their implementation and enforcement (Alston et al, 1999). The trade-off between the costs and benefits of institutional development focuses on the factors that alter this trade-off and swing the balance of incentives towards new institutional development and entrepreneurship. Transaction cost reductions can also act as a fundamental motivator of institutional change (North, 1990, 2005). Changes in demand and supply create incentives for entrepreneurs to engage in institutional framework and when demand rises and resources become scarcer, individuals find stronger incentives to delineate and enforce property rights over constrained resources (Alston et al, 1999).

Technological change can also drive entrepreneurs to establish new institutional regimes. For example, Rutten (2006) suggests that technological change in the form of double-cropping and high-yielding rice varieties during the 1950s in India led to the replacement of the institution of shared tenancy contracts with sub-tenancy arrangements. Anderson and Hill (1975) describe how the development of barbed wire allowed for lower cost enforcement of property rights in the American West motivated ranchers to promote the legal institutions necessary to define and secure those rights. When certain cultural resources are available, institutional entrepreneurship actions may be less costly and therefore, more likely to take place. For example, the conventional moral obligation to cooperate in communal infrastructure made the implementation of rural development programmes less costly and therefore, more likely to succeed (Rutten, 2006). Lastly, transaction costs represent the costs associated with the transfer, capture and protection of property rights (Barzel, 1997) and can dissuade or inhibit economic activity. Transaction costs can be a function of the nature of economic institutions and as such a central motivating factor in institutional development.

Institutional entrepreneurs have been alternatively defined as actors with social skills, where these skills refer to the ability to motivate cooperation of other actors by providing them with common meanings and identities (Fligstein, 1997). They are responsible for sustaining a collective identity and finding ways to bring together the interests of different groups, acting as arbitrageurs that intervene to find common solutions to collective problems. They also work in collaboration with other actors, taking advantage of convergent interests and relying on collective action to influence macro-level institutions (Zucker, 1988).

Collective institutional entrepreneurship is the process of overcoming collective action dilemmas and achieving collaboration among dispersed actors to create or transform institutions. Levy and Scully (2007) characterise institutional entrepreneurship as a strategic act, utilising Machiavelli's conception of power. As modern princes, the institutional entrepreneurs act as organisers and expression of a collective group moves it towards action. In doing so, they alter and shape the material, organisational and discursive forces that make up the politically contested fields in which they operate. Rao (1998) found that framing had a powerful legitimising effect in the establishment of consumer watchdog associations. Similarly, the US chemical industry sought to align the creation of self-regulatory institutions with ideas of environmental protection and improved efficiency (King and Lenox, 2000). Such framing tactics tie back to the goal of creating legitimacy for new forms and practices by closely integrating new ideas and processes with commonly accepted narratives. As the poor and disadvantaged fishermen outnumbered the concentrated businesslike fishermen, the highly productive technology of the latter was substituted by more labour-intensive, but less productive, techniques. In this case, the more concentrated interest group did not prevail. Instead, social beliefs coupled with the size of the aggrieved group influenced the direction of the institutions that guided fishing practices. Goldberg (1974) speaks of the importance of resource endowments of firms in helping them to alter the rules of the game, but is concerned, however with the marginal contribution of resources that an individual firm should invest in a particular institutional initiative, given the associated free-rider problems that may arise. There is a relationship between the study of property rights and power, since the distribution of such rights determines the relative power that some individuals have over others.

8.6 Women Entrepreneurship

Women's entrepreneurship development in developing countries has a tremendous potential in empowering women and transforming society. However, this potential remains largely untapped. Sinha (2003) remarks that there are three categories of women entrepreneurs based on chance, forced or created entrepreneurship. These categories are based on how their businesses got started or the main reasons or motivations behind starting their own businesses. Chance entrepreneurs are those who start a business without any clear goals or plans. Their businesses probably evolved from hobbies to economic enterprises over time. Forced entrepreneurs are those who were compelled by circumstances to start a business and their primary motivation tends to be financial. Created entrepreneurs are those who are located, motivated, encouraged and developed through entrepreneurship development programmes. Within the developing countries, the degree varies by country, depending on many factors, including level of economic development, reflected by the level of income per capita and social, cultural and political factors. Gender development index and gender empowerment measure indicate the level of development of women and the extent to which women are free from discrimination in building their capabilities and in gaining access to resources and opportunities.

With respect to sectoral distribution within the manufacturing industry, most of the women entrepreneurs are in the food, beverages and tobacco industry, followed by textile, garment and leather and non-metallic mineral products. In basic metal and fabricated metal products, the proportion of women entrepreneurs is very small. This indicates that women entrepreneurs in manufacturing industry tend to do businesses that do not require high skills and expertise. Within SMEs, majority of women entrepreneurs are found in enterprises employing five or less workers (and in many cases are non-employing). They choose these enterprises because this economic activity is characterised by an easy entry and exit and low capital, skills and simple technology requirements. In non-manufacturing sectors, the percentage of female entrepreneurs is higher than that of their male counterparts in trade, hotel and restaurant. Beyond the manufacturing industry, women entrepreneurs are more likely than male to be involved in these sectors, mostly as own account traders having small shops or as owners of small restaurants or hotel (Tambuan, 2009). A major factor sequence being discovered as a result of the deep-extending value chain networks is the hitherto invisible and unacknowledged power of women. For instance, in late 1990s, about six per cent of those in managerial positions were women and this percentage has since more than doubled. India has been dealing with two generations of gender issues, the first defined by the lack of managerial opportunities for women, because of an assumption that they were only good for easy jobs.

The second generation issue concerns oppression of women using subtle barriers, even in the face of equal opportunity policies. These barriers include paucity of mentors and role models and the masculine policies such as working late nights and rigid hours. However, the introduction of flexible work conditions and other gender-sensitive policies have allowed women to enter in non-traditional jobs and sectors. As a third generation issue, women's need for varying work-life balance over their careers has remained unaddressed. Insensitivity about this need has resulted in a growing new perception that the gender sensitisation policies are over-hyped. It has made many men uncomfortable about working with women bosses, feeling that they will be asked to do extra work while the women bosses will have it easy. Women are addressing this issue by becoming entrepreneurs, both within and outside the corporations.

This parallels the development in the US, where the rate of women entrepreneurship is growing twice as fast as male entrepreneurship and the number of women business owners is now about the same as male business owners (National Association of Women Business Owners). In India, women are pioneers in cultural entrepreneurs and women have always been the stewards of cultural knowledge, and are in charge of cultivating this knowledge amongst children and other family members. In the new India, women are also taking charge of culturally-embedded opportunities outside the traditional male domains. They are doing so in a diverse array of organisations: multinational firms, large private sector, family businesses, their own start-ups and micro-ventures. Multinational firms in India have set aggressive percentage goals for hiring, retaining and advancing women as a means of addressing a rapidly expanding work force requirement. All concerns about the business case for such initiatives have been put to rest by women like Indira Nooyi, ranked by Fortune as the world's most powerful businesswomen in 2006. Non-cola beverages are culturally preferred over the cola beverages in India for health reasons and sensing health conscious in the West, she co-authored Pepsi's 21st century transformation by successfully moving it into non-cola beverages.

Many private sector firms have been prodded by diverse teams of overseas clients to include women amongst their top teams. The senior vice president of Satyam, a top Hyderabad computer firm, notes that it will be awkward if the company has not a single woman leader, while there may be many women customers. As they face intensified competition, the family businesses are calling upon their daughters and daughter-in-laws to take charge of exploiting new opportunities using their culturally sensitive insights. For instance, Hero group called upon Shefali Munjal to champion a new firm offering IT solutions to small and medium auto businesses and in a short period of time, she successfully made this new firm a market leader. Not surprisingly, the group thereafter decided to diversify into the scooters segment and to accomplish this goal, the company developed women-only showrooms, women friendly product designs and women supervisors and sales executives. Kiran Mazumdar Shaw wanted to be a master brewer following her father. However, she was denied entry into the male bastion and then resolved to start Biocon, a biotech firm, in her garage with a budget of $1000. Shaw brought in biotech research and clinical trials from overseas firms. Within time, her firm achieved a first-day market cap of $1 billion, making her the wealthiest woman of India.

Women are leaders in micro ventures as well, leveraging on key cultural resources such as the one exemplified by the rag picker story. Women account for more than 90 per cent of all micro loans and have more than 95 per cent repayment rates. As cultural entrepreneurs, women are guided by socially sensitive leadership. They focus on sustainability, as opposed to short term profits and are acutely aware of the impact of their decisions on various participants in the cultural system, including suppliers, buyers and employees, in addition to the members of their families and communities. Federation of Indian Chambers of Commerce and Industry (FICCI) has established its Ladies Organisation (FLO) with the objective of women empowerment to encourage them exploit the maximum of their potential as entrepreneurs. FLO has around 1000 members comprising entrepreneurs, professionals and executives and has many chapters in important cities. At the basic level, it holds entrepreneurship development programmes for women, working with them in advising on how to start a business and following it with vocational training. At the middle level, it holds seminars and workshops for women who run small-scale businesses, such as computerisation and financial management. At the senior level, FLO has sophisticated programmes for women in marketing and finance. Besides undertaking several business oriented activities for women through entrepreneurship development programmes, workshops and panel discussions, FLO has an active business consultancy cell where free professional guidance is offered; besides, it serves as a single window stop for all information on diversified statutory compliances, procedures and obligations. It advises women entrepreneurs on subjects such as company incorporation, registration, preliminary documentation, taxation and policies of government. FLO has recently launched Young FLO, a forum of career women and has also started giving awards to recognise outstanding women in various walks of life.

The Federation of Indian Women Entrepreneurs, established in 1993, provides networking, technical know-how, industry research and expertise, skill development and training to women entrepreneurs. The Association of Women Entrepreneurs of Karnataka (AWAKE), founded in 1983 in Bangalore, provides business development services. AWAKE's mission is to empower women through entrepreneurship development and improve their economic condition. To achieve this mission, it conducts various activities, such as business counselling, entrepreneurship awareness, entrepreneurship development training, management development training and business incubation. With growing membership, an affiliate member of Women's World Banking, AWAKE's activities are formulated and managed by an executive prising voluntary members who design and ensure the mentation of all its programmes. Apart from motivating nen entrepreneurs, it conducts growth-oriented r sustaining the businesses of existing entrepreneurs in of garments, electronic components, printing, injection onents, machinery manufacturers to services in catering, tionery and business incubation for food processing. as developed its own 4s module of stimulus, start-up, ance and support. The common function of the support agencies to provide opportunities for building knowledge and skills and networking with other women entrepreneurs, besides policy advocacy and business counselling. Like in Bangladesh, access to reliable and reasonably priced telecom facilities maybe a constraint and a common facility has been established providing subsidised services. Mentoring and peer group support has been found to be an effective support device in western industrialised countries. This presupposes the existence of a critical mass of successful entrepreneurs who may be willing to offer their time. There is considerable scope for support agencies to learn from each other. For example, the idea of a directory, institution of awards for successful women entrepreneurs and business opportunity identification are activities which can benefit women entrepreneurs irrespective of their culture or business environment. Tamil Nadu has promoted industrialisation of Hosur region (near Bangalore) as part of an industrial dispersion programme. The resulting rapid industrialisation created a demand for both labour as well as services.

Myrada is an NGO working with rural women from poor households in the Mysore region. The collaboration between Titan and Myrada into self-help groups (credit and lending groups) began in 1992, with a contract given to a group of women to launder uniforms of the Titan factory workers (UNDP, 2010). This collaboration stimulated Myrada and Titan to work together on more programmes that could employ the rural poor productively. In 1995, a collaborative venture resulted engagement of girls from poor households in the assembly of watch straps. Meadow (Management of Enterprises and Development of Women) started in 1996 became Meadow Rural Enterprises Private Limited in 1998. When Meadow started its job of bracelet link assembly to obtain individual metal components, it linked them to form bracelets and return the linked pieces to Titan for compaction, polishing and further use. Meadow realised right from the beginning the need to build up its fund base and for th took an early decision to surrender a part of their cumulative to build up a fund for the company.

Both Myrada and Titan are regularly approached with re to see the experiment. Titan received an international award for s development that it attributes at least in part to its involvement w Meadow. Women entrepreneurs are encouraged, taking pride in th fact that they have been involved every step of the way in building and running their company. They have reached levels of capability where they can directly negotiate with Titan in the annual revision of piece rates, handle all purchases, control the movement of their vehicles, draw up work schedules, calculate payments, follow up on receivables and do the base work for meeting all statutory requirements. Besides training them to become entrepreneurs, Meadow has also had the expected impact of improving their incomes. Women have often become the most important wage earners and their social status within their families and communities has changed dramatically, allowing them more social freedom (UNDP, 2010).

Network of Entrepreneurship and Economic Development (NEED) is a non-profit organisation that creates and supports grassroots and networking initiatives designed to empower very poor people. Based in Lucknow, Uttar Pradesh, NEED conducts training, creates tools, mobilises grassroots organisations, sells handicrafts and conducts projects in nearly 1,000 villages in that state (NEED, 2010). NEED aims to uplift marginalised communities and to alleviate poverty in general, but its main focus is on the economic and socio-political empowerment of women. Its focus is on forming self help groups (SHGs) for credit and social mobilisation and has designed a training model called Entrepreneurship Linked Income Generation for Self Employment Programme. This strategy represents a movement away from managing quantifiable mechanisms such as credit, thrift to issues of developing human capital. NEED facilitates ecological development through projects to reclaim waste land and has created partnerships between villages and government organisations in which stakeholders can work together towards land reclamation. NEED publishes learning documentation and conducts training programmes for the functionaries of other NGOs, governmental departments, banks and leaders of the SHGs. NEED has launched specific projects like poorest area civil society project called empowering the rural poor, especially women, through building local women owned organizations, creation of network platforms and opportunity and enhancing human resource development in a sustainable manner. NEED opened remedial centres to equip women with the skills needed to directly enter the next level in the formal school system (NEED, 2010).

Self-Employed Women's Association (SEWA) is a trade union for poor, self-employed women workers, established in 1972. SEWA Trade Facilitation Centre (STFC) is a company, owned and managed by more than 15,000 women artisans pursuing craft activities, in traditional hand embroidery, in the drought affected and disaster prone districts of Gujarat. The aim of STFC is to strengthen the position of women workers in the informal sector and promote their enterprises in global markets through efficient marketing, with a view to providing them economic security and full employment. STFC was established by the artisan members of SEWA to turn their activity into a commercial venture with the main objective of promoting access to national and global markets, through capacity-building and product development. STFC delivers a range of services ranging from marketing support, product development, quality standardisation, information systems and access to capital (SEWA, 2009). Kiran Mazumdar Shaw founded Biocon in her garage in 1978 with the initial operation to extract an enzyme from papaya. Currently, her company is the biggest biopharmaceutical firm in the country. Ekta Kapoor, creative head of Balaji Telefilms has been equated synonymous with soap operas in Indian TV. Neelam Dhawan has been the managing director of Microsoft India. She wanted to join FMCGs like Hindustan Unilever and Asian Paints, but the companies rejected her as they did not wish to appoint women for marketing and sales. Naina Lal Kidwai was the first Indian woman to graduate from Harvard Business School. *Fortune* magazine listed Kidwai among the world's top 50 Corporate Women from 2000 to 2003. According to the *Economic Times,* she is the first woman to head the operations of a foreign bank in India. Indu Jain has been the chairman of the Times Group and is known as a spiritualist, humanist, entrepreneur and educationalist. Priya Paul entered her family business and is currently the chairperson of Park Hotels. Simone Tata has been instrumental in changing a small subsidiary of Tata Oil Mills into the largest cosmetic brand Lakme. She became a part of Lakme during 1961 and has been responsible for turning the company into one of the biggest brands of fashion in India. At present, she is the chairperson of Trent Limited, a subsidiary of Tata group. Mallika Srinivasan, the director of Tractors and Farm Equipment was honoured with the title of Businesswoman of the Year during 2006 by *Economic Times*. She joined the company in 1986 and has been responsible for accelerating its turnover. When the Government of India appointed Anjana Kumar as the chairperson and managing director of The Indian Bank, she became the first woman to become head of a public sector bank in India.

8.7 Conclusion

An individual entrepreneur sets up an enterprise, adopts latest techniques, arranges finance and takes up all types of risks with a view to earn profit. Institutional entrepreneurs are entrepreneurs who inherit the business of family through inheritance. As the entrepreneurs inherit family business, these are sometimes called as second generation entrepreneurs. Circumstances compel some persons to become entrepreneurs, who are called forced entrepreneurs, but these may not be successful because of lack of proper training and understanding. Entrepreneurs who estimate customers' needs and undertake production to cater them are called industrial entrepreneurs. Corporate entrepreneurs promote corporations having separate legal entity. Agricultural entrepreneurs engage in the process of raising and marketing crops, fertilisers and other inputs of agriculture. Entrepreneurs motivated by government or other non-government agencies are called motivated entrepreneurs. Professional entrepreneurs make entrepreneurship as a profession. Whatever the type of entrepreneur, an individual creates a business with the ultimate goal of reaching the largest available market, whilst making profit. These build businesses like Google, Microsoft, Sony, Apple and Facebook and make the Forbes list of wealthiest persons in the world over and over again. They can be extremely innovative businesses that change the way Facebook and Twitter see the world and they can be more than Wal-Mart or Toyota. Lifestyle entrepreneurs create businesses around their passions but their primary goal is not vast profits but rather a rich and flexible lifestyle. The business allows them to work extremely flexible hours, travel the world and afford a life that is associated with millionaires. A sub-category that has become quite popular with the establishment of the internet is the internet is lifestyle entrepreneur. He or she builds a business on the internet that allows him or her to work from anywhere at any time. This has manifested itself in the form of pro-blogging where one makes a business out of one's blog and earns income from advertising or selling through blog.

A social entrepreneur recognises a social problem and uses entrepreneurial principles to organise, create and manage a venture to induce social change. Whereas a wealth creation entrepreneur typically measures performance in terms of profit and return, a social entrepreneur assesses success in terms of the impact on society as well as in profit and return, operating through non-profits or charities from a private standpoint. Just as entrepreneurs change the face of businesses, social entrepreneurs act as the change agents for society, seizing opportunities others miss and improving systems, inventing new approaches and creating solutions to change society for the better. Different classes of social, institutional, political and ecological and women entrepreneurs have emerged to showcase the varied phases of entrepreneurial action towards sustainable development. All these developments usher in an innovative entrepreneurial conclave which would enable the emergence towards global leadership.

9

Innovation and Entrepreneurship: India's Emergence in Business Leadership

9.1 Introduction

This chapter showcases the growth of innovative culture leading to entrepreneurial development, in which different types of innovations are encountered. Following the cue from the flying geese theory and innovation enhancement, it is shown how in select sectors the country is able to have global leadership. It compares the entrepreneurial acumen of Japan, China and India and how the Indian entrepreneur is poised to be the future gladiator and discusses the characteristics of innovative entrepreneurs, especially in the IT sector.

Entrepreneurs in Japan, China and India have pursued business opportunities in different ways peculiar to their own environment (Gupta, 2008). Japanese entrepreneurs took control of both peripheral physical and intellectual assets discarded by Western firms. In this endeavour, they found opportunities for redeploying and repacking the assets into popular products. They demonstrated how such products could be produced using peripheral assets, through transplanting them into factories in Asia and other less attractive regions. The use of peripheral assets is depicted by the Japanese in the 1950s as they bought scrap steel from Western junkyards and reprocessed it in their mini steel plants. Later, during the 1980s, the Japanese partnered with the auto parts suppliers who were subject to huge bargaining pressures from the US assemblers. In this partnership, the Japanese had transformed from being suppliers of basic functional vehicles to suppliers of augmented high end vehicles (Gupta, 2002).

In the beginning of the last century, the UK was still one of the world's largest producers but in decline. Characteristic of the changing economic fortunes was a deal signed by Sakichi Toyoda, a Japanese inventor and entrepreneur, and Platt Brothers, the world's leading manufacturer of textile equipment (Bernstein, 1997). The deal was a licensing agreement giving Platt Brothers the right to make and distribute Toyoda's automatic loom. That such an international company should agree to sell a Japanese innovation was a huge achievement for the entrepreneur. His fast-growing business was a foundation company that helped transform the textile industry and enabled Japan to overtake the UK as the world's largest exporter of cotton goods. Toyoda achieved his success after many failed attempts. Trained as a carpenter, he built loom after loom from wood but when he set up in business to sell his patented invention, he closed down his first business after only a couple of years. He persisted and began designing steam-powered looms but left the business that had been founded to make the product when sales fell. Benefiting from a textile boom during the First World War, he found the necessary investment and time to develop a loom that automatically replenished the yarn when it ran out and was thus more productive. By 1929, when he signed the deal with Platt, Toyoda had a large group of companies involved in textile manufacturing that was an integral part of the fast-growing Japanese textile industry. His son Kiichiro Toyoda wanted to make cars not looms and in 1933 he established an automobile division within Toyoda Automatic Loom Works. It was a risky diversification as the Japanese automobile market was small and dominated by Ford and General Motors. Changes to the market environment endorsed Kiichiro's decision however. In 1936, driven by military considerations, the Japanese government restricted motor manufacturing to domestic producers only, thereby removing all foreign competition. Kiichiro understood the changing market so as to develop not only cars but trucks which the military needed. Kiichiro ran a competition to re-brand the car company. The winning entry was 'Toyota'. During the Second World War the Japanese government converted most textile firms into armament producers while the need for trucks and buses boomed (Bernstein, 1997). Thus, Kiichiro's diversification proved a wise business decision and led to the emergence of a successful car company from the old textile conglomerate. After the war, the company became one of the great innovators of modern production techniques like lean manufacturing. By the 1980s, Japan had the highest productivity in the world in the sector, a major aspect of economic miracle.

9.2 The Chinese Experience

China is the leading iron and steel producer of the world. Experiencing an economic transition from central planning system to market-oriented economy, its entrepreneurship development can be viewed in different phases (Zhang and Duysters, 2010). Before the 1980s, its economic activities were planned, controlled and distributed by the government rather than by market. Entrepreneurship was hardly developed during that period and the number of private enterprises declined to 150,000 in 1978 compared to nine million in 1949. China's economic reform has initiated a long term institutional transition, which was marked by many comprehensive changes (Pang and Heath, 1996). They have led to many changes like economic liberalisation, permitting private enterprises to be involved into economy and allowing them as one of important components of economic growth.

The first generation of Chinese entrepreneurs emerged during the reform programme to encourage different entrepreneurial activities in the early 1980s. With this, light industry grew rapidly from 1979 till 1984 (Wong, 1988). Since the mid-1980s, the second phase emerged, characterised by the organisational mode of township and village enterprises. These kinds of enterprises have been owned by privates or collectively owned by local governments. Along with the newly started private enterprises, the commune and brigade enterprises of the first phase were also incorporated into them. The third phase of entrepreneurial activities was stimulated by the entry of foreign investment in the late 1980s. Since for many years private enterprises were restricted to develop only in rural areas, a new organisational mode called *getihu* emerged, promoting entrepreneurial activities in many urban sectors. After the era of *getihu,* entrepreneurship development was remarked by the emergence of private sectors and another organisational mode called *si ying qiye* (Zhang and Duysters, 2010), by which private enterprises were recognised to coexist with stated-owned enterprises.

The emergence of socialist market economy mitigated the low esteem showed on entrepreneurship and narrowed down the differences between state and private-owned businesses. Large state-owned enterprises were converted into independently run companies and many state owned enterprises were privatised. The central government provided the Innovation Fund for Technology Small and Medium Enterprises to be invested in hi-tech zones, which in turn created science parks and technology business incubators. Technology-oriented entrepreneurs were encouraged to invest in start-ups in science parks with incentives of reduced corporate income tax, exemption of income tax in the first three years and no restrictions being levied on local residence permit. By 2006, China had already six thousand industrial parks and fifty eight national level science parks (Cai, 2008). China's entrepreneurship development has been characterised by its relationship-based network, which not only included an association with business partners such as suppliers, customers and competitors but also political interactions with government (Peng and Heath, 1996). In the pre-1999 period, the entrepreneurs relied on informal, interpersonal relationship and had to establish contacts in professional networks with other entrepreneurs and government officials.

China has been recognised as an opportunity-oriented entrepreneurial country (60 per cent as contrasted to 40 per cent necessity-oriented) and ranked 10th in the world according to Global Entrepreneurship Monitor report (Zhang and Duysters, 2010). Perceptions of entrepreneurs are improving and people are rushing to *xiahai,* whereas successful entrepreneurs are considered as role models and idols. When India and China are compared, a tradition of dissent and pluralism identifies India's culture heritage, whereby China's heritage has developed with order, harmony and hierarchy (Fuller, 2010). Indian workers tend to have an internal locus of control and are passive avoiders of control that motivates entrepreneurial tendencies in emerging economies like China, where the cultural roots in Confucianism seems to contradict such an orientation. The Chinese exhibit collectivist tendencies with loyalty geared to the group rather than individual effort. Hofstede (1980) describes China as a culture that has strong uncertainty avoidance, large power distance (a high tolerance for unequal relationships), feminism (a focus on harmony and relationships) and collectiveness (focus on group accomplishment).

Lee and Peterson (2000) suggest that countries with specific cultural tendencies experience more entrepreneurial competitiveness. The Indian culture consists of characteristics that project a strong entrepreneurial orientation towards Hofstede characteristics of weak uncertainty avoidance, small power distance, masculinity and individualism. The positive aspects of these characteristics provide favourable conditions towards the emergence of entrepreneurial activities. However, the Chinese culture, which exhibits the opposite characteristics on each of these dimensions, a strong uncertainty avoidance, large power distance, feminity and collectivism are less likely to support entrepreneurial activity. This would support that within a culture, whether Chinese or Indian, there are cultural characteristic that dominate and influence entrepreneurial behaviour. However, when entrepreneurs exhibit characteristics of high individualism, high power distance, low uncertainty avoidance and high masculinity, entrepreneurs are alike regardless of their cultural background, but may have traits that differentiate them from non-entrepreneurs (Fuller, 2010).

In the case of China, the entrepreneurs took control of their previous generation's physical and intellectual assets, which had been transferred by the Western firms. Specifically, several Western firms were transferring their older generation's assets into the consumer electronics, auto and other sectors to China since the cost of losing intellectual property rights was relatively limited (Gupta and Wang, 2004). During this period, the entrepreneurs found opportunities for redeploying the assets more cost-effectively using a range of popular products. In discovering such opportunities, the entrepreneurs demonstrated their negotiation skills for huge premiums from the Western firms. These Western firms were seeking to acquire their big share in the joint ventures, while willing to give up their own share for a huge discount. The Chinese economy has registered a rapid growth, but at the same time, the central government continues to resist the adoption of privatisation policies that favour entrepreneurial activity. This has resulted in the co-existence of two systems of the command economy of the past and the free-market economy of the future.

Indian entrepreneurs are taking control of their current generation's physical and intellectual assets since Western firms are finding them costly to deploy. In this endeavour, the entrepreneurs are transforming the next generation's assets by making them accessible to grassroots markets. As Indian entrepreneurs make assets accessible to a variety of markets, they are also examining how grassroots can serve global markets. They are discovering how grassroots can use their unique culturally-embedded knowledge. India's innovators are coming up with many new products to solve many problems by boosting exports and reducing the poverty level (Goering, 2007). An example of these entrepreneurs is Conserve in New Delhi, which employs poor urban rag-pickers to collect, sort, weigh and clean the plastic bags that litter the streets. The bags are melted together to create a thicker material with different designs using strips and cut-outs of bags. This recycled trash is then turned into chic handbags that are sold for $50 in European boutiques. By tapping rag-pickers for their business, Conserve helps grassroots women earn three times what they previously made (World Resources Institute, 2007).

The three distinct pathways to becoming a business leader include a pioneering pathway, the inheritance pathway and the professional pathway (Ramani and Mukherjee, 2010). The pathway each leader experiences stamps him or her with lasting personal and business values, tastes and managerial styles and professionalism. One of the striking features of China is that despite nearly half a century of socialism, with campaigns against capitalism and the bourgeoisie, the spirit of private entrepreneurship has managed to stay alive. China's consumer spending is rising with an urbanisation boom resulting in the spread of new personal services, which have enabled many entrepreneurs to exploit property development, retail and manufacturing. However, many of these entrepreneurs, especially those from the generation whose education was interrupted by the Cultural Revolution, are not well educated. Most operate with an extremely short time horizon focusing on making sure that the bank account is not in the red at the end of the month. They act more on gut instincts than on reasoned and sophisticated business planning and face intense, cut throat competition daily. The environment in which they operate, which includes the need to deal with bureaucracy and the confrontation with state-owned enterprises as competitors, shapes their behaviour and outlook. They still need to tread carefully and to demonstrate their contributions to development wherever they can (Jia, 2007).

Being a successful corporate leader may have less to do with business strategy and visions than with managing government relations. Zhang Yue, founder of Broad Ltd, a Changsha-based maker of giant cooling systems that has successfully marketed its products worldwide, conspicuously displays in his office certificates attesting that Broad has paid more taxes than any other private company in China. Not far from his office is a hangar that houses his private helicopter and jet. This juxtaposition of on the one hand being a champion taxpayer and on the other having a private helicopter and jet is highly illustrative of how Chinese entrepreneurs have chosen to travel on the pioneering pathways to an affluent society (Jia, 2007).

The children of China's top leaders and officials are known as 'princelings' (Ramani and Mukherjee, 2010). Before the 1980s, most princelings were given priority in schooling and many ended up being readied for high positions in the government. Starting in the 1980s, many princelings opted to go into business instead of government. Through their personal connections and family traditions, these princelings have been able to pursue the inheritance pathway to becoming business leaders. Many such princelings grew up in relative comfort and had privileged access to higher education and other opportunities, such as international travel. Because of the still sizable and influential state sector, their connections and pedigrees continue to carry weight and remain valuable assets. It is therefore not difficult to imagine that their conception of corporate leadership is closely tied to the role of government authority.

The professional pathway started to operate in China relatively late, with the arrival of foreign multinational companies in the 1980s (Wong et al, 2005). Foreign businesses, including some from Hong Kong, created a market for skilled business professionals and paid competitive market wages, typically a high multiple of what could be earned working for a government enterprise. Such professional employment in turn stimulated the supply side Chinese institutions of higher learning started to develop a capability to meet the demand for graduates in business administration, finance, marketing and IT. Even before Chinese educational institutions started to respond to the new demand, enterprising Chinese students took to studying overseas. Fudan University in Shanghai has curricula developed in partnership with leading international institutions, such as the Massachusetts Institute of Technology's Sloan School of Management. In a society that is still characterised by seniority and hierarchy, not many of them have reached leadership positions. In many a way, this may bridge the gap between entrepreneurial energy and corporate leadership in China (Wong et al, 2005). In India, the inheritance pathway could not be more different from China's. If there is a business aristocracy in India, it would have to be the Tatas. Jamsedji Tata started in textiles, then expanded into trading, quickly establishing a stronghold in Bombay. Jamsedji Tata introduced pensions for workers in his textile mills in 1886 and accident compensation in 1895. In this respect he was way ahead of his time and other Indian business enterprises.

9.3 Innovativeness in Different Frontiers

In India, over 80 per cent of the R&D has been financed by the government, especially in strategic sectors like atomic energy, defence and space research (Forbes, 1999). The government created a network of laboratories under the leadership of Council of Scientific and Industrial Research, but the links of these laboratories with the industrial sector remained rather lowly; further, technological capabilities so created remained largely confined to the laboratories themselves. An effort was made in the early 1970s to formulate a national science and technology plan that would dovetail with the economic planning process and help integration of the government's technology development efforts with industrialisation, but this was short-lived. Earlier, the central government had created a strong infrastructure of institutions of higher technical education. At the state-level, many governments created and funded government colleges of engineering and private involvement in higher technical education. The IITs recruited good faculty who had obtained doctoral degrees from the United States and provided a good environment for academic pursuits. The quality of IIT education is excellent, the research output from its faculty good but not outstanding but, as in the case of the national research laboratories, IITs had limited interaction with industry. IIT graduates found few opportunities to use their technical knowledge in the industrial sector and tended to emigrate in large numbers, principally to the United States. Those that stayed behind went into the government research establishments or to management positions in the private sector. There are many programmes to support the absorption of imported technologies by industry, develop and demonstrate indigenous technologies, help individual innovators to become technology-based entrepreneurs and commercialise indigenous technologies. There are also programmes to support collaboration between technical institutions and industrial enterprises. The New Millennium Indian Technology Leadership Initiative has the objective of ushering in global leadership in selected niche areas by supporting scientific and technological innovations. In spite of these support measures, the national expenditure on R&D remains at around 0.8 per cent of GNP after dipping to 0.7 per cent in the mid-1990s.

However, private sector industry's share of national R&D expenditure has gone up from13.8 per cent in 1990-91 to 28.6 per cent in 2009-10 according to Global R&D Funding forecast. While the government's investment in R&D has not kept pace with the growth of the economy, the private sector's investments have clearly been increasing at a much higher rate. This can be discerned by the research efforts in the iron and steel industry, automobiles and biotechnology.

Brush (1952) points out that India has been a major leader and exporter of pig iron in spite of World War II, but in respect of steel production, it lacked the technology and had to import one-third of its requirement. With severe restrictions on FDI and thereby technology adoption, coupled with the licence raj, India was not able to emerge as global leader in iron and steel manufacturing for long. It was only after 1991 that foreign collaboration and new technology absorption became possible. Moreover, as Giriappa (2003) remarks, the Indian iron and steel making are relatively high energy intensive (consuming 7.5 to 13 giga calories of energy per tonne) as compared to less than five giga calories in Japan and other advanced countries. However, recent energy conservation measures have greatly reduced energy intensity in the industry and the country is slated to be number two producer after China in the near future. India could not cope with the technological change satisfactorily in the field of iron and steel making. While India's adoption of sophisticated steel making technology was almost at the same time with many developed and rapidly industrialised countries, it could not achieve the full benefits due to improper assimilation. In spite of abundance of iron ore and many other raw materials and availability of cheap labour and a large pool of technically qualified employees, productivity of Indian steel industry remained low. The major bottlenecks were protectionism and administrative control over prices and distribution. Till India adopted the liberalisation policy in 1991, steel industry was not able to grow. Inadequate technology policy, less emphasis on R&D, government bureaucracy and poor socio-economic background are reasons for which the steel industry could not attain technological advancement. With adequate ore and other raw materials, a good technology base and a well-framed technology policy, India can become highly competitive in iron and steel making in the global scenario.

India's use of basic oxygen process is 54 per cent and it is comparable to many leading steel manufacturers in the world like

United States and Republic of Korea, but it is better than Mexico and Egypt. However, 14 per cent steel is still produced using the obsolete Open Hearth Process in India. This has reduced the overall competitiveness of Indian steel manufactures in the global platform according to Tata Steel website. Out of the major steel producers in the world, only erstwhile USSR countries still use Open Hearth furnaces for making 33 per cent of its total production, followed by India (14.3 per cent) and People's Republic of China (4.9 per cent). As regards the use of Electric Arc Process, which is 32 per cent, India is placed in the middle. While all 9 integrated steel plants are operating at their total capacity, only 67 Electric Arc Furnaces are working out of 184 and these are operating at 60 per cent of their total capacity. EAP has lower capital costs, greater production flexibility, lower environmental impact and more efficient small-scale operations. Some of the important reasons for the reduction in the use of EAP include the requirement of high quality scrap and its vulnerability to rising prices. The quality of steel produced using BOP can attain much higher quality at reduced cost as compared to EAP route. Many large manufacturers nowadays are producing special steel items, where many of those items were being produced earlier by smaller units. Large units get the advantage of economy of scale. The high cost of electrical power is also a reason for switching over to the other processes from EAP. Due to upgradation of technology from EAP to BOP, many of the Electric Arc Furnaces became idle. Because of the government policies of reserving the development of new integrated steel plants to the public sector, many EAP-based smaller units were closed down.

Developing economies need to import many technologies from developed nations (De, 1999). After 1950s, many steel producers went for technical collaborations and many public sector steel plants were built with collaboration from countries like United Kingdom, Germany and erstwhile USSR. In earlier years, many of these plants faced problems in their collaboration projects. Due to elements of secrecy and other reasons, India had to deviate from what considered suitable by the countries aiding the project. Indian Iron and Steel Company (collaboration with British, Soviet and Japanese firms), Rourkela (collaboration with West Germany), and Bokaro (collaboration with Russia) had many teething problems during execution of the projects (Krishnamurthy, 1987). Hence, most of the state-owned plants and some private ones have gone for large capital-intensive modernisation programmes, mostly with foreign collaborations.

In the case of new plants, the electrical power consumption has been higher than many other countries. New plants in India consume an average of 450-575 kwh/tonne of billet in EAF, whereas the figures for Japan, Germany and the USA are 378, 410, and 430 respectively. Heating time is more and the furnace size used in India is also relatively small as compared to those countries. The cost of major raw materials like iron ore, coking coal, and other raw materials is less in India among the countries mentioned. The labour cost is low, but it is neutralised by its low level of productivity. The financial cost and the cost of power, oil and some other materials are high. Energy accounts for about 35 to 40 per cent of the cost of steel production in India, whereas it is about 28 per cent in the developed countries (Das, 2008). All these make the pre-tax cost of steel making in India higher than that of South Korea, Australia, Mexico and CIS countries. However, considering the low wage rate and other economic factors, the labour cost in India is around 15 per cent of the cost of the steel as compared to around 30 per cent in many developed countries like Japan and United States. In spite of these advantages Indian firms could not become cost-effective and also due to the following advantages. Because of liberalisation, licensing requirement for capacity creation has been abolished and steel industry has been removed from the list of industries reserved for the state sector. Automatic approval granted for foreign equity investment in steel has been increased upto 74 per cent. Price and distribution controls were removed from 1992 and restrictions on external trade, both in import and export, have been removed. Import tariff was reduced from 105 per cent in 1992-93 to 30 per cent in 1996-97. Other policy measures adopted included convertibility of rupee on trade account, permission to mobilise resources from overseas financial markets and rationalisation of existing tax structure.

The new entrants and the existing manufacturers went for technical tie-ups with leading steel producers of the world. For many decades since independence, the steel industry in India grew in protected and controlled environment with administrative control over prices, distribution and allocation of imports resources and high tariffs. The productivity levels of state-owned large integrated steel plants remained low and on the other hand private sector firms were deprived of many of the opportunities to grow. Due to inadequate growth of infrastructure sectors, the overall demand of steel remained low. In 1996, the per capita consumption of steel in India was low when compared to western countries. Import of certain types of steel products due to liberalisation has further reduced the demand of in-house steel products. India took a long time to develop its first technology policy in 1958. It lacked direction during the early formative years after independence. The next notable technology policy came only in 1983 but could not generate the desired thrust for a sustainable technological growth (De, 1999). The low level of R&D expenditure by steel manufacturers has impact on the technological growth of steel sector. Except a very few companies, the overall focus on R&D is too low. In 1997-98, Tata Steel and Reliance spent only 0.14 per cent and 0.29 per cent of their sales value respectively on R&D.

Some of the major problems for this under-development include inadequacy of knowledge and skill to exploit the results and lack of confidence in the successful exploitation of the projects on commercial basis. Bureaucratic efficiency, controls of royalty, inadequate price of technology, import restrictions are some of the major impediments considered serious by the technology suppliers (Desai, 1998). Impact of poor infrastructure like high cost of electrical power, poor reliability of the availability of electrical power, inadequate transport facilities and less-developed logistic network decelerated the growth of steel industry. Further, the manufacturing industry was not able to provide adequate technological support to the steel sector and the manufacturers had to import many of their equipments and technology. Cumbersome procedures to comply with the series of statutory requirements and the corresponding poor efficiency of administrative machinery retarded the growth of steel industry. Technical aspects like high alumina content in raw materials, adverse alumina to silica ratio in iron ore and high content of ash in coal increased the cost of production. In medium and smaller size steel producers, initial high cost of adoption of newer technologies is also a major barrier to their technology adoption.

India has adopted IT Mark Three (iron making technology mark three), a unique technology developed and owned by Kobe Steel Limited, Japan for smelting iron ore fines using non-coking coal to produce premium grade iron in the form of nuggets. Unlike traditional technologies of iron making, this process represents a revolutionary change in the way iron is made and in the product quality. This is a new source of iron particularly, for electric steel making (Das, 2008). India produced nearly 67 mt steel in 2010 and aims to produce 100 mt in the near future to become, after China, the second largest steel maker. To do this, India benefits from large iron ore reserves, especially of high-grade hematites, which presently constitute for domestic consumption exports. India has large coal resources but mainly in non-coking coal and often with high ash content. Hence, the iron and steel industry has to choose between the conventional route based on the Blast Furnace and Oxygen Converter, which implies increasing the imports of high-grade coking coal, mainly from Australia. Various routes are also available based on local Indian coals like Corex or Finex processes to produce liquid hot metal and through direct reduction processes, based on natural gas or on local coals, mainly in rotary kilns or based on coal gasification processes. Another feature of Tata, Essar and Jindal is their development outside India, which means the control of some 18 mt steel/year.

The best example of a company that has transformed itself into a globally competitive organisation is Tata Steel. One of India's oldest companies, its future viability was in doubt at the onset of liberalisation as it had outdated processes, a large workforce and an inward-looking mindset. However, by 2001, it had been ranked number one in a survey of steelmakers conducted by World Steel Dynamics, a US-based research firm. While its main advantage came from historical and locational advantages such as ownership of low-cost iron ore and coking coal, it was number two in terms of operating costs. This transformation came about as a result of nearly ten years of concerted effort to control costs, improve operational efficiency, modernize the plant, and develop a high margin downstream product mix and increase labour productivity. Introduction of a flatter structure (only three levels against the eleven existing previously) in new parts of the plant, in-house fabrication of specialised equipment, and a shift to an external focus on the customer were important managerial decisions adopted by Tata Steel in becoming a global leader. Raw material consumption efficiency improved from 4.81 tonnes per tonne of saleable steel in 1990-91 to 3.71 in 2000-01 and labour productivity improved from 79 tonnes of saleable steel per man-year in 1995 to 189 in 2001 (Kanavi, 2001).

Tata Motors (formerly Tata Engineering and Locomotive Company) progressively diversified into the design and manufacture of passenger cars in the 1990s. Starting with products derived from their light commercial vehicles, the company launched a small passenger car, the Indica, to compete with small cars produced by Maruti Udyog (then a joint venture between the Indian government and the Suzuki Motor Company of Japan), Hyundai and Daewoo. The car was a success in the market and has established Tata Motors as a significant player. The company has subsequently entered into an arrangement whereby the car will be sold under the Rover brand name in Europe. Another vehicle manufacturer, Mahindra and Mahindra has launched a new sports utility vehicle, the Scorpio, which is competing successfully with vehicles from Tata and Toyota.

Other prominent loci of product innovation have been the two-wheeler industry and the pharmaceutical industry. The Indian two-wheeler industry is one of the largest in the world and has grown at a compounded annual growth rate of 10 per cent in the last seven years, caused by a rising demand for affordable personal transportation. In this industry, product innovation and frequent product launches has become the key to competitive success (Krishnan and Prabhu, 1999). One of the most successful companies has been the TVS Motor Company, which was formerly a joint venture between the TVS group and Suzuki Motor Company. Even before it broke the joint venture with Suzuki, the company had developed a stream of successful mopeds and scooterettes (Krishnan, 2001). It has launched the Victor, one of the successful motorcycles that have sold more than one million units since its launch in 2001. Other two-wheeler companies like Bajaj Auto and Kinetic Motors have also launched products designed and developed in-house.

Tata's Nano uses a modular design that enables a knowledgeable mechanic to assemble the car in a suitable workshop. Tata can outsource assembly to independent workshops that can then assemble the car on buyers' orders. This innovation not only removes costly labour from the manufacturer's side but also allows for distributed entrepreneurship on the dealer's side. Further, the low cost of the Nano comes from a combination of its exclusion of frills and luxuries and its inclusion of numerous lighter components, from simple door handles and bulbs to the transmission and engine parts. The lighter vehicle enables a more energy efficient engine that gets about 28 kms per litre. Moreover, the Nano's novel design incorporates a much smaller footprint at three metres long and it is one of the shortest four-passenger cars on the market, yet allowing for ample interior space.

Tata Motors successfully developed and launched a range of light commercial vehicles in the 1980s to combat the entry of Indo-Japanese joint ventures in the market. The company invested resources in the development of a strong engineering capability even at a time when due to regulatory constraints they were unable to leverage this in the market. Similarly, the TVS group's efforts at designing two-wheelers go back to the late 1970s when they launched a two-wheeler moped, the TVS 50. For these companies, liberalisation allowed them to use their own technological capabilities, fill gaps through imports and integrate these abilities with understanding of the market.

Tata Motors, Mahindra and Mahindra and TVS Motor have backed up their efforts in design and engineering by major investments in plant and machinery to produce their new products in large volumes with the latest manufacturing practices. They have all demonstrated a production capability, an investment capability and an innovation capability (Dahlman et al, 1987). Their innovation capability centres on understanding user needs, conceptualising distinctive products to meet these needs, system and industrial design and system integration. They have outsourced technologies and designs for sub-assemblies but managed the integrity of the design and the product.

The Indian pharmaceutical industry has been one of the high performance industries of the 1990s. About one-third of its 2002 production of $5.2 billion was exported to other countries. Among the ten entities based in India with the largest number of US patents. These pharmaceutical companies are seeking to move from imitative research and reverse engineering to the discovery of new molecules and drug delivery systems. The average R&D intensity of large Indian pharmaceutical firms is two per cent (OPPI, 2002) but the R&D intensity of these innovative firms is substantially higher. Joint R&D initiatives with multinational drug companies, licensing of new discoveries to MNCs, sponsored research projects at national laboratories with government support and the creation of international marketing networks in the hope of future exploitation of such networks to sell newly developed novel drugs are some of the developments in this area. One of the most successful pharmaceutical companies has been Dr. Reddy's Laboratories Ltd (DRL). Starting a full-fledged R&D laboratory in 1992, DRL invested about Rs.1.12 billion in R&D over an eight-year period. It filed 55 US patents of which 19 have been granted. It licensed three molecules to foreign drug firms (two to Novo Nordisk and one to Novartis) for revenue of $8 million till 2001 (Business Today, 2001) and increased its R&D intensity from 5.5 to eight per cent. Ranbaxy, Cipla, Wockhardt and Sun Pharma are some other pharmaceutical companies with ambitious new drug discovery programmes.

The evolution of innovation capabilities in the two-wheeler and pharmaceutical industries has been driven by regulatory changes, demand conditions, competitive forces and entrepreneurial initiative. While both have been high growth industries, regulatory changes have played an important role in the two-wheeler industry, stringent new emission norms required upgradation of products and since sourcing new designs from outside India would be too expensive, companies created their own designs. In the pharmaceutical industry, the changes in the patent laws following the government's acceptance of the WTO agreement put pressure on companies to move away from imitative research. In the two-wheeler market, the need to be able to differentiate products in the marketplace has influenced the creation of innovation capabilities. Both the two wheeler and pharmaceutical industries have also had visionary entrepreneurs who were willing to make the investments and take the risks involved in creating and launching new products. These entrepreneurs became role models for the other companies in the industry. Many of the companies that have demonstrated innovative capabilities in the 1990s had a tradition of innovative behaviour.

CSIR laboratories filed 310 Indian patent applications in 1998-99 against 120 in 1987-88 and were awarded 133 Indian patents in 1998-99 against 76 in 1987-88. While no international patents were granted in 1987-88, the CSIR was awarded 38 international patents in 1998-99. External cash flows had reached Rs. 2040 million in 1998-99 with about Rs. 370 million (18.1 per cent) coming from private industry and Rs. 150 million (7.3 per cent) coming from foreign sources. Following a review in the mid-1980s, the CSIR adopted a target of achieving at least one-third of its revenue from sources outside the government (Krishnan, 2002). This target was implemented with effect from 1989, but laboratories took the target more seriously after the onset of economic liberalisation. The government also created a proxy for profitability by allowing laboratories to retain net earnings from externally sponsored projects in a separate laboratory reserve fund with the laboratories being given greater freedom to spend the proceeds from the laboratory reserve. Economic liberalisation also created an environment in which laboratories could target customers outside India and also obtain contract research projects without being accused of violating their mandate (Krishnan, 2002).

The most prominent case of a laboratory that was able to reorient itself taking advantage of the policy changes was the National Chemical

Laboratory (NCL) (Krishnan, 2002). NCL succeeded in transforming itself into a global R&D platform, both licensing technologies and undertaking contract research for multinational corporations. The NCL leadership found that contract research allowed them to overcome the problem of having to provide complete production technologies, a requirement of Indian companies. This in turn avoided the need to set up pilot plants, scale-up technologies or provide performance guarantees. NCL became the trailblazer in obtaining US patents, accounting for more than 90 per cent of the patents obtained by the CSIR and propelling the CSIR to the position of the largest holder of US patents from India. To make this transformation, NCL's top management made a number of organisational changes including the creation of separate business planning and scientific information system divisions, medals for obtaining US patents, awards for technology development and support functions and a scheme to support innovative ideas from scientists. To fund the awards, a separate NCL Research Foundation was created using funding obtained from well wishers of the laboratory. The revenue from sponsored projects at the IIT, Kanpur has increased tenfold while the consultancy income has gone up about sixteen times between 1993-94 and 2002-03. In IIT, Madras, revenue from sponsored projects increased 3.5 times and that of consultancy projects almost doubled over the same period, though from a larger base Indian software companies entered the industry by providing low-cost, skilled manpower to clients in developed markets. This manpower provided skilled labour at the customer's site, typically under the direction of an external consultant or the firm's own information systems department. Starting with low value adding jobs like maintenance and testing, the software companies graduated to reengineering existing pieces of code to new operating systems and platforms. Demand for the latter was created by the shift of users from mainframes to client-server systems. In the years immediately preceding 2000, Indian software companies obtained many projects to solve the Y2K problem (Arora et al, 2001). The internet and e-commerce explosion helped companies to develop into large-scale coding assignments that actually developed new applications. Simultaneously, Indian software companies developed good project management and quality processes that enabled them to manage large projects whether at the customer's site or back in India (offshore) at their own development centres. The declining cost of telecommunication links and the wider diffusion of internet combined with the good track record of the companies, have led to a steady increase in the proportion of offshore revenues (Nasscom, 2002).

9.4 Conclusion

While Indian companies are globally challenged, they have to find ways to continually reinvent themselves through widespread radical innovations. Companies have to re-skill at all levels in order to meet the challenge of value creation and this may facilitate in the creation of an innovative culture. Process-related challenges and mindset changes are to be properly comprehended. The starting point for innovation is innovation in the educational sector and a fundamental retooling in the educational system would be required to successfully exploit global opportunities. Focusing on intrapreneurship, there are factors that are relatively more under control and others that not so. What drives every intrapreneur is a clear sense of purpose or mission of life. Another important prerequisite for effective intrapreneurship is communication with stakeholders. Finally, the image of the intrapreneur in the perception of the people who matter is a key driving force in the intrapreneurial innovation. However, with a few exceptions, the public sector failed to drive the industrial sector on to a higher growth trajectory and got bogged down by cost and time overruns, high costs and a lack of technological dynamism. Though private industrial activity by both Indian firms and multinational companies flourished, there were tight regulations on inward capital flows, expansion, diversification and the import of capital goods and technology. Technology imports were regulated on a case-to-case basis and companies permitted to import technology were often required to commit to progressive indigenization through a phased manufacturing programme. The high effective rate of protection coupled with industrial licensing meant that local industry felt little need to innovate (Forbes, 1999).

Constraints on growth also acted as a disincentive to innovative behaviour. With a protected market and a high cost structure, very few firms pursued exports or targeted external markets. R&D as done by industry was concentrated on import substitution and the creation of local sources for inputs. The small scale sector was provided reservation in many sectors and implicitly encouraged to make imitative products through reverse engineering and improvisation (Tyabji, 2000). Since small-scale industries enjoyed fiscal benefits like lower rates of excise duties and were outside the purview of industrial regulation, there was a tendency to fragment capacities and no incentive to grow in exploiting economies of scale or scope. It was only after the liberalisation that foreign direct investment and collaboration and less regulated regime has emerged, thus facilitating the emergence of global entrepreneurship in India. The World Bank and International Finance Corporation's report Doing Business 2012 ranks India at 166 out of 183 countries for ease of starting a business, putting it in the company of the West Bank, Gaza and Nigeria. In 2011, India ranked the same, demonstrating miniscule improvement in the enabling environment. According to the report, it takes 29 days to register and start a business, whereas it took 89 days to do the same thing in 2004. India has stayed the same in the categories of enforcing contracts, dealing with construction permits and trading across borders. A Legatum Institute 2011 survey found that Indian entrepreneurs are increasingly optimistic about their country's future, though they are far less approving of the government. The top five constraints in starting a business in are mostly within the purview of the government, namely energy, corruption, tax administration, labour regulation and labour skills. Across industry surveys, the biggest constraint in creating and growing a small business is lack of infrastructure, power, roads, water and public transportation.

Laura Parkin, cofounder of National Entrepreneurship Network explains that a lack of governance makes it difficult for entrepreneurs and lack of infrastructure disproportionally affects businesses. For example, the cost of back-up power equals four to eight months of salary for a junior programmer. That is a lifetime in a start-up and start-ups cannot generally afford to buy back-up generators or spend hours in the dark. Endemic corruption is another constant handicap of the entrepreneurs. Local officials reportedly request bribes, seek a lengthy list of approvals and licences and even cite rules to follow, which they often cannot explain or produce. Hiring lawyers to deal with opaque procedures consumes valuable time and income of start-ups. The recent protests against corruption might affect local officials' behaviour temporarily, but a sustained effort to eradicate low and high level corruption would benefit not only the entrepreneurs, but the entire society. Venture capital, angel investors, innovation incubators and programmes for skill-building all contribute greatly to economic activity, but unless the basic infrastructure is improved, the entrepreneurial gold rush that many foresee for India will take much longer to be realised.

10

The Prospects of Entrepreneurship Development in India

10.1 Introduction

Starting a business is either driven by necessity and the exploitation and creation of an opportunity. Everyone has an invisible sign hanging from their neck saying, 'make me feel important.' Hence we shall not forget this message when working with people. Business is not just doing deals. It is producing great products and providing tremendous service to customers. It is a 'cobweb of human relationship.' as HR Perot remarks. Successful entrepreneurs are not born business leaders but they are made and became great leaders because they desire it and humble themselves by learning the art and science of leadership. Today, they are leaders in their game with a huge number of followers. An entrepreneur's success depends on his or her power of getting people to believe he or she has something they want. Development of entrepreneurial skills provides an understanding of creative thinking processes and the ability to use creative thinking techniques. It enhances the ability to identify and sort out opportunities that will enable individuals to act entrepreneurially. Further, it develops skills in functional areas such as finance, marketing and human resources that are essential for the realisation of innovative ideas. Finally, it advances the leadership attributes in the articulation of vision and stamina needed for the realisation of entrepreneurial ventures. Personal skills are those skills that are attached to personality, more like habits. These are the characters possessed by successful entrepreneurs. As Warren Buffett says, it takes 20 years to build a reputation and only five minutes to ruin it. If we think about that, we will do things differently.

From this perspective, the concluding chapter focuses on the status of entrepreneurship in India and its prospects. it deliberates on the general aspects of entrepreneurship that requires an evaluative discussion in terms of global competition and discusses the relevance of global competitiveness index, comparing the competitive performance of countries like the US, Singapore, Japan, Korea, China and India. The chapter focuses on global entrepreneurial assessment in different stages of economic development in terms of global entrepreneurship monitor reports and compares different countries as to the global entrepreneurial development index as reported by the GEM report for 2010-11. The pertinent questions pertaining to the arguments indifferent chapters are summarised, extending the thread towards the assessment of Indian entrepreneurship in terms of its crucial role, innovativeness, global presence and to societal contribution.

10.2 Entrepreneurship Development in Retrospective

In an economy characterised by higher values of the aggregate elasticity of substitution, a higher level of development with more entrepreneurs and smaller firms may be expected. In recent years, economists have come to recognise the input-completing and gap-filling capacities of entrepreneurial activity in innovation and the significant contribution of innovation and growth to prosperity and economic welfare (Acs and Armington, 2006). While most developed countries are in the innovation-driven stage, many developing economies, including Brazil, Russia, India and China are in the efficiency-driven stage (Acs et al, 2008). In addition to differences in the nature of competition across stages, there are also differences in the degree of integration of countries into the global economic system. In particular, since innovation contributes to competitive advantage in foreign markets, developed economies are better integrated globally (UNCTAD, 2006) and tend to have higher levels of export-oriented entrepreneurship than developing economies. To move into the innovation-driven stage, it is necessary for the countries to develop environmental conditions conducive to entrepreneurship. Bill Gates became the richest man in the world in his thirties because he strategically negotiated a deal with IBM in his early 20s. If he had lacked persuasion skills, his name may not have been made that famous. When confronted by a lady, Picasso had this to say: 'yes dear, it took only 30 seconds to draw your picture; but 30 long years to achieve this skill'. Business is all about relationship with people and entails them with different backgrounds, beliefs and skills to a common cause. Finally, as the adage goes: 'if you cannot sell, you will be sold'.

This chapter continues with the deliberations of the last section of the preceding chapter in assessing the entrepreneurial capability of India in the world scenario in terms of global competitiveness index and global entrepreneurship development index, considering the different stages of entrepreneurial development in which the countries are categorised. Further, it focuses on the future prospects of entrepreneurship in the light of the conclusions presented in all the chapters and the questions raised therewith. Jeffrey Timmons, a professor at Harvard Business School, summarised entrepreneurship as commitment and determination to overcome obstacles and compensate for others' weaknesses, where successful entrepreneurs are self-starters with an internal locus of control, transmitting vision and passion to the management team and other employees (Timmons, 1989). They are market-driven and obsessed with value creation and enhancement and have a high tolerance for risk and uncertainty, thriving on chaos and able to resolve problems and integrate solutions. They adapt to change and solving problems creatively and motivate to excel, with a high need for achievement (Prasad, 2003). Drucker judges entrepreneurship to be a practice as a state of being, characterised by making plans that are not acted upon. According to him, entrepreneurship begins with action (creation of a new organisation) and when individuals create a new organisation, they enter the entrepreneurship paradigm. The entrepreneur considers change as rules and always pursues change, responds actively and utilises it as an opportunity (Prasad, 2003).The Global Entrepreneurship Monitor defines entrepreneurship as an attempt at new business or new venture creation, such as self-employment, new organisations or the expansion of an existing business, by an individual, a team of individuals or an established business (Prasad, 2003).

We can enlist five streams of research which are at the roots of entrepreneurship (Minniti and Levesque, 2008), namely, boundary rationality, rule following, institutions, cognition and evolution. At the macro level, studies in entrepreneurship are either on the impact of entrepreneurship on issues such as job creation, economic growth and poverty reduction (Parker, 2004) or on entrepreneurial performance (Audretsch and Thurik, 2001) or on the determinants of entrepreneurship such as culture, access to finance and R&D technology (Schramm, 2006). With regard to entrepreneurial performance and entrepreneurial impact, a majority of studies applied data from World Bank, Eurostat and GEM databases, looking at entrepreneurship development mostly in the OECD countries or focused on entrepreneurship comparison between high income and low-income economies. It is evident from the studies that entrepreneurship contributes to economic development by introducing innovation, enhancing rivalry and creating competition (Wong et al, 2005) and developing countries have higher levels of necessity entrepreneurial activities (starting a business because of being pushed into it), while high-income countries have lower levels of necessity entrepreneurial activities, but higher level of opportunity entrepreneurship (starting a business to exploit a perceived opportunity). From this angle, an attempt is made to evaluate entrepreneurial performance in India when compared to other countries.

10.3 Global Competitiveness Index

Development of entrepreneurship depends on the competitive nature of an economy. According to Global Competitiveness Index (Sala-I-Martin et al, 2011; Schwab, 2012), basic requirements which are key for factor-driven stage of an economy comprise of institutions, infrastructure, macroeconomic environment, health and primary education. Development factors that are essential for efficiency-driven stage include higher education and training, general market competency, labour market efficacy, financial market development, market size and technological capability. During the innovation-driven stage, business sophistication and innovation become crucial.

Switzerland, which occupies the firat place in 2011 and 2012, is characterized by an improving capacity for innovation and a very sophisticated business culture. According to Sala-I-Martin et al (2011), Switzerland's scientific research institutions are among the world's best, and the active collaboration between academic and industry, combined with high R&D has resulted in an innovative market and strong intellectual property. Public institutions in Switzerland are termed as very effective and transparent. Competitiveness is fortified by a good infrastructure, a well-functioning goods market and highly developed financial and labour markets. Switzerland's macroeconomic environment is among the most stable in the world when many European countries are struggling in this area.

Singapore is in the second place, having improved from third place and its institutions noted for the lack of corruption, besides an efficient government. Singapore occupies first for the efficiency of its goods and labour market and second for its financial market sophistication, indicating efficient allocation of these factors to their best use. Singapore has a developed infrastructure, with excellent roads, ports, and air transport facilities. Its competitiveness is enabled by a strong impetus on education and technical skills.

The United States was in the the fourth position, but has slided to seventh place during 2012. The US companies are highly sophisticated and innovative, supported by an excellent university system that interacts with industry in R&D. Labour markets are well developed, characterised by flexibility of hiring workers. Entrepreneurs like Andrew Carnegie, the Rothchilds, the Rockefeller family and Henry Ford are celebrities and school children are raised on stories about inventors like Benjamin Franklin, Alexander Graham Bell and Thomas Alva Edison. Many educational institutions promote garage business and create heroes out of dropouts. Entrepreneurs like Bill Gates, Steve Jobs and Marc Zuckerberg have been eulogised. The US has grown to become the world's most mature venture capital industry and the spirit of enterprise has been a core constituent of state policy. The country respects entrepreneurs, risk takers and innovators who work towards destroying old certainties to create new opportunities.

Japan, positioned at sixth has slided to tenth, but enjoys a competitive edge in the areas of business sophistication and innovation. The country's overall competitive performance has experienced macroeconomic weaknesses, with high budget deficits over several years, which have led to the build-up of one of the highest public debt levels in the world. The Republic of Korea has improved from 19th from 22nd position and remains one of the world's innovation power houses. China with a rank of 29 (down by two rankings when compared to 2011) remains stable in most variables with strengths in large and growing market size, macroeconomic stability and relatively sophisticated and innovative businesses. It has a low technological readiness with low ICT penetration. Although labour market is efficient, it is characterised by a lack of flexibility.

India has experienced a slide-down in the rankings, from 56 to 59 in 2012 and its competitiveness is based on its large market size and improving financial markets, business sophistication and innovation. However, the country has failed to improve significantly on any of the basic drivers of competitiveness, ranking low in health and education. Infrastructure requires up-gradation, especially with respect to quality of roads, ports and power. The macroeconomic environment is characterized by persistent budget deficits, high public debt and high inflation. especially in innovation, its achievement has been deteriorating.

10.4 Global Entrepreneurship Assessment

The Global Entrepreneurship Monitor (GEM) focuses on the level of social and business entrepreneurship among and to uncover factors determining national levels of entrepreneurial activity, besides identifying policies that may enhance the level of social and business entrepreneurial activity (Acs and Szerb, 2008). GEM defines entrepreneurship as any attempt at new business or social enterprise by an individual, teams of individuals or established businesses or social enterprises. GEM considers not only the economic contribution of large and small businesses and social enterprises but also the behaviour of the individuals behind them, linking a country's economic activity to the interplay of established and new firms (Acs and Szerb, 2008). The national expert component of GEM focuses on the factors that constrain entrepreneurial activities and the factors that promote entrepreneurship and to recommend areas that can be improved in promoting. The level of entrepreneurship has been evaluated by quantitative measures like the self-employment rate, business ownership rate or business start-ups. GEM's Total Early-stage Entrepreneurial Activity (TEA) ratio has become a widely used measure of entrepreneurship (Acs and Szerb, 2010; 2012). OECD and European Union have provided sophisticated measures of entrepreneurship encompassing areas of the determinants of entrepreneurship (regulation, R&D, entrepreneurial capabilities, culture, access to finance and market conditions), entrepreneurial performance (firms, employment and wealth) and impact of entrepreneurship. While these indicators and ratios have undergone some modification and change to incorporate qualitative measures, like education and high growth firms, they are basically limited to measuring the quantity of existing or nascent businesses.

Rostow (1960) suggests that countries go through five stages of economic growth. Porter (1990) defines competitiveness according to the nature of economic development, distinguishing among factor-driven, efficiency-driven and innovation-driven stages, with two transitions between these stages (Acs et al, 2008). While Rostow focuses on the age of high mass consumption, Porter's model encompasses recent developments in the economics of knowledge and hence the focus is on innovations. Countries in the factor-driven stage compete through low cost efficiencies in the production of commodities or low value-added products. This stage is marked with high rates of non-agricultural self-employment and sole proprietorships (self-employed) account for most small manufacturing and service firms. Economies experiencing this neither create knowledge for innovation nor use knowledge for exporting. To move into the second efficiency-driven stage, countries must increase their production efficiency and educate the workforce to be able to adapt in the subsequent technological development phase. To compete in this stage, countries must have efficient productive practices to tackle large markets, which allow companies to exploit economies of scale. Industries in this stage are manufacturers or provide basic services (Syrquin, 1988).

The efficiency-driven stage is marked by decreasing rates of self-employment. There may be several reasons for entrepreneurial activity to decline as economies become more developed (Kuznets, 1966). If individuals have different endowments of managerial ability, then as economy becomes wealthier, the average firm size should increase as better managers run the companies. Average firm size is an increasing function of the wealth of the economy if capital and labour are substitutes. An increase in the capital stock increases returns from working and lowers returns from managing. In other words, marginal managers find they can earn more money when employed by somebody else. Increases in the capital stock (through private enterprise, direct foreign investment or government ownership) will increase returns to wage work, relative to entrepreneurial activity and the relationship between entrepreneurial activity and economic development would be negative. As the economy becomes more developed, fewer persons may be pursuing entrepreneurial activity. Sala-I-Martin et al (2007) point out that the first two stages of development are dominated by institutions. In fact, innovation accounts for only about five per cent of economic activity in factor-driven economies and rises to 10 per cent in the efficiency-driven stage. However, in the innovation-driven stage, when opportunities for productivity gains from factors and efficiency have been exhausted, innovation accounts for 30 per cent of economic activity. The innovation-driven stage is marked by an increase in entrepreneurial activity. Firm size distribution in developed countries began to shift away from larger corporations and towards entrepreneurial activity.

There are three reasons entrepreneurial activity rises in the final stage of economic activity (Acs and Szerb, 2010; 2012). First, the innovation-driven stage is marked by decreases in the share of manufacturing sector in the economy. Many industrialised market economies experienced a decline in manufacturing over the last 30 years. The business service sector expanded relative to manufacturing. Service firms are smaller on average than manufacturing firms and in this case, the average firm size may decline. Moreover, service firms provide better opportunities for entrepreneurship, which is clearly the case in the US and several EU countries. Second, technological change during the post-war period has been biased towards industries in which entrepreneurial activity has become very crucial (Jorgenson, 2001) as in the case of improvements in information technologies towards increased returns to entrepreneurship. Express mail services, photocopying, personal computers, the internet, web services and mobile phone services make it less expensive and less time consuming for geographically separated individuals to exchange information. Third, a high value of the elasticity of factor substitution not only leads to more per capita capital, but makes it easier for an individual to become an entrepreneur, if the aggregate elasticity of substitution is also negative.

GEM programme is an annual assessment of the national level of entrepreneurial activity. Initiated in 1999 with 10 countries, it was expanded to 21 in 2000 and to over 60 countries in 2008 (Acs and Szerb, 2010; 2012). The programme is based on an assessment of the level of national entrepreneurial activity for all participating countries and involves exploration of the role of entrepreneurship in national economic growth. Representative samples of randomly selected adults ranging from 1,000 to 27,000 are surveyed annually in each participating country to provide harmonised measures of the prevalence of entrepreneurial activity. Though the GEM project is unique in that while all countries collect official data on self-employment, the size distribution of firms, census data on all or most plants and firms, almost none of these registry sources are comparable across countries. Official data sources differ in the way they define when an establishment enters a file, when it leaves and how they handle self-employment, making cross-national comparisons almost impossible.

Therefore, one of the major strengths of the GEM project is the application of uniform definitions and data collection across countries for international comparisons. The purpose of GEM data is to systematically assess the level of start-up activities or the prevalence of nascent firms that have survived the start-up phase (Acs and Szerb, 2010). Start-up activity is measured by the proportion of the adult population (18-64 years of age) in each country that is engaged in the process of creating nascent businesses. The proportion of adults in each country who are involved in operating a business that is less than 42 months old, measures the presence of new firms. The distinction between nascent and new firms is made to determine the relationship of each to national economic growth. For both measures, the focus is on entrepreneurial activity in which the individual involved has a direct, but not necessarily full ownership interest in the business. The GEM model serves as a vehicle to interpret both the data collection process and provide a framework for theory and policy (Levie and Autio, 2008). A shortcoming of GEM data has been the fact that it has not been able to effectively deal with the issue of how to compare entrepreneurial activity in developed and developing countries. For example, low-income countries, such as Uganda, Peru and Ecuador, have very high levels of self-employment and therefore, have high levels of entrepreneurial activity as measured by the GEM programme. High income countries like Japan, Sweden and Germany have much lower levels of entrepreneurial activity as measured by GEM. In order to address this issue for developing countries, GEM started to collect data on both opportunity entrepreneurship (starting a business to exploit a perceived business opportunity) and necessity entrepreneurship (starting a business, pushed into it).

However, both measures show higher levels in developing countries than in developed countries. Many respondents state they are pursuing an opportunity rather than being involved in entrepreneurial activities because they have no other option for work. Moreover, the relationship between necessity entrepreneurship and economic development is most likely negative in low-income countries, while in high-income countries it may be positive. Countries like India and China have high levels of opportunity entrepreneurship, while countries like Japan have very low levels (Acs and Szerb, 2010). Therefore, in economies in the early or middle stage of economic development, the efficiency-driven stage, entrepreneurial activity would be negatively related to economic development, since many would be trying to move from self-employment to wage employment. In developed economies, entrepreneurial activity may be positively related to economic development as individuals shift from wage work to entrepreneurial activity, indicating a U-shaped relationship may exist between entrepreneurial activity and economic development in the global economy. Countries like Uganda, Peru and Ecuador are all countries with high levels of entrepreneurial activity but low levels of per capita income. Countries with much lower levels of entrepreneurial activity, Brazil and Argentina have higher levels of per capita income and are moving towards lower levels of entrepreneurial activity. The middle represents a set of countries that appear to be transitioning from a middle-income level to a higher income level and some have rising levels of entrepreneurial activity. High-income countries have relatively low levels of entrepreneurial activity Japan, with one of the lowest levels of entrepreneurial activity and the United States, with one of the highest levels of entrepreneurial activity are exceptions.

The situation in developed countries is different and has its origins in the work of Blau (1987), who documents the upturn in self-employment rates after they declined. A major explanation for the diversity in the level and time series pattern of entrepreneurship is the stage of economic development and the negative relationship between entrepreneurship and economic development. Although economic development is essential for entrepreneurship development, the convergence of several factors in the 1970s tended to stem the secular decline in entrepreneurship for many countries. Of 23 OECD countries examined by Acs et al (1994), 15 had a U-shaped relationship during the 1970s and 1980s, wherein sources of inter- and intra-country variations in self-employment included stages of economic development, bias of technological change, changes in industry composition, changes in female labour force participation, unemployment and cultural factors. The development of new technologies and the emergence of new business models have shifted from large corporations to small and new ventures (Jorgenson, 2001).

Entrepreneurship contributes to economic performance by introducing innovation, enhancing rivalry and creating competition.

As regards economic development and business ownership in OECD countries, the existence of a U-shaped relationship is witnessed (Wennekers et al, 2005). The U-shaped approach is useful in understanding the decline in self-employment in developing countries both across countries and over time, but is less useful in explaining entrepreneurship. The U-shaped approach is not very useful in explaining the role of entrepreneurship in developing countries in the efficiency-driven stage of development, either as they enter the efficiency-driven stage or leave the efficiency-driven stage (Acs and Amoro, 2008). While the U-shaped framework was originally developed to understand the increase in entrepreneurship in high-income OECD countries, the model is only of limited value. Carree et al (2007) suggest that the S-shaped or L-shaped or U-shaped relationship between entrepreneurship and economic development could not be distinguished empirically. For example, the U-shaped relationship does not provide an adequate explanation for the relationship between entrepreneurial activity and economic development (Carree and Thurik, 2003). Total Entrepreneurial Activity measures reflect various activities or components related to entrepreneurship in both developed and developing countries (Acs et al, 2008) and can independently be inadequate for policy planning. The 2004 Global Entrepreneurship Report (Acs et al, 2005) started to pursue the idea of using the opportunity-necessity ratio as a composite indicator of entrepreneurial activity and economic development. GEM data are used to identify the type of activity in countries at different levels of development.

Opportunity entrepreneurship represents the voluntary nature of participation and necessity, reflecting the individual's perception that such actions presented the best option available for employment. Opportunity entrepreneurship differs from necessity by sector of industry and with respect to growth aspirations. Opportunity entrepreneurs expect their ventures to grow more and provide more new jobs. A clear trend occurs between the ratio of opportunity to necessity entrepreneurship and the per capita income of a country. Opportunity to necessity entrepreneurship ratio describes the importance of the desirable, opportunity entrepreneurship relative to the necessity-induced entrepreneurship. In this case, countries with high levels of necessity entrepreneurship will be ranked with low levels of entrepreneurship. Countries, where more entrepreneurship is motivated by an economic opportunity recognised than by necessity have higher levels of income. Brazil with an opportunity: necessity of 1.1 is at the bottom, Japan is in the middle next to New Zealand and Denmark is near the top (Acs and Szerb, 2008). The development of measures like the World Bank Group Entrepreneurship Survey and the Complex Entrepreneurship Context Index can be helpful in providing a broader and more encompassing picture of entrepreneurship. In this case, the relationship between entrepreneurship and economic development is S-shaped and not U-shaped The CEC index is consistent with the three stages of development (Porter et al, 2002). In the efficiency-driven stage, entrepreneurial activity is mildly increasing or relatively flat as necessity entrepreneurship is steadily reduced and innovation comes from outside.

The role of foreign direct investment becomes critical in creating efficiency in the efficiency-driven stage and knowledge spillovers to move a country to the technological frontier, which is synonymous with the innovation-driven economy (Baumol, 2006). In the early days of GEM, a conceptual model including various Entrepreneurial Framework Conditions (EFCs) was developed, indicating various conditions in which entrepreneurship may flourish. It includes aspects such as access to finance, existence of government support policies for entrepreneurship, presence of entrepreneurship-specific training and education and access to and transfer of R&D and technology. Various EFCs affect entrepreneurial activities by enhancing opportunity recognition and skills perception. Recent GEM reports of 2007 and 2008 (India has not participated subsequently) indicate India as emerging major economy in the world, the outlook of its potential entrepreneurs is relatively becoming very optimistic. The estimates of the GEM Report 2007 of perceptions about entrepreneurship among even the non-entrepreneurially active population in the age group of 18-64 years are quite positive. On potential entrepreneurship activity, India scores 52 per cent compared to 17 per cent in China, four per cent in Russia and 25 per cent in Brazil and in the case of perceived opportunities, the score is 70 per cent; in perceived capabilities, 69 per cent and 50 per cent on entrepreneurial intentions (Bosma et al, 2008). The GEM Report 2008 has worked out entrepreneurial attitude and perception in 43 GEM member countries, by the phase of economic development. India scores quite high on almost all the parameters. Though India is among the low income countries and is factor-driven country, its economic and entrepreneurial performance has been better than most of its peers, owing to a high growth rate of 7.5-9.7 per cent since 2000. During the global economic meltdown, India's economy performed much better than the major world economies. India's comparison with some of the countries as regards entrepreneurship development is deliberated in the following section.

10.5 Global Entrepreneurship Development Index

Global entrepreneurship and development index (GEDI) captures the essence of the contextual features of entrepreneurship by focusing on entrepreneurial attitudes, entrepreneurial activities and entrepreneurial aspirations (Acs and Szerb, 2010; 2012). Entrepreneurial attitudes indicate the society's basic attitudes towards entrepreneurship through education and social stability. Entrepreneurial activity implies what individuals are actually doing to improve the quality of human resources and technological efficiency. Entrepreneurial aspirations showcase how much of the entrepreneurial activity is being directed towards innovation, high-impact entrepreneurship and globalisation. Entrepreneurial aspirations incorporate the efforts of the early-stage entrepreneurs to introduce new products and services, develop new production processes, penetrate foreign markets, substantially increase the number of firm employees and finance the business with either formal or informal venture capital or both.

During 2012, many countries have experienced a decline especially in high growth entrepreneurship (Acs and Szerb, 2012). The US is the most enterprising economy, maintaining its lead, followed by Australia, Sweden, Canada and Denmark. Acs and Szerb (2012) calculate the GEDI taking into consideration different indicators. Domestic market size that is the sum of gross domestic product plus value of imports of goods and services, minus value of exports of goods and services, normalised on a 1-7 scale data from the World Economic Forum Competitiveness Index. Urbanisation indicates the percentage of population living in urban areas and the data are from the population division of the United Nations. Market size indicates a combined measure of the domestic market size and the urbanisation that later measures the potential agglomeration effect. The business climate rate assesses the overall business environment quality in a country and reflects whether corporate financial information is available and reliable, whether the legal system provides fair and efficient credit or protection and whether a country's institutional framework is favourable to inter-company transactions. The number of internet users in a particular country per 100 inhabitants and the corruption perceptions index measures the perceived level of public-sector corruption in a country and the performance is measured on a ten point Likert scale. Business freedom is a quantitative measure of the ability to start, operate and close a business that represents the overall burden of regulation and the efficiency of government in the regulatory process. The business freedom score for each country is a number between zero and 100, with 100 equalling the freest business environment. The score is based on 10 factors, all weighted equally, using data from the World Bank's Doing Business. Firm level technology absorption indicates in the scale 1-7, from the capability not to absorb new technology to aggressively absorb new technology. The extent of staff training indicates to what extent companies invest in training and employee development.

The extent of market dominance indicates corporate activity dominated by business groups. Gross domestic expenditure on R&D is taken as a percentage of GDP, whereas innovation index points from GCI and is a complex measure of innovation including investment in R&D by the private sector, the presence of high-quality scientific research institutions, the collaboration in research between universities and industry and the protection of intellectual property (Acs and Szerb, 2012). It refers to the ability of companies to pursue distinctive strategies, which involves differentiated positioning and innovative means of production and service delivery. Globalisation Index measuring the economic dimension of globalisation involves the actual flows of trade, foreign direct investment, portfolio investment and income payments to foreign nationals as well as restrictions of hidden import barriers, mean tariff rate, taxes on international trade and capital account restrictions. Another measure is the capacity for the entrepreneurs with innovative but risky projects to find venture capital. The indices show significant and high correlations with one another and with the GDP purchasing power parity per capita values. While measures of competitiveness, red tape, economic freedom and corruption are available, a vital aspect of wealth creation and development, entrepreneurship has been missing from the picture.

GEI fits into the picture and may be capable of providing valuable insight to understand entrepreneurship and its components and their role in economic development (Acs and Szerb, 2010). A more detailed picture emerges when we examine the average values of the indicators for countries grouped according to the three stages of development. The entrepreneurial performance of the innovation-driven countries is significantly different from the efficiency-driven countries in all indicators but one, the exception being the opportunity perception potential. Factor-driven and efficiency-driven countries are more similar regarding entrepreneurship indicators, but the differences are higher in the cases of the attitude indicators of non-fear of failure and cultural support. It implies that attitude development is vital for those countries that transit from the factor-driven stage to the efficiency-driven stage. Aspiration related internationalisation is a key to forward to the efficiency driven stage. The largest differences between the stage two and three countries are in new product, non-fear of failure, internationalisation and risk capital. The three groups of the countries are the most similar to each other, besides the previously mentioned opportunity perception in high growth. This may imply that there are other sources of high growth than entrepreneurship in the lower phases of economic development. Examining the attitude sub-index pillars, opportunity perception and start-up skills are the highest in the case of the leaders. However, factor drivers are second, followed by innovation challengers. Comparing resource based and efficiency based, it seems that institutional improvement, increased internationalisation and technological progress is not followed by opportunity and skill development.

Lacking individual characteristics of opportunity recognition and managerial start-up skills and not institutional deficiencies cause the low level of attitudes in the cases of efficiency driven and innovation followers. This finding underlines the general beliefs that changing institutions is relatively easier than changing individual characteristics. Hence, efficiency driven and innovation followers need to improve opportunity perception and start-up skills while not to decrease other indicator values. Though aspiration is increasing in terms of economic development, the aspiration related pillar values do not necessary follow this trend. New product is the highest in the innovation follower cluster, as is internationalisation. Innovation challengers lead in high growth, followed by innovation followers and the innovation leaders are only in third place implying that gazelle type of fast growing start-ups is the weakest pillar in leading entrepreneurial countries. Innovation challengers have a low level of new technology, lower than that of the efficiency driven economies. Innovation challengers are good in industries that require relatively old technology and product innovation as opposed to innovation followers. Leaders are ahead of the followers and challengers because of the formal and informal venture finance, technology application and adaptation and a more balanced performance over the aspiration pillars.

While the institutional and individual variable averages are very close to each other, it is balanced only in the innovation challenger cluster. In the cases of the innovation followers and efficiency transformers individual variable, averages are higher than institutional ones. However, efficiency driven countries improved more in institutions than in individual characteristics. Therefore, the key factor in the case of lower level of development is to enhance institutions. This is particularly true in the innovation follower cluster, where the difference between institutional and individual means is almost ten times as compared to the individual developers. While the difference between the individual and institutional variables is the same in the leaders as in the institutional developers, the relative difference is the same. To reach a higher level of development and capture the leading entrepreneurial nations, institutional developers should improve in individual characteristics while individual developers should enhance their institutions. The innovation leaders are the same countries that lead the GEDI rank, wherein thirteen out of the first fourteen countries constitute the leader group. These are the Anglo-Saxon and Nordic countries together with the Netherlands and Switzerland. Most Latin American countries are factor-driven, save Jamaica and Chile which are efficiency-driven. Eastern European and Balkan countries, except Serbia, the Czech Republic, Slovenia and Latvia are efficiency transformers.

Asian countries are the most diverse nations in terms of entrepreneurship, found in four groups. Many Asian countries are in the resource driven clusters (five) and the factor driven (four) clusters. The most populous Asian nations, China, India and Indonesia belong to the efficiency-driven cluster. The most entrepreneurial Asian nations Hong Kong, Saudi Arabia and the United Arab Emirates are innovation challengers. Israel, Japan, Korea and Singapore are innovation followers and none are innovation leaders (Acs and Szerb, 2012). With this assessment, an attempt is made to summarise the different chapters so as to bring in the crucial questions that arise in the study of entrepreneurship.

India's entrepreneurial performance in 2012 has been weak when compared to the preceding year, since it has slided back in its world rankings from 68 to 73, while has maintained its ranking at 54. While many developed countries have had a slowing down of economic growth when compared to India, it is a paradox that India could not maintain its entrepreneurial tempo in recent years, whether in doing business, venture capital or in innovation, its record has been rather disappointing, though it ranks high in self-employment quotient, the quality of entrepreneurship in that regards is very poor.

10.6 A Resume

Entrepreneurship is not treated as a serious stimulant of development in India in spite of the important role played by entrepreneurship in the transformation of the west. India is in a state of transition, striving to move from a subsistence-oriented, tightly integrated, inward looking local economy to a surplus seeking, market-led, outward looking economy. Entrepreneurship is an evolving phenomenon and successful entrepreneurship depends on dedicated, talented, creative entrepreneurs, irrespective of the nature of an economy. In India, a pattern of entrepreneurship, distinct from early Japanese and Chinese styles appears to be emerging. The Japanese model of entrepreneurship was based on the use of globally discarded materials and manpower, while the Chinese model has been based on the cost-effective use of earlier generation's global machinery and methods. The emerging Indian model is based on the making of the next generation's products and services accessible to the grassroots (Prahalad and Hammond, 2002) and creating new products and services by leveraging the intellectual properties of the grassroots.

Intrapreneurship involves taking ownership and operating with an entrepreneurial mindset. In the corporate context, since the person leading the reinvention is not an autonomous entrepreneur, he/she is more appropriately referred to as an intrapreneur. As an example, Tata Steel accomplished many new projects by setting up the Cold Rolling Mill (CRM) to manufacture high value cold rolled products for use in the automobile and white goods industry from hot rolled coils. After the completion of the CRM project was started the revamping Blast Furnace-F. The old furnace had outlived its utility and had to be totally upgraded. However, resource constraints (especially R&D) and time pressure have been the major factors inhibiting intrapreneurship. In the iron and steel industry, the new entrants and the existing manufacturers went for technical tie-ups with leading steel producers of the world. In 2001, Tata Steel had been ranked number one in a survey of steelmakers conducted by World Steel Dynamics. While its main advantage came from historical and locational advantages such as ownership of low-cost iron ore and coking coal, it was number two in terms of operating costs. This transformation came about as a result of nearly ten years of concerted effort to control costs, improve operational efficiency and modernise the plant. The example of Tata Motors in modernisation and introducing the first cheap people's car may also be cited. The pharmaceutical companies are seeking to move from imitative research and reverse engineering to the discovery of new molecules and drug delivery systems. One of the most successful pharmaceutical companies has been Dr. Reddy's Laboratories, which has invested about Rs.1.12 billion in R&D over an eight-year period. It has filed 55 US patents of which, 19 have been granted. It licensed three molecules to foreign drug firms for $8 million till 2000 and has increased its R&D intensity from 5.5 to eight per cent in recent times. Ranbaxy, Cipla, Wockhardt and Sun Pharma are some other pharmaceutical companies with ambitious new drug discovery programmes.

The success of the Indian software industry can be attributed to factors on both the demand and supply sides (Krishnan et al, 2003). The software companies have provided role models for entrepreneurship. Three out of the top five software companies were started after 1980 by individuals who were not from Indian business families. Their success and the status enjoyed by their founders have attracted many persons to start new ventures. While Indian companies are globally challenged, they have to find ways to continually reinvent themselves through widespread innovations. In spite of development, India's overall performance in the global scenario is not in the top order. The World Bank and International Finance Corporation's report *Doing Business 2012* ranks India at 166 out of 183 countries for ease of starting a business. In 2013, the ranking has been better at 132 out of 183 countries. A Legatum Institute 2011 survey found that Indian entrepreneurs are increasingly optimistic about their country's future, though they are far less approving of the government. The top five constraints to starting a business in India are mostly within the purview of the government, namely energy, corruption, tax administration, labour regulation and labour skills.

10.7 Some Questions

The first chapter poses the question as to whether entrepreneurship is crucial to economic development in the developing countries as in the advanced countries. Entrepreneurial opportunities may be created through demographic, regulatory and institutional changes, wherein some of these changes result from entrepreneurial drivers. Also, even when opportunities may originate in demographic, regulatory and technological changes, they can pre-exist the process itself (Sarasvathy and Venkataraman, 2011). It may be possible to conceptualise opportunities in different ways so that what appears as discovered at one point in time may be shown to have been co-created at another. The entrepreneurial process and models theorises the varied nature of entrepreneurship emergence and development in different economic situations.

The second chapter, while assessing the evolution of entrepreneurship in India, questions whether it may emerge as a world leader. Visionary entrepreneurs had to build their markets systematically. The Kirloskar brothers could not sell their six metal ploughs even though they clearly increased productivity ten-fold over wooden ploughs. They worked with social reformers and the independence movement to educate the farmers on the links between economics and patriotism and could grow their venture into the enduring firm it is today. Successful entrepreneurs become visionaries after the fact, single-minded in pursuit of their vision in the face of criticism and in the absence of resources within their control (Sarasvathy and Venkataraman, 2011).

The third chapter compares the iron and steel industry establishment in Korea and India as a transition towards global leadership. Entrepreneurship becomes a specific set of skills and becomes a generalised method (Sarasvathy and Venkataraman, 2011). Given the necessary economic incentives, it is shown how a low-ranking steel producer can become a global leader over time.

The fourth and fifth chapters fortify this by showcasing the experiences of the software and biotech industries respectively. Entrepreneurs operate continually creating a world in which no particular set of conditions is necessary for the success and progress. Their job is to implement sufficient even if unnecessary conditions arise. Each solution they implement may be focal and temporary, but successful solutions are usually stable and profitable enough to fix the objectives to a new signpost (Sarasvathy and Venkataraman, 2011).

The sixth chapter presents the profiles of some of the major business houses in different sectors that have characterised the companies in the forefront of global business environment. Success depends on building on past successes and reshaping parts of the present that do not work well. Entrepreneurial action has been described as an interaction over time, between stakeholders and through local transformation of every kind of environment. Rationality embedded in these interactions not only reshapes economic and social landscapes, also it reconstitutes individual preferences and values.

The seventh chapter analyses the performance of small and medium enterprises on which the bulk of future entrepreneurial development hinges upon. Knight emphasised the importance of entrepreneurial judgment in creating the notion of profit and Schumpeter and Baumol have questioned the lack of a central role for the entrepreneur in economic theory. Entrepreneurship is not merely an instrument of free markets, but uses both markets and governments as instruments in formulating and achieving new ends (Sarasvathy and Venkataraman, 2011).

The eighth chapter focuses on different types of entrepreneurship and the progress made in India in respect of social, public, institutional, ecological and gender entrepreneurship, citing many case studies. Entrepreneurs may be characterised by heterogeneity, wherein they may be very different from one another. Further, they may change over time, wherein not only behaviours, but traits and preferences also change. They may play multiple roles, wherein both risk taking and risk aversion activities may be undertaken at the same time.

The ninth chapter devotes some space in the development of innovativeness in the case of Tatas and pharmaceutical and software companies. This chapter assesses the global competitiveness and global entrepreneurship development indices in respect of India's emerging trend. Why it has taken so many years for India to emerge into the current position and whether it can be a global leader in select sectors? Is entrepreneurship in India showing a convergence to the western-type or can there being a definite Indian model? Answers to these and other questions may be had from the assessment of entrepreneurship attempted as in the Indian case, which necessitate reformulation of entrepreneurship as a method of human action, comparable to social forces such democracy and the scientific method to tackle developing problems.

10.8 An Assessment of Indian Entrepreneurship

Four ethnic Indian entrepreneurs appear in the 2008 Forbes list of the top 10 billionaires (Minqiu, 2010). Private enterprises have provided the foundation for India's economic growth. Among the 47 Indians included in the 2008 Forbes list are Mukesh Ambani (fifth) and Anil Ambani (sixth) of Reliance group, Azim Premji (60th) of Wipro, Kumar Birla (76th) of Aditya Birla Group, Shiv Nadar (277th) of Hindustan Computer Limited and N.R. Narayana Murthy (843rd) of Infosys Technologies. India has reached its goal of becoming a global centre for manufacturing, trade and service and many enterprises have expanded their foreign investments through various mergers and acquisitions. It is no longer unusual to encounter an Indian chief executive officer at multinational companies like PepsiCo and Citigroup and many top management positions at many Fortune 500 companies are occupied by Indian nationals. Entrepreneurs with a strong sense of mission, steadfast values, self-confidence and determined actions according to Minqiu (2010) include Jamsetji Tata, Azim Premji and Narayana Murthy, who rather than focusing solely on generating personal income, aimed to create wealth for the country and society. These entrepreneurs always set large goals and explored ways to achieve them and develop values for their enterprises and incorporate into them a code of conduct to guide their employees, the codes of conduct addressing integrity, honesty, trust, equality, responsibility, understanding, excellence and unity.

As regards innovative entrepreneurs, Dhirubhai Ambani, the founder of Reliance Industries created a massive industrial conglomerate in his lifetime. His focus was on providing shareholder value to India's multitude of small retail investors through the relentless pursuit of growth and profits through diversification, backward integration and creation of economically viable large scale industrial units. Azim Premji, the chairman of Wipro, stressed that 'innovation is Wipro and Wipro is innovation'. When government policy restricted foreign capital, causing International Business Machines Corporation to withdraw from India in the late 1970s, Premji entered the domestic computer market and propelled Wipro into becoming a leading information technology company.

Entrepreneurs maintain an international perspective, stressing adoption of the most advanced technologies and equipment, absorbing best talent in the world and following modern systems to keep pace and occasionally to surge ahead of international competition. India's enterprises are influenced by those in developed countries and they seek cooperation to keep pace with advanced technologies and to enter the world market. International cooperation generally involves importing technology, equipment and talent during the company's initial development stage, exporting products and launching joint ventures when the company gains strength and pressing their advantage by expanding beyond the homeland and establishing sole proprietorships and joint ventures to cooperate in technology and sales.

When Jamsetji Tata opened a modern textile mill over 100 years ago, he recruited engineers, machines, technologies and various textile inventions from the United Kingdom. When he entered the steel industry, experts from the United States guided the entire process, from exploration of iron ore and coal mines to site selection and construction. When the steel plant began production, the company imported new technologies and processes from the international steel industry, becoming the most technologically efficient steel enterprise in India. Upon entering the automobile manufacturing industry in 1954, Tata group reached a cooperative agreement with Daimler-Benz of Germany. During the 1990s, the group imported technologies from leading automotive companies in Germany, Japan and the United States and began manufacturing sedans. In 1998, it independently produced the Tata Indica hatchback.

JRD Tata believed that excellence requires a goal of perfection and that achieving perfection requires strict attention to detail. For Ratan Tata, quality means that consumers not only purchase Tata products but also choose them over and over again. He designed the Tata business excellence model to mirror quality standards in the United States, enabling Tata group companies to reach the highest international product standards. His view of a global company is that it has to be internationally competitive and must draw its assets and employees from all over the world. Global consumers must demand Tata products and global investors must buy its shares. A global company must obtain its raw materials, funds and talents from the best and most competitive sources and gain customers and markets in all areas to deliver superior value to its customers, suppliers and business partners. After entering markets in other countries or areas, the company must accept the local culture, merge into society and contribute to local economic development.

Tata Consultancy Services has created a new offshore operation method, changing from body shopping to business process outsourcing, bringing overseas projects to India for work. It developed new software programmes, most notably for financial services. It generates 90 per cent of its income from overseas businesses. Infosys Technologies derives more than half of its revenue from the United States and about a quarter from Europe. Shiv Nadar's Hindustan Computer Limited developed India's first microcomputer and initiated technology cradles where new, high-potential and cutting-edge technologies are incubated and developed. HCL Technologies has over 500 clients around the world and conducts business in 17 countries.

Mahindra and Mahindra Limited purchased a franchise from Willys-Overland, the American Jeep producer, which allowed it to import, assemble and sell Jeep parts in India. This strategy allowed the company to sell various types of vehicles to consumers in different market segments. Hero group, after becoming India's largest bicycle producer in 1975, targeted the western market and imported modern equipment from Europe and Taipei, China, updating its technologies and manufactured high-standard products. Technological support from developed countries played an important role in Wipro's business expansion, which earns 60 per cent of its sales revenue in the US and 30 per cent in Europe. Wipro imported technologies from Switzerland when it was still a hydraulic cylinder producer and later forged a strategic relationship with Apple, IBM, Intel Corporation, Seiko Epson Corporation, Sun Microsystems and Tandem Computers.

Infosys sells its products on the basis of value rather than cost, while providing an image of a local company. Kumar Birla of Aditya Birla group believes that the greatest challenge to the globalisation of India's enterprises comes from culture and global expansion requires not only geographical reach but also a mindset. Several Tata companies have completed more than 20 overseas acquisitions in recent years. Wipro employs workers from over 40 countries and its 53 research centres are located throughout the world. Aditya Birla group owns 85 companies and maintains service centres in 20 countries. Infosys operates offices or research centres in 20 countries. Tata Consultancy Services has established research and development centres in 10 countries. Infosys and Wipro joined NASDAQ in 1999, and Dr. Reddy's Laboratories joined the New York Stock Exchange in 2001. In the mid-1990s, Reliance Industries raised funds through global depository receipts and later issued euro convertible bonds in Europe and the first Indian company to issue 50-100 year bonds in the United States. JRD Tata opined that Tata group companies should recruit the best and most dedicated personnel. Wipro operates by the principle of employing the best and invest in them. Infosys Technologies identifies the best learners among skilled applicants, because they generally are modest, often to the point of shyness, and have a deep respect and hunger for knowledge which is the key to personal progress (Ghoshal and Bartlett, 1994). Training programmes at Reliance Industries reflect the company's belief that thoughts, behaviour and management should mirror the world's best training methods. Tata group's strict rules encourage and discipline employee behaviour, and its companies offered generous salaries and benefits before they were required by law. Tata's code of conduct includes stringent requirements for services, skills, ethics and values. Wipro stresses trust and encourages its employees to create synergistic efficiency through joint efforts. GD Birla indicates that the wealth one generates should benefit multiple stakeholders. Aditya Birla group invests part of its profits outside its business to improve society, notably healthcare, education and infrastructure. The group also developed a concept of sustainable livelihood, channelling resources to ensure that people can sustain themselves. In 1995, Kumar Birla institutionalised the concept of triple accountability of economic success, environmental responsibility and social commitment. The Aditya Birla Centre for Community Initiatives and Rural Development was established to provide strategic direction and thrust areas for their work ensuring performance management. All Aditya Birla companies have rural development cells that implement various sustainable livelihood programmes and all are subject to internal performance assessment and external auditing. Reliance Industries helps in construction of public infrastructure and is also involved in environmental safety, energy conservation and provides local communities with drinking water, healthcare, schools, scholarships and hospitals.

Premji's management model includes replacing intrusive judgment with objective fact, guiding the development of enterprise with measurement standards and achieving objectives by combining data, intention and measurement. This involves establishing a target pole management model that recognises excellent management to implementing the targets and result and purpose management to combine strategic objectives with root performance, automating business processes and improving the scientific basis of programmes, besides encouraging the employees to eliminate extravagance and encourage thrift (Hamm, 2007). Premji recognises a strong relationship among the accumulation and development of human resources, the development of an enterprise and power of a nation. In the modern world, the key difference between advanced and developing countries involves their ability to release human capacity and translate human capital into economic activities.

10.9 Scope of Entrepreneurship in India

In India, there is a dearth of quality personnel and demand for higher levels of entrepreneurship generates new scopes for growth. Results of the 66th round of the National Sample Survey Organisation show that unemployment figures in 2009-10 were as high as 8.9 million, one million more Indians joining the rank of the unemployed between 2007 and 2010. The rate of employment generation has declined from 2.7 to 0.8 per cent during the period. This slowdown in employment generation is evident across both rural and urban areas, though it was especially marked in rural India, requiring an upping of rural entrepreneurship. The rising unemployment rate (9.2 per cent) has resulted in growing frustration among the youth. In addition there is always problem of underemployment. As a result, increasing the entrepreneurial activities in the country is the only way out. The report of Planning Commission to generate employment opportunities for 10 crore workers over the next ten years has recommended self-employment as a way-out for teaming unemployed youth. The success of Indian entrepreneurs in Silicon Valley is evident and the only thing that is lacking is confidence and mental preparation. What is more important than the skill and knowledge base is the courage to take the plunge. However, it is appreciative that the current generations of youth do not have hang-ups about the previous legacy and are willing to experiment. For example, Vikas Kedia was only 21 when he had turned his back on a possible $100,000 a year job. He has also created history of sorts in the IIM circuit by starting his own dot.com company in Bangalore, now he has his own company which is a California and Kolkata based GRMtech.

Various government departments and chambers of commerce have started organising seminars and workshops to promote entrepreneurship. Many management colleges have incorporated entrepreneurship as part of their curriculum. In India, where over

300 million persons are living below the poverty line, it is simply impossible for any government to provide means of livelihood to everyone. Such situations surely demand for a continuous effort from the society, where people are encouraged to come up with their entrepreneurial initiative. Encouragement has to be provided in the shape of venture capital and infrastructural support, like the export processing zones. About 35 per cent of the start-ups in Silicon Valley are by Indians and similar risk-taking ability has to be cultivated within the country. Entrepreneurs need more than technical talent, more than business savvy. Entrepreneurs must learn how to overcome the risk of failure or of vulnerability. The institutions can give them valuable insights and also support them in this. Entrepreneurship will determine technical innovations, status of social institutions and political management systems. On the basis of these factors, we can expect the future to be a place where basic needs will remain and only the wants will change. India will overcome the barriers of infrastructure with a strong manufacturing and agricultural sector. Entrepreneurs and not managers will be in demand, as only they will be equipped to find order in chaos. The focus of entrepreneurial energy will shift from achieving volume sales to fulfill a specific requirement.

Governance will become more transparent and will be willing to accept changes necessary for growth and development with more autonomy becoming the basis of all issues. Technological obsolescence will become order of the day and there will be more space for leisure and new businesses will be credited with innovating and providing new jobs. There may be technological upheavals in quick succession, social value systems and cultural issues undergoing slow but dynamic transformation. For transformation to happen there needs to be support both at the governmental and societal level. For the government, it is important to realise that the goal of small business owners will be to remain self-employed and may not need financial assistance but they will need marketing and legal assistance in order to sustain themselves. Practical and cost effective programmes need to be developed to address their needs because self-employed persons will represent an important segment in economic revitalisation.

Entrepreneurship development is the key factor to fight against unemployment, poverty and to prepare the country for global competitive advantage. The lack of effective entrepreneurship may be one of the causes of poverty in developing countries, though they may have many entrepreneurs. Many in advanced countries are not entrepreneurs, mostly working for companies, doing highly specialised and narrowly specified jobs, implementing someone else's entrepreneurial vision and people are entrepreneurial in the developing countries than in the developed countries (OECD, 2007). According to that OECD study, in most developing countries, 30-50 per cent of the non-agricultural workforce is self-employed. In some of the poorest countries, the ratio of those working as one-person entrepreneurs is high at 66.9 per cent in Ghana, 75.4 per cent in Bangladesh and 88.7 per cent in Benin. In contrast, only 12.8 per cent of the non-agricultural workforce in developed countries is self-employed and the ratio is only 6.7 per cent in Norway, 7.5 per cent in the USA and 8.6 per cent in France. The difference is 10 times, if we compare Bangladesh with the USA (7.5 per cent versus 75.4 per cent). And in the most extreme case, the chance of someone from Benin being an entrepreneur is 13 times higher than the equivalent chance for a Norwegian (88.7 per cent versus 6.7 per cent).

Entrepreneurs like Edison and Gates became what they are only because they were supported by a whole host of collective institutions and the scientific infrastructure that enabled them to acquire their knowledge and experiment with it. Company and other commercial laws made it possible for them subsequently to build companies with large and complex organisations, while educational institutions supplied highly trained personnel that manned those companies. The financial institutions enabled them to raise huge amounts of capital when they wanted to expand, while patent and copyright laws protected their inventions. Besides institutional support, cooperation amongst the entrepreneurs also matters. As in the case of dairy industry in Denmark, the Netherlands and Germany which has become what it is because farmers organised themselves, with state help into co-operatives and jointly invested in processing facilities and export marketing. In contrast, the dairy sectors in the Balkan countries have failed to develop, despite quite a large amount of microcredit channelled into them, mainly because the farmers tried to make it on their own. Many small firms in Italy and Germany jointly invest in R&D and export marketing, which are beyond their individual means, through industry associations, whereas developing country firms do not invest in these areas because there is not such a collective mechanism.

The engine of development for developing countries is the informal sector, fuelled by microcredit. Microcredit allows the poor to get out of poverty through their own efforts, by providing them with the financial means to realise their entrepreneurial potential. In the process they gain independence and self-respect, as they are not relying on hand-outs from the government and foreign aid agencies for their survival any more. Women are empowered by microcredit, as it gives them the ability to earn an income and thus improve their bargaining positions when compared to their male partners. Unfortunately, there are criticisms of microfinance since little evidence is available on its positive impact. In short, it is not the lack of raw individual entrepreneurial energy, but it is the inability to channel the individual entrepreneurial energy into collective entrepreneurship that matters.

Finally, at the firm level, entrepreneurship has become highly collective in the advanced countries, manned by professional managers. The increasing scale of modern technologies was making it increasingly impossible for a large company to be established and run by a visionary individual entrepreneur and displacement of heroic entrepreneurs by executive types. In the case of Japan, the firms have even developed institutional mechanisms to exploit the creativity of even the lowliest production line workers. Similar institutional support and entrepreneurial initiatives are required for countries like India.

10.10 Conclusion

There is no doubt entrepreneurs respond to incentives in their pursuit of self-survival and accumulation of wealth. The nature of this response depends on the economic and social climates and the policy of government. The economy has to face many problems due to government regulations and little interaction with outside world. It was only after the economic reforms of post-1991 era that Indian economy began a course with the rest of the world. In this, entrepreneurial efforts have generated many social and economic benefits, including new businesses, new jobs, innovative products and services and increased wealth for future community investment (Kayne, 1999). According to Global Entrepreneurship Monitor model, the social-cultural-political context within a country must foster certain general national framework conditions, which can generate not only the opportunities for entrepreneurship but also the capacity for entrepreneurship. The important framework conditions are the availability of financing, the need for supportive government policies and the opportunities for education and training in entrepreneurship

(Lal and Clement, 2005) and providing opportunities for education in entrepreneurship is critical in this. Foreign capital has been pumped into India to exploit software development and technology services. Networking and exchange among both new and established entrepreneurs and providing venture capital to the start-ups are to be the focus, besides an emphasis on high-tech manufacturing, which is very low at present. Though India has a good industrial base (never it had an industrial revolution) its export structure is still dominated by low-tech products. A hi-tech export structure relies on complex products like electronic machinery, precision instruments and fine chemicals, which yield competitive advantage. Hence, encouragement of hi-tech entrepreneurship is required, especially of the intra, eco and technopreneur types leading to strengthening of entrepreneurial skills and improvement of entrepreneurial framework conditions.

Nations cannot exist without establishing competitive advantage in certain aspects and in this regards, increase in competitiveness is the only criterion to establish an effective entrepreneurial system. Global competitiveness necessarily involves hi-tech innovations and organisation of labour towards increasing productivity. Proper attention has to be laid to employment generation also, so that in addition to poverty alleviation, unemployment, underemployment and disguised unemployment, so characteristic of the Indian economy, are annihilated. Entrepreneurs may fall on accumulation of capital or transfer of technology, but an innovation-driven scenario beats them all. At the macro level, effective measures to develop entrepreneurship by strengthening entrepreneurial research with education and industry collaboration and at the micro level by offering specialised training courses to bring in the entrepreneurial potential of the students, would be required. Modernising the small and medium industry sector towards sustainability and case studying success stories of entrepreneurship in other systems would provide a new lease of life to the live and practice of entrepreneurship in the country. It was Adam Smith's petty 'bakers and butchers' who gave rise to the emergence of bigger day capitalists and it was the Schumpeterian entrepreneur who gave rise to radical innovations. All the more, the future of industrial prospects in India largely depends on the self-interested small capitalists and radically innovative entrepreneurs. When we look at the breathtaking scope of entrepreneurial innovations, ordinary consumers are now able to pay their bills and purchase goods and services using their cellular phones instead of cash, thanks to innovations by telecommunications companies. The concept of micro-lending has been transformed into micro-saving, providing poor people with a low-cost, secure way of saving money and sending money back home to their families. Also, entrepreneurs make use of knowledge of the tastes and preferences of local consumers to challenge the long-standing dominance of multinationals. Entrepreneurs in the developing countries often start from a clean slate and engage in leapfrogging strategies. A time has come where innovation is no longer considered synonymous with Silicon Valley and other icons of Western success. Hence the Look south parody!

Lastly, the problem of unemployment which daunts not only India but many other countries can be removed only if people understand the reason behind the problem and the options available to become an entrepreneur. Entrepreneurs can fulfill the dream of any country that does not have any kind of unemployment problems. They also help the governments in implementing several plans by funding the schemes through the different taxes that their businesses pay to the government treasury. Most of these plans are aimed towards benefit of the residents thereby helping them in living a utopian dream. As has been mentioned in the preface, the drama is unfolding! Look south!! Invent in thy future fortunes!!!

Further Reading

Acharya, Shankar. 2001. *India's Macroeconomic Management in the Nineties*, New Delhi: Indian Council for Research on International Economic Relations.

Acs, Z.J. and Szerb, 2012. *The Global Entrepreneurship and Development Index,* London: Imperial College.

Acs, Z.J. and Szerb, L. 2010. *Global Entrepreneurship and the United States*, Ruxton, MD: Small Business Administration.

Acs, Z.J. and Szerb, L. 2008. "A complex global entrepreneurship context index (CEC)". Faculty of Business and Economics, University of Pecs, mimeo.

Acs, Z.J. and Amoros, J.E. 2008. "Entrepreneurship and Competitiveness Dynamics in Latin America". *Small Business Economics,* 31:3, 305-322.

Acs, Z.J., Desai, S. and Hessels, J. 2008. "Entrepreneurship, Economic Development and Institutions", *Small Business Economics,* 31:3, 219-234.

Acs, Z.J. and Armington, C. 2006. *Entrepreneurship, Geography and American Economic Growth,* Cambridge: Cambridge University Press.

Acs, Z.J., Arenius, P., Hay, M., and Minniti, M. 2005. *2004 Global Entrepreneurship Monitor:* London U.K. and Babson Park, MA: London Business School and Babson College.

Acs, Z.J. and Audretsch, D.B. 2003. 'Innovation and technological change', *Handbook of Entrepreneurship Research: an Interdisciplinary Survey and Introduction*. Z. J. Acs and D. B. Audretsch. Kluwer, Boston, 55-79.

Ahluwalia, I.J. 1985. *Industrial Growth in India*, Delhi: Oxford University Press.

Ahmad, A. and Dhillon, A.S. 1991. "Energy Management Tata Steel's Approach", *Tata Tech*, 1, 19.

Akamatsu, Kaname (1961). "A Theory of Unbalanced Growth in the World Economy", in *Weltwirtschaftliches Archiv*, Hamburg, 86, 196-217.

Amsden, A.H. 1989. *Asia's Next Giant: South Korea and Late Industrialization,* New York: Oxford University Press.

Alston, L J, Libecap, G.D. and Mueller, B. 1999. *Titles, conflict, and land use: The development of property rights and land reform on the Brazilian Amazon frontier:* Ann Arbor: University of Michigan Press.

Alvarez, S.A. and Barney, J. 2007. "How entrepreneurs organize firms under conditions of uncertainty" *Journal of Management.* 31:5, 776-93.

Andersen, E.S. 2008. "A note on Erik Reinert's Listian–Schumpeterian Development Economics", Workshop on Institutions, Innovation and Development, Department of Business Studies, Aalborg University, May 6.

Andersen, T.L. and Hill P.J.1975. "The Evolution of Property Rights: A Study of the American West", *Journal of Law and Economics,* 18: 163-175.

Anstey, V. 1952. *Economic Development of India*, London: University Press.

Arora, A. and Athreye, S. 2002. "The Software Industry and India's Economic Development," *Information Economics and Policy*, 14:253-273.

Arora, A, Arunachalam, V.S., Asundi, J.B. and Fernandes, R.C. 2001. "The Indian software services industry", *Research Policy,* 30, 1267-1287.

Ashby, J., Heinrich, G., Burpee, G., Remington, T., Wilso, K., Qhiros, C.A., Aldana, M. and Ferris, S. 2009. "What farmers want: collective capacity for sustainable entrepreneurship", *International Journal of Agricultural Sustainability*, 7:2, 130-146.

Ashoka Innovators for the Public. 2000. *Selecting leading social entrepreneurs,* Washington DC.

Asian Productivity Organization. 2007. *Development for Competitive Small and Medium Enterprises*, Tokyo: APO.

Athreye, S. 2010. "Economic Adversity and Entrepreneurship-led Growth Lessons from the Indian Software Sector", United

Nations University - Maastricht Economic and Social Research and Training Centre on Innovation and Technology, Keizer Karelplein, Maastricht, The Netherlands.

Athreye, S. 2005. "The Indian software industry and its evolving service capability". *Industrial and Corporate Change,* 14:3, 393-418.

Athreye, S. 2002. "The Indian Software Industry and its Evolving Service Capability," mimeo, Open University, U.K., June 2002.

Arora, A., Gambardella, A. and Torrisi, S. 2004. "In the Footsteps of Silicon Valley?" in Bresnahan, T. and Gambardella, A. (eds). *Building High-Tech Clusters:Silicon Valley and Beyond*, Cambridge: Cambridge University Press.

Audretsch, D.B. and Thurik, A.R. 2001. "What is new about the new economy: sources of growth in the managed and entrepreneurial economies", *Industrial and Corporate Change,* 10, 267-315.

Audretsch, D.B., Thurik, A.R., Verheul, I. and Wennekers, A.R.M. (eds). 2002, *Entrepreneurship: Determinants and Policy in a European-US Comparison*, Boston/Dordrecht: Kluwer Academic Publishers.

Audretsch, D.B. and Lehmann, E., 2006. "Location and new venture creation", *Handbook of Entrepreneurship Research*. S.C. Parker III, Kluwer.

Avant, D.A. 2005. *The Market for Force: The Consequences of Privatizing Security*. Cambridge, UK: Cambridge University Press.

Awasthi, D. 2011. "Approaches to Entrepreneurship Development: The Indian Experience", *Journal of Global Entrepreneurship Research,* 1:1, 107-124.Bala subrahmanya, M.H. 2007. "Development strategies for Indian SMEs: promoting linkages with global transnational corporations", *Management Research Review,* 30:10, 762-774.

Balasubramanyam, V.N. and Balasubramanyam, A., 2010. "Human Capital and Development A Tale of Two Cities; Software Sector in Bangalore and Hyderabad", Lancaster, UK: Lancaster University Management School.

Bagchi, S. 2005. "Lessons in Entrepreneurship from the Indian IT Industry". Bangalore: MindTree Consulting.

Bandura, Albert. 1982. "Self-Efficacy Mechanism in Human Agency," *American Psychologist* 36,122-147.

Barzel, Y. 1997. *Economic Analysis of Property Rights*. Cambridge, UK: Cambridge University Press.

Basu, K. 2006. "Globalization, poverty, and inequality: what is the relationship? What can be done?" *World Development,* 34: 1361–1373.

Baumol, W.J. 2006. "Entrepreneurship and Invention: Toward Their Microeconomic Value Theory," Special Session on Entrepreneurship, Innovation and Growth I: Theoretical Approach, American Economic Association Meetings.

Baumol, W.J. 2002. *The Free-market Innovation Machine: Analyzing the Growth Miracle of Capitalism*. Princeton: Princeton University Press.

Baumol, W.J. 1990. "Entrepreneurship: productive, unproductive and destructive", *Journal of Political Economy*. 98: 893-921.

Baumol, W J. 1988. *Entrepreneurship, Management, and the Structure of Payoffs*. Cambridge, MA: MIT Press.

Baumol, W.J. 1986: "Entrepreneurship and a Century of Growth", *Journal of Business Venturing*, 1:2, 141-145.

Beckert, Jens. 1999. "Agency, entrepreneurs, and institutional change: The role of strategic choice and institutionalized practices". *Organization Studies* 20:5, 777-799.

Berna. 1960. *Industrial Entrepreneurship in Madras State*, Bombay: Asia Publishing House.

Bernhardt, D. 2000. "Credit rationing?" *American Economic Review*. 90: 235-39.

Bernstein, J.L. 1997. "Interindustry R&D Spillovers for electrical and electronic products: The Canadian Case", *Economic Systems Research*, 9:1, 67-80.

Bhalla, G.S. 2000. "Political economy of Indian development in the 20th century: India's road", in Bhatia Anju, *Women Development and NGOs*. New Delhi: Rawat Publication.

Bianchi M. and Henrekson M. 2005. "Is neoclassical economics still entrepreneurless?" *SSE/EFI Working Paper No. 584,* Stockholm School of Economics.

Binswanger, H.P. and Deininger, K. 1997. "Explaining agricultural and agrarian policies in developing countries", *Journal of Economic Literature,* 35: 1958-2005.

Biospectrum. 2009. *BioSpectrum-ABLE industry overview*, June.

Birch, D.L. 1979. "MIT Programme on Neighbourhood and Regional Change," *The Job Generation Process,* Cambridge, MA.

Blau, D. 1987. "A time-series analysis of self-employment in the United States". *Journal of Political Economy,* 95:3, 445-67.

Bosma, N., Jones, K., Autio, E. and Levie, J. 2008. *Global Entrepreneurship Monitor, 2007 Executive Report*, Babson Park, MA: Babson College and London: London Business School.

Brush, J.E. 1952. "Iron and Steel Making in India", *Geographical Review",* 42:52-58.

Buckley, P., Clegg, J., Cross, A. and Tan, H. 2005. "China's inward foreign direct investment success: Southeast Asia in the shadow of the dragon". *Multinational Business Review*, 13, 3-30.

Burgelman, R.A. 1983: "A Model of the Interaction of Strategic Behavior, Corporate Context and the Concept of C Strategy", *Academy of Management Review*, 8:1, 61-71.

Bygrave, W.D. 2004. 'The entrepreneurial process', in W.D. Bygrave and A. Zacharakis (eds), *The Portable MBA in Entrepreneurship*. Hoboken, NJ: John Wiley and Sons.

Cai, F. 2008. *Approaching a triumphal span: how far is China towards its Lewisian turning point?*, UNU-WIDER Research Paper, no. 2008/09, Helsinki: World Institute for Development Economics Research of the United Nations University.

Cantillon, R. 1755. *Essai sur la nature du commerce en général*, London: Fetcher Gyler. edited in an English version by Henry Higgs, C.B., London: MacMillan (1931).

Carree, M.A., Thurik, R. and Wennekers, S. 2007. "The relationship between economic development and business ownership revisited," *Entrepreneurship and Regional Development*, 19:3, 281-291.

Carree, M.A. and Thurik R.A. 2003. "The Impact of Entrepreneurship on Economic Growth". in Z.J. Acs and D.B. Audretsch (eds). *Handbook of Entrepreneurship Research,* Boston: Kluwer Academic Publishers, 437-471.

Carroll, G. and Khessina, O. 2005. "The Ecology of Entrepreneurship", *Handbook of Entrepreneurship Research: Disciplinary Perspectives,* Sharon A. Alvarez, Rajshree Agarwal and Olav Sorenson (eds). Springer, Chapter 8: 167-200.

Casnocha, B. 2011. "The four types of entrepreneurship", *Entrepreneurship*, February: 2-8.

Casson M., 1990. *The Entrepreneur: An Economic Theory*. 2nd Edition, Cheltenham: Edward Elgar.

Chandra, A. 2009. "India: Country replete with phenomenal innovation and entrepreneurship potential", available on the web at http://www.knowledgeportal-in/contents/node/445.

Chaminade, C. and Vang, J. 2008. "Globalization of Knowledge Production and Regional Innovation Policy: Supporting Specialized Hubs in Developing Countries". *Research Policy*, 37 (10), pp. 1684-96.

Chaminade, C. 2004. "Social capital and innovation in SMEs: a new model of innovation? Evidence and discussion" Paper presented at SPRU/CENTRIM Seminar series.

Christensen, C.M. 1997. *The Innovator's Dilemma: When New Technologies Cause Great Firms to Fail*, Mass: Harvard Business School Press.

Coase, Ronald. 1974. "The Lighthouse in Economics", *Journal of Law and Economics,* 17:2, 357-376.

Cole, Arthur H. 1959. *Business Enterprise in its Social Setting*. Cambridge, MA: Harvard University Press.

Dahlman, C.J., Ross-Larson, B., and Westphal, L.E. 1987. "Managing Technological Development: Lessons from the Newly Industrializing Countries," *World Development*, 15:6, 759-775.

Das, A.C.R. 2008. "ITmk3 Technology: An overview in the Indian perspective", New Delhi: Ministry of Steel.

Das, K. 2009. "Broad-basing rural industrialization in India: approaches and challenges", International Research Development Council, Canada, SIID-01/2009.

D'Costa A.P. 2011. "Institutional Change, Industrial Logics, and Internationalization: Growth of Auto and IT Sectors in India", Asia Research Centre, Copenhagen Business School.

D'Costa, A.P. 2008. "The international mobility of technical talent: trends and development implications", in A. Solimano (ed.). *International Mobility of Talent and Development Impact*, Oxford: Oxford University Press, 44-83.

Department of Biotechnology, 2006. Annual Report, Department of Science and Technology, New Delhi: Govt. of India.

Department of Science and Technology. 2006. *R&D Statistics*, New Delhi: Department of Science and Technology, Government of India,

De, P.K. 1999. "Managing Technological Change: The Case of Iron and Steel Manufacturing in India", Jamshedpur: Xavier Labour Research Institute.

Dees, G. 1983. *Social enterprise: Private initiatives for the common good*, Working paper series No. 9-395-116, Harvard Business School.

Dejean, F., Gond, J.P. and Leca, F. 2004. "Measuring the unmeasured: An Institutional Entrepreneur Strategy in an emergent industry". *Human Relations*, 57:6, 740-765.

Desai, Sameeksha and Acs, Zoltan J. 2007. "A theory of destructive entrepreneurship", *Jena Economic Research Papers*, No. 2007, 085, 1-42.

Dossani, R. 2006. "The Origins and Growth of India's Software Industry", in *Offshoring White-Collar Work*, Collins, S. and Brainard, L., (Eds.), Washington DC: Brookings Institution.

Dossani, R. and Kenney, M. 2002. "Creating an Environment for Venture Capital in India", *World Development,* 30:2, 227-253.

de Meza, D. and Webb D.C. 1999. "Wealth, enterprise and credit policy", *Economic Journal,* 109:153-63.

DiMaggio, P. 1988. "Interest and agency in institutional theory", in L. Zucker (Ed.), *Institutional Patterns and Organizations,* Cambridge, MA: Ballinger., 3-22.

DiMaggio, J. and Powell, W. 1983. "The iron cage revisited: Institutional isomorphism and collective rationality in organizational fields", *American Sociological Review,* 48:2, 147-160.

Downing, S. 2005. "The social construction of entrepreneurship: Narrative and dramatic processes in the coproduction of organizations and identities", *Entrepreneurship Theory and Practice*, 29:2, 185-204.

Drucker, P.F. 1985. *Innovation and Entrepreneurship*. New York: Harper & Row Publishers.

Dutta, S. 1997. *Family Business in India*, New Delhi: Response Books.

Enos, J. and Park, U.H. 1987. *The Adoption and Diffusion of Imported Technology: The Case of Korea*. London: Croom Helm.

Evans, D.S. and Jovanovic, B. 1989. "An estimated model of entrepreneurial choice under liquidity constraints", *Journal of Political Economy*. 97: 808-27.

Fan, P. and Watanabe, K.N. 2008. "The Rise of the Indian Biotech Industry and Innovative Domestic Companies", *International Journal of Technology and Globalization*, 4:2, 148-169.

FAO, 2006. *The safety match industry in India*, in Case studies in forest-based small scale enterprises in Asia, Rome: FAO Corporate Document Depository.

Fligstein, N. 1997. "Social skill and institutional theory". *American Behavioral Scientist*, 40, 397-405.

Forbes, N. 1999. "Technology and Indian Industry: What is Liberalization Changing?" *Technovation*, 19, 403-412.

Freeman, John R. and Duvall, Raymond D. 1984. "International Economic Relations and the Entrepreneurial State", *Economic Development and Cultural Change,* 32:2, 373-400.

Frew, S.E., Sammut, S.M., Shore, A.F. and Ramjist, J.K. 2007. "India's health biotech sector at cross roads". *Nature Biotechnology*, 25: 403-417.

Frew, S.E., Al-Bader, S., Rezaie, R, Daar, A.S. and Singer, P.A. 2008, "Chinese health biotech and the billion-patient market", *Nature Biotechnology*, 26:1, 37-53.

Friedman, T.L., 2006. *The World is flat: A Brief History of the Twenty-First Century*, New York: Farrer, Straus and Girox.

Fuller, D.B. 2010. "How law, politics, and transnational networks affect technology entrepreneurship: Explaining divergent venture capital investing strategies in China". *Asia Pacific Journal of Management,* doi:10.1007/s10490-009-9149-0.

Gadgil, D.R. 1959. *Origins of the Modern Indian Business Class*. New York: Institute of Pacific Relations

Garud, R., Hardy, C. and Maguire, S. 2007. Institutional entrepreneurship as embedded agency, *Organization Studies*, 28: 957-969.

Gartner, W.B. 1988. "Who is an entrepreneur is the wrong question". *American Journal of Small Business* 12:4, 11–32.

Ghoshal, S. and Bartlett, C.A. 1994. "Linking organizational context and managerial action: The dimensions of quality of management". *Strategic Management Journal, 15*, 91-112.

Giriappa, Somu. 2003. "Steel Infrastructure in India", in *Facets of Development Ethos, New Delhi:* Mohit Publications.

Global Industry Analysts, 2012. *Global Biotechnology Industry: Market Research Reports, Statistics and Analysis*, Los Angeles, CA.

Godrej, A.B. 2005. "The Family Concern", *Business Today,* January 16.

Goldberg, V.P. 1974. "Institutional change and the quasi-invisible hand", *Journal of Law and Economics*, 17: 461-492.

Gopakumar, K.1995: "The Entrepreneur in Economic Thought: A Thematic Overview," *Journal of Entrepreneurship,* 4:1, 1.

Gopalakrishnan, R. 2009. "India and Tata National Development and the Corporation", *Innovations*, 1-13.

Goering, L. 2007. "India nurturing home-grown ideas" *The Chicago Tribune*, August 6.

Government of India. 2003, *Annual Report 2002-03*. New Delhi: Ministry of Commerce and Industry, Department of Industrial Policy and Promotion.

Greenwood, R. and Suddaby, R. 2006. "Institutional Entrepreneurship in Mature Fields: The Big Five Accounting Firms", *Academy of Management Journal*, 49:1, 27- 42.

Greif, A. 1998. "Historical and comparative institutional analysis", *American Economic Review*, 88: 80-84.

Greiner, L.E. 1972. "Evolution and revolution as organisations grow", *Harvard Business Review*, 50:55-67.

Gupta, A. 2002. 'Indian Experience on Promoting Business and Technology Incubation for Improved Competitiveness of Small and Medium-sized Industries through Technological Developments", National Workshop on Promoting Business and Technology Incubation for Improved Competitiveness of Small and Medium-sized Industries through Application of Modern and Efficient Technologies, Phnom Penh, November 26-28.

Gupta, V. 2008. 'An Enquiry into the Characteristics of Entrepreneurship in India', *Journal of International Businesss Research*, 7:1, 13-31.

Gupta, V. and Wang, J. 2004. "From corporate crisis to turnaround in East Asia: A study of China's Huajing Electronics Group Corporation", *Asia Pacific Journal of Management*, 21, 213-233.

Hagen, Everett. 1962. *On the Theory of Social Change*. Homewood, IL: Dorsey Press.

Hamel, G. 1999. "Bringing Silicon Valley inside". *Harvard Business Review,* 77:5, 70-76.

Hamm, S. 2007. "Bangalore Tiger: How Indian Tech Upstart WIPRO is Rewriting the Rules of Global Competition", translated by Zhao Xue. New York: McGraw–Hill.

Hansemark, O. 1998. "The effects of an entrepreneurship programme on need for achievement and locus of control of reinforcement", *International Journal of Entrepreneurship Behaviour and Research*, 4:1, 28-50.

Hannan, M.T. and Freeman, J. 1987. "The ecology of organizational founding: American labor unions, 1836-1985", *American Journal of Sociology,* 92: 910-943.

Hatten, T. and Ruthland. 1995. "Student attitudes toward entrepreneurship as affected by participation in an SBI programme. *Journal of Education for Business*, 7:4, 224-227.

Hayward, M.L.A., Shepherd, D.A. and Griffin, D. 2006. "A Hubris Theory of Entrepreneurship", *Management Science*, 52:2:160-72.

Heeks, R. 2010. "Do information and communication technologies (ICTs) contribute to development?" *Journal of International Development,* 5.

Hertz, N. 2002. *The Silent Takeover: Global Capitalism and the Death of Democracy*. New York: Free Press.

Hisrich, Robert. 1990. "Entrepreneurship/Intrapreneurship", *American Psychologist*, 45:2, 209-222.

Hofstede, G. 1980. *Culture's Consequences: International Differences in Work-Related Values*, Beverly Hills, CA: Sage.

Holcombe, R. 1992. "Political entrepreneurship and the democratic allocation of economic resources". *Review of Austrian Economics*, 15: 143–59.

Holmes, T.J. and Schmitz, J.A., 1990. "A theory of entrepreneurship and its application to the study of business transfers", *Journal of Political Economy*. 98: 265-94.

Hopkins, Anthony, G. 1987. "Big Business in African Studies." *Journal of African History,* 28: 119-140.

Hoselitz, B.F. 1952. "Entrepreneurship and Economic Growth", *American Journal of Economic Sociology*, 97-106.

Hosseini, H. (1990). "The Archaic, the Obsolete and the Mythical in Neoclassical Economics", *American Journal of Economics and Sociology,* 49 (1), 81-92.

Huggett, B., Hodgson, J. and Lahteenmaki, R. 2011. "Public biotech 2010-the numbers", *Nature Biotechnology*, 29: 585-591.

Ingram, P. and Rao, H. 2004. "Store wars: The enactment and repeal of anti-chain-store legislation in America," *American Journal of Sociology,* 110:446-487.

Ito, Takatoshi. 2001. "Growth, Crisis, and the Future of Economic Recovery in East Asia". in: Stiglitz, Joseph E. and Shahid Yusuf (eds). *Rethinking the East Asian Miracle*. New York: Oxford University Press, 55–94.

Japan Information Technology Services Industry Association, 2008. *IT Services Industry in Japan*. Tokyo: Japan Information Technology Services Industry Association.

Jia, H. 2007. "China syndrome – a regulatory framework in meltdown?" *Nature Biotechnology*, 25:8, 835-837.

Jones, G. and Wadhwani R.D. 2007. "Entrepreneurship and Business History: Renewing the Research Agenda", Harvard business School: 07/007.

Johnson, S., McMillan, J. and Woodruff, C. 1999. "Contract Enforcement in Transition". Discussion Paper 2081, London: Centre for Economic Policy Research.

Johnson, S, McMillan, J and Woodruff, C. 2000. "Entrepreneurs and the ordering of institutional reform". *Economics of Transition,* 8:1, 1-36.

Jovanovic B. 1982. "Selection and the evolution of industry", *Econometrica*. 50: 649-70.

Kahar, S. 1978. *The Inner World.-A Psycho-Analytic Study of Hindu Childhood and Society*. London: Oxford University Press.

Kamesam, V. 2003. "Identifying the Real Policy Issues" in the Session on "Improving Financing for Entrepreneurship and SMEs": OECD "Workshop on Entrepreneurship in a Global Economy: Strategic Issues and Policies", September 9, Budapest.

Kanungo, R.N. and Bhatnagar, J.K. 1978. "Achievement orientation and occupational values: A comparative study of young French and English Canadians", *Canadian Journal of Behavioral Science,* 12:384-392.

Kanavi, S. 2001. "New Steel in an Old Bottle" *Business India,* July 23, 54-60.

Kaplan, S. and Murray, F. 2009. "Entrepreneurship and the construction of value in bio-technology". *Research in the Sociology of Organizations*.

Kaye, J. 2004. *Coca-Cola India*. Dartmouth College: Tuck School of Business.

Kayne, Jay. 1999. *State Entrepreneurship Policies and Programs,* Kansas City: Kauffman Center.

Khanna, T. and Palepu, K. 2000. "Is Group Affiliation Profitable in Emerging Markets? An Analysis of Diversified Indian Business Groups". *Journal of Finance*, 55:2, 867-891.

Kilby, Peter (ed). 1971. *Entrepreneurship and Economic Development*. New York: Free Press.

Kilhstrom, R.E. and Laffont, J.J., 1979. "A general equilibrium entrepreneurial theory of firm formation based on risk aversion", *Journal of Political Economy*. 87: 719-49.

King, A and Lenox, M. 2000. "Industry self-regulation without sanctions: The chemical industry's responsible care programme". *Academy of Management Journal,* 43: 698-716.

Kirzner, I. 1997. "Entrepreneurial Discovery and the Competitive Market Process: An Austrian Approach", *Journal of Economic Literature* 35, 60-85.

Kirzner, I., 1973, *Competition and Entrepreneurship*, Chicago: University of Chicago Press.

Klepper, S., 1996. "Entry, exit, growth and innovation over the product life cycle", *American Economic Review*. 86: 562-83.

Knight, F.H., 1921. *Risk, Uncertainty and Profit*. Houghton-Mifflin. New York.

Kojima, K. 2000, "The "flying geese" model of Asian economic development: origin, theoretical extensions, and regional policy implications", *Journal of Asian Economics*, 11, 375-401.

Kondaiah, C. 2007. "Development strategy and overview of small-scale industries (SSIs) in India", in *Entrepreneurship Development for Competitive Small and Medium Enterprises,* Report of the APO Survey on Entrepreneur Development for Competitive SMEs (05-RP-GE-SUV-41-B), Tokyo: Asian Productivity Organization.

Kraatz, M.S. and Moore, J.H. 2002. "Executive migration and institutional change". *Academy of Management Journal,* 45: 120-143.

Krishnamurthy, K. 1987. *Technology Transfer: India's Iron & Steel*. Madras: Technology Books.

Krishnan, R.T. 2002. "Bangalore as High-tech Cluster: where does it stand?" Proceedings of the R&D Management Conference, New Delhi: Council of Scientific & Industrial Research, 105-112.

Krishnan, R.T. and Prabhu, G.N. 1999. "Innovation in the Indian Information Technology Industry: A Study of the Software Product Development Process." *Science, Technology and Society*, 7:1, 91-115.

Krishnan, R.T., Gupta, A. and Matta, V. 2003. "Biotechnology and Bioinformatics: Can India Emulate the Software Success Story?" Paper presented at Workshop on the Indian Development Experience, Department of Management Studies and Indian Institute of Science, March 3-5.

Krueger, Anne O. 1993. *Political Economy of Policy Reform in Developing Countries,* Cambridge: MIT Press.

Krugman P. 1991. *Geography and Trade*. Cambridge, Mass: MIT Press.

Kumra, G., Mitra, P. and Pasricha, C. 2011. *India Pharma 2015: Unlocking the Potential of the Indian Pharmaceutical Market*, New Delhi: McKinsey & Co.

Kuhnert, S. 2001. "An evolutionary theory of collective action: Schumpeterian entrepreneurship for the common good". *Constitutional Political Economy,* 12: 13-29.

Kuznets, S. 1966. *Modern Economic Growth,* New Haven: Yale University Press.

Lal, A.V. and and Clement, R.W. 2005. 'Economic Development in India: The Role of Individual Entrepreneur', *Asia-Pacific Development Review*, 12:2, 81-99.

Lall, S. 1985. "Trade in technology by a slowly industrializing country: India", in Rosenberg, N. and Frischtak, C. (eds). *International Technology Transfer*, New York: Praeger, 45–76.

Lall, S. 1987. *Learning to Industrialize: The Acquisition of Technological Capability by India*, Hampshire: MacMillan Press.

Lamb, Helen B. 1955. "The Indian Business Communities and the Evolution of an Industrialist Class." *Pacific Affairs,* 28:2, 101-116.

Lansberg, Ivan. 1998, "Succession Conspiracy", *Family Business Review*, Summer.

Lateef, A. 1997. *Linking up with the global economy: A case study of the Bangalore Software Industry*, Discussion paper 96/1997, Geneva: International Institute for Labour Studies.

Lawrence, T.B. 1999. "Institutional strategy", *Journal of Management*, 25: 161-187.

Lazear, E.P., 2002. "Entrepreneurship", *NBER Working Paper No. 9109*. Cambridge, MA.

Lee, S. and Peterson, S. 2000. "Culture, Entrepreneurial Orientation, and Global Competitiveness". *Journal of World Business*, 35:4, 401.

Leeuwen, B.V. 2007. "Human Capital and Economic Growth in India, Indonesia, and Japan: A quantitative analysis, 1890-2000". Unpublished Ph.D. Dissertation, Amsterdam, Netherlands: International Institute of Social History.

Leff, N.H. 1979. "Entrepreneurship and economic development: the problem revisited", *Journal of Economic Literature*, 17:1, 45-64.

Leibenstein, H. 1968, "Entrepreneurship and Development". *American Economic Review,* 58:2, 72-83.

Levy, D. and Scully, M. 2007. "The institutional entrepreneur as modern prince: The strategic face of power in con-tested fields", *Organization Studies*, 28: 971-991.

Lockwood, W. W. 1954. *The Economic Development of Japan, Growth and Structural Change 1868-1938,* Princeton: Princeton University Press.

Lucas R.E., 1978. "On the size distribution of business firms", *Bell Journal of Economics*. 9: 508-23.

Mani, S. 2009. *The growth of knowledge-intensive entrepreneurship in India, 1991-2007 analysis of its evidence and the facilitating factors*, Thiruvananthapuram: Centre for Developing Studies.

McClelland, David. 1965. "Need achievement and entrepreneurship, A longitudinal study". *Journal of Personality and Social Psychology*, 1, 389-392.

McClelland, David. 1961. *The Achieving Society*. Princeton, NJ: Van Nostrand.

McClelland, David and Winter, D.G. 1969. *Motivating Economic Achievement*, New York.

Medhora, Phiroze B. 1965. "Entrepreneurship in India" *Political Science Quarterly* 80:4, 58-59.

Minniti, M., Bygrave, W.D. and Autio, E. 2006. *Global Entrepreneurship Monitor executive report 2005,* Babson Park, MA: Babson College and London: London Business School.

Minqiu, Z. 2008. *Tata Group: A Successful Model in Emerging Markets*. Beijing: Tsinghua University Publishing House. von Mises, L. 1998 (1949). *Human Action: A Treatise on Economics*, Auburn, AL: Ludwig von Mises Institute.

Morris, M.H. 1998. *Entrepreneurial Intensity: Subtitle Sustainable Advantages for Individuals, Organizations, and Societies*. Verenigde Staten: Greenwood Publishing Group.

Morris, Morris David. 1967. "Values as an Obstacle to Economic Growth in South Asia: An Historical Survey", *Journal of Economic History,* 27: 588-607.

Moskowitz T.J. and Vissing-Jorgensen, A. 2002. "The returns to entrepreneurial investment: A private equity premium puzzle?", *American Economic Review*. 92: 745-48.

Murphy, P., Liao, J. and Welsch, H.P. 2006. "A Conceptual History of Entrepreneurial Thought", *Journal of Management History,* 1-41.

Nafziger, Wayne E. 1971. "Entrepreneurship and Economic Development." Ed. Peter Kilby. New York: The Free Press.

Nafziger, W .E. and Terrell, D. 1996. "Entrepreneurial human capital and the long-run survival of firms in India". *World Development* 24:4, 689-696.

Nakra, N. 1996. "Changing Trends in Iron and Steel Industry in World and its Impact on Indian Steel Scenario". *Metal News*, 18:5, 12-18.

NASSCOM. 2010. *Indian IT Industry Factsheet*. New Delhi: National Association of Software and Service Companies.

NASSCOM-Deloitte. 2008. *Indian IT/ITES Industry: Impacting Economy and Society 2007-08*. New Delhi: NASSCOM Foundation.

NASSCOM. 2004. *Indian IT industry*. Available online at: http://www.nasscom.org.

Natesh, S. and Bhan, M.K. 2009. "Biotechnology sector in India: strengths, limitations, remedies and outlook", *Current Science*, 97:2, 157-69.

Nayyar, D. 2008. "Internationalization of Firms from India: Investment, Mergers and Acquisitions", in *Trade and Globalization*, New Delhi: Oxford University Press.

Neelakantan, S. 2005. "Scouting for Homegrown Ingenuity", *The Chronicle for Higher Education*, 52:6, A 43.

Network for Entrepreneurship and Economic Development. 2010. "Banking with the poor network", Lucknow.

Neumann, P.J. and Greenberg, D. 2012. "Is the United States ready for QALYs?"*Health Affairs,* 31:6, 366-371.

Nikkei, 2012. "Indian pharmaceuticals to expand marketing in Japan", *Japan Economic News*, March 16.

Nigam, V. 2001. *Venture Capital in India*. New Delhi: ICRA Information Services.

North, D.C. 1990. *Institutions, Institutional Change, and Economic Performance*, Cambridge: Cambridge University Press.

North, D.C. 2005. *Understanding the Process of Economic Change*, Princeton: Princeton University Press.

OECD. 1998. *Fostering Entrepreneurship*. Paris: Organization for Economic Cooperation andDdevelopment.

OECD. 2009. *Measuring Entrepreneurship, A Digest of Indicators,* OECD Statistics Directorate, Eurostat Entrepreneurship Indicators Programme.

Ogilvie, S. 2007. "Whatever is, is right? Economic institutions in pre-industrial Europe". *Economic History Review,* 60: 649-684.

Oliver, C. 1997. "Sustainable competitive advantage: Combining institutional and resource-based views". *Strategic Management Journal* 18, 697-713.

Oliver, C. and Holzinger, I. 2008. "The effectiveness of strategic political management: A dynamic capabilities framework". *Academy of Management Review*, 33: 496-520.

Oonk, G. 2007. "South Asians in East Africa (1880-1920) with a particular focus on Zanzibar: Toward a Historical Explanation of Economic Success of a Middleman Minority." *African and Asian Studies*, 5:1, 1-32.

Ostrom, E. 2005. *Unlocking public entrepreneurship and public economies*. Helsinki, Finland: EGDI.

Ostrom, E. 1990. *Governing the Commons: The Evolution of Institutional Forms of Collective Action*. Cambridge, UK: Cambridge University Press.

Ozawa, Terutomo. 2009. *The rise of Asia The 'Flying Geese' Theory of Tandem Growth and Regional Agglomeration,* Cheltenham: Edward Elgar.

Pacheco, D.F., York, J.G., Dean, T.J. and Sarasvathy, D. 2010. "The Coevolution of Institutional Entrepreneurship: A Tale of Two Theories", *Journal of Management,* 36:4, 974-1010.

Panagariya, Arvind, 1994. "India: a new tiger on the block?" *Contemporary Issues in World Trade*, 48:1, 193-221.

Parker, Simon. 2004. *The Economics of Entrepreneurship,* Cambridge, UK: Cambridge University Press.

Parker, S.C. and van Praag, C.M. 2004. "Schooling, capital constraints and entrepreneurial performance: the endogenous triangle", Discussion Paper No. 04-106/3, Tinbergen Institute, University of Amsterdam.

Peng, M.W. and Heath, P.S. 1996. "The growth of the firm in planned economics in transition: Institutions, organizations, and strategic choice". *The Academy of Management Executive*, 14:1, 113-151.

Penrose, E.T. 1959. *The Theory of the Growth of the Firm.* New York, NY: John Wiley & Sons.

Pinchot, G. 1985. *Intrapreneuring,* New York: Free Press.

Piramal, Gita, Bartlett, Christopher A. and Ghoshal, Sumantra. 2000. *Managing Radical Change: What Indian Companies Must Do to Become World Class,* New Delhi: Viking.

Pistrui, David and Huang W .V. 2006. "Family and Cultural Forces: Shaping Entrepreneurship and SME Development in China", in Panikkos Zata Potziouris and others (ed). *Handbook of Research on Family Business* (ed), Edward Elgar, USA.

Porter, M. 1990. *The competitive advantage of nations*. New York: Free Press.

Porter, M. 1980. *Competitive Strategy: Techniques for Analyzing Industries and Competitors,* New York: The Free Press.

Porter, M., Sachs, J. and McArthur, J. 2002. "Executive summary: competitiveness and stages of economic development", in Porter, M., Sachs, J., Cornelius, P.K., McArthur, J.W. and Schwab, K. (eds.), *The Global Competitiveness Report 2001-2002, New York:* Oxford University Press,16-25.

Prahalad, C.K. and Hammond, A. 2002. "Serving the World's Poor Profitably", *Harvard Business Review*, 80:9, 48-58. Port and Hammond, 2002.

Pursell, Gary, 1992. "Trade Policies in India," in Dominick Salvatore, ed National Trade Policies: *Handbook of Comparative Economic Policies*, Vol. 2, New York: Greenwood Press.

Ramani, S.V. and Mukherjee, V. 2010. *CSR and market changing product innovations: Indian case studies,* United Nations University - Maastricht Economic and Social Research and Training Centre on Innovation and T hnology, Maastricht, The Netherlands.

Rao, H. 2008. *Market Rebels: How Activists Make or Break Radical Innovations*. Princeton: Princeton University Press.

Rao, Niranjan, 2009. "Information Technology Sector In Andhra Pradesh" in Mahendra Dev S., Ravi C. and Venkatanarayana M. (ed), *Human Development in Andhra Pradesh; Experiences, Issues and Challenges,* Hyderabad: Centre for Economic and Social Studies.

Rao, T.V. 1985. "The entrepreneurial orientation inventory: measuring the locus of control", *The 1985 Annual: Developing Human Resources*, 129-135.

Raman, V. 2010. "Emerging trends in entrepreneurship, National Seminar on Paradigm change in Global Business Environment", Thakur Institute of Management Studies and Research, Mumbai, 30 January.

Ray, Rajat Kanta. 1992. "Introduction." In *Entrepreneurship and Industry in India, 1800-1947*, Rajat Kanta Ray (ed), New Delhi: Oxford University Press.

Reynolds, P., Bosma, N., Autio, E., Hunt, S., De Bono, N., Servais, I., Lopez-Garcia, P. and Chin, N. 2005. "Global Entrepreneurship Monitor: Data collection design and implementation 1998-2003". *Small Business Economics,* 24:3, 205-231.

Robinson, P.B., Stimpson, D.V. Huefner, J.C., Hunt, H.K. 1991. "An attitude approach to the prediction of entrepreneurship", *Entrepreneurship Theory and Practice*, 15:4, 13-31.

Rostow, W.W. 1960. *The Stages of Economic Growth: A Non-communist Manifesto,* Cambridge: Cambridge University Press.

Rungta, R.S. 1970, *Rise of Business Corporations in India 1851-1900,* Cambridge: Cambridge University Press.

Ruttan, V.W. 1997. "Induced Innovation, Evolutionary Theory and Path Dependence: Sources of Technical Change", *Economic Journal,* 107, 1520-1529.

Rutten, M. 2006. "The Study of entrepreneurship in India: In need of a comparative Perspective", in *The Oxford India Companion to Sociology and Social Anthropology*, eds. Veena Das, New Delhi: Oxford University Press.

Sala-I-Martin, X., Blanke, J., Hanouz, M.D. and Geiger, T. 2011. *The Global Competitiveness Index 2010-2011: Looking Beyond the Global Economic Crisis,* World Economic Forum, IRENE MIA

Sala-I-Martin, X., Blanke, J., Hanouz, M.D., Geiger, T., Mia, I. and Paua, F. 2007. "The Global Competitiveness Index: Measuring the productive potential of nations", The Global Competitiveness Report 2007-2008, Hampshire: Palgrave Macmillan, 3-40.

Sarasvathy, S.D. and Venkataraman, S. 2011. "Entrepreneurship as Method: Open Questions for an Entrepreneurial Future", *Entrepreneurship Theory and Practice,* January, 113-135.

Saxenian, A. 2006. *The New Argonauts: Regional Advantage in a Global Economy*. Cambridge, MA: Harvard University Press.

Say, J.B. 1964. *Traité d'économie politique: ou, simple exposition de la manière dontse forment, sedistribuent et se consomment les richesses*, Translation: Treatise on Political Economy: On the Production, Distribution and Consumption of Wealth, Kelley, New York, (1st edition: 1827).

Schneider, M. and Teske, P. 1992. "Toward a theory of the political entrepreneur: Evidence from local government". *American Political Science Review*, 86: 737-47.

Schramm, C.J. 2006. *The Entrepreneurial Imperative,* New York: Harper Collins.

Schwab, K. 2012. *The Global Competitiveness Report 2012-13*, World Economic Forum, IRENE MIA.

Schumpeter, J.A. 1934. *The Theory of Economic Development*, Cambridge, MA: Harvard University Press.

Schumpeter, J.A. 1950, *Capitalism, Socialism and Democracy*, New York: Harper and Row.

Schumpeter, J.A. 1961, *The Theory of Economic Development: An inquiry into profits, capital, credit, interest, and the business cycle*, New York: Oxford University Press.

Schumpeter, J.A. 1969. "Economic theory and entrepreneurial history" in *Essays on Economic Topics of J.A. Schumpeter*, ed. R.V. Clemence, New York: Kennikat Press, 248-266.

Seshadri, D.V.R. and Tripathy, A. 2006. "Innovation through Intrapreneurship: The Road Less Travelled", *Vikalpa,* 31:1, 17-29.

Sethi, S.O. 1994. *Multinational Corporations and the Impact of Public Advocacy on Corporate Strategy: Nestle and the Infant Formula Controversy*. The Netherlands: Kluwer.

SEWA. 2009. "Social protection and shelter", *Social Protection Newsletter,* 4:1-5.

Sinha, D.K. 1990. "The Contribution of Formal Planning to Decisions." *Strategic Management Journal,* 11, 479-492.

Sinha, D.K. 1984. "A Model of Effective Leadership Style in India" *International Studies of Management and Organization*, 14, 86-98.

Sinha, Jai B.P. 1978. "Superior Subordinate Relationship and Alienation," *National Labour Institute Bulletin* 4, 209-223.

Shane, S. and Venkataraman, S. 2000. "The promise of entrepreneurship as a field of research", *Academy of Management Review*, 25: 217-26.

Shapero, A. and Sokol, L. 1982. "The Social Dimensions of Entrepreneurship", in C. Kent, D.

Sexton, and K.H. Vesper (eds). *The Encyclopedia of Entrepreneurship*. Englewood Cliffs, NJ: Prentice-Hall, 72-90.

Shim, W.S. and Steers, R.M. 2001. "The Entrepreneurial Basis of Korean Enterprise: Past Accomplishments and Future Challenges", *Asia Pacific Business Review*, 7:4, 22-43.

Shivani, S., Mukherjee, S.K. and Saran, R. 2006. "Socio-Cultural Influences on Indian Entrepreneurs: The Need for Appropriate Structural Interventions". *Journal of Asian Economics*, 17:1, 5-13.

Singh, A., Hallihosur, S. and Rangan, L. 2009. "Changing landscape in biotechnology patenting", *World Patent Information*, 3, 219-225.

Singh, J.B. 1990. "Entrepreneurship education as a catalyst of development in the third world", *Journal of Small Business and Entrepreneurship*, 7:4, 56-63.

Singhal, A. and Tagore, A. 2002. *Big Industry Before Independence: 1860-1950*, Working Paper No. 25, State, Market and Economy, New Delhi: Centre for Civil Society, 61-69.

Siti-Maimon, K. 1993. "Intrapreneurship and Exopreneuring as critical Success factors for Competitive advantage", *SME Proceeding of the international symposium on gaining competitive advantage through marketing: Current issues and future challenges,* Kuala Lumpur: University of Kebangsaan.

Smith, B., Matthews, C. and Schenkel, M. 2005. "The search for and discovery of entrepreneurial opportunities: The effects of taciτness and codification". *Frontiers of Entrepreneurship Research*, 25: 283-293.

Software Technology Parks of India. 2011. *Annual Report 2010-2011*, New Delhi: STPI.

Stiglitz, J.E. 2004. "Information and the change in the paradigm in economics, part 2", *The American Economist*, 48:1, 17-49.

Stiglitz, J.E. 1998. "The private uses of public interests: Incentives and institutions". *Journal of Economic Perspectives,* 12: 3-22.

Stiglitz, J.E. and Weiss, A. 1981. "Credit rationing in markets with imperfect information", *American Economic Review,* 71: 393-410.

Streefkerk, H. 1985. *Industrial Transition in Rural India: Artisans. Traders and Tribals in South Gujarat*. Bombay: Sangam Books.

Stuart, T. and Sorenson, O. 2005. "Social Networks and Entrepreneurship", in H*andbook of Entrepreneurship Research: Disciplinary Perspectives*, New York: Springer Science Business Media.

Suchman, M.C. 1995. "Managing legitimacy: Strategies and institutional approaches". *Academy of Management Review*, 20: 571-610.

Suddaby, R. and Greenwood, R. 2005. "Rhetorical Strategies of Legitimacy". *Administrative Science Quarterly*, 50: 35-67.

Suresh, N. 2009. "Today's biotech industry in India", *Biotechnology Journal*, 4, 291-294.

Surie, G. 2007. *Knowledge, Organizational Evolution and Market Creation: The Globalization of Indian Firms,* Northampton, MA: Edward Elgar.

Surie, G. and Torras, M. 2007. "The co-evolution of technology and entrepreneurship: lessons for development from India and Korea", *International Journal of Technoentrepreneurship,* 1:2, 183-206.

Syrquin, M. 1988. "Patterns of structural change". in *Handbook of Development Economics*, Amsterdam and New York: North-Holland, 203-273.

Tabe, Noboru. 1970. *Indian Entrepreneurs at the Cross Roads - A Study of Business Leadership,* Tokyo: Institute of Developing Economies.

Tambuan, T. 2009. "Women entrepreneurship in Asian developing countries: Their development and main constraints", *Journal of Development and Agricultural Economics*, 1:2, 27-40.

Teske, P. and Schneider, M. 1994. "The bureaucratic entrepreneur: The case of city managers", *Public Administration Review*, 54: 331–40.

Thurik, R. 1999. "Entrepreneurship, industrial transformation and growth", *The Sources of Entrepreneurial Activity,* G.D. Libecap, Stamford, CT: JAI Press.

Thornton, Patricia. 1999. "The Sociology of Entrepreneurship." *Annual Review of Sociology*. 25: 19-46.

Times of India. 2007. "Young Indians happiest in the world: Survey", September 20.

Timmons, J.A. 1994. *New Venture Creation: Entrepreneurship for the 21st Century*, 4th edition, Burr Ridge: Irwin Press.

Timmons, J. A. 1989. *The Entrepreneurial Mind*, Harvard: Brick House Publishing.

Tripathi, Dwijendra. 2004. *The Oxford History of Indian Business/ Dwijendra Tripathi*. Reprint. New Delhi: Oxford University Press.

Tripathi, D. 1971. "Indian Entrepreneurship in Historical Perspective: A Re-Interpretation", *Economic and Political Weekly*, 6:22.

Trivedi, C. 2012. "Towards a Social Ecological Framework for Social Entrepreneurship", *The Journal of Entrepreneurship*, 21:1, 63-80.

Trivedi, P., Lakshmanan, I. and Jain, R. 2011. *Productivity, efficiency and competitiveness of the Indian manufacturing sector,* Mumbai: Reserve Bank of India.

Tuli, R., Samir V.S., Prabodh, K.T., Pradhyumna, K.S. and Nath, P. 2009. "Agricultural Biotechnology in India: Prospects and Challenges", *Biotechnology Journal,* 4:319-328.

Turner, P. 2007. "Entrepreneurship: Riding growth in India and China". knowledge@Insead.com.

Tyabji, N. 2000. *Industrialisation and Innovation: The Indian Experience,* New Delhi: Sage.

UNCTAD, 2006. *World investment report 2006:FDI from developing and transition economies: implications for development.* New York/Geneva: United Nations.

UNCTAD, 2004. *Entrepreneurship and Economic Development: the Empretec Showcase*, Geneva: UNCTAD.

UNDP, 2010. *Ready Reckoner on Microfinance*, New Delhi: United Nations Development Programme.

UNDP, 2010. *Human Development Report 2010*, New York: Oxford University Press.

UNDP, 2001. *Human Development Report 2001*, New York; Oxford University Press.

US Department of State. 2009. "US Department of State Foreign Affairs Manual", Vol. 9 Visas.

Varadarajan, R. 2011. "Conjectures on innovation drivers in an emerging market: India", in *Handbook of Research International*, Google Books, chapter 6.

Varaprasad, S.D. 2011. "Technology Trade in Indo-Chinese Relations: Divergent Dynamics and Implications", *Journal of International Affairs,* 64:2, 125-141.

Venkataraman, S. 1997. "The Distinctive Domain of Entrepreneurship Research," in *Advances in Entrepreneurship, Firm Emergence and Growth*. Eds. J. Katz and R. Brockhaus. Greenwich, CT: JAI Press, 119-138.

Veen, J.H. van der. 1976. "Commercial Orientation of Industrial Entrepreneurs in India," *Economic and Political Weekly*, 11:35: M91- M94.

Vernon, R S. 1966. "International investment and international trade in the product cycle," *Quarterly Journal of Economics*, 80:2, 190-207.

Wade, R. 1990. *Governing the Market: Economic Theory and the Role of Government in East Asian Industrialization*. Princeton, NJ: Princeton University Press.

Ward, J.L. 2004. "Is Google a Family Business?" *Families in Business,* May-June. 14: 83-84.

Watanabe, S. 1970. "Entrepreneurship in small enterprises in Japanese manufacturing". *International Labour Review*, 102:6, 531-576.

Weber, Max. 1930. *The Protestant Ethic and the Spirit of Capitalism*, translated by Talcott Parsons, London: Allen & Unwin.

Weber, Max. 1958. *The Religion of India - The Sociology of Hinduism and Buddhism*. New York: The Free Press.

Weik, E. 2011. "Institutional Entrepreneurship and Agency", *Journal for the Theory of Social Behaviour*, 41:4, 466-481.

Wennekers, Sander. 2006. *Entrepreneurship at Country Level; Economic and Non-Economic Determinants*, Rotterdam: ERIM.

Westphal, Larry E, Linsu, K. and Dahlman, C.J. 1985. "Reflections on the Republic of Korea's Acquisition of Technological Capability," in Nathan Rosenberg and C. Frischtak (eds). *International Technology Transfer: Concepts, Measures and Comparisons,* Praeger: New York, 167-221.

Williamson, O.E. 2000. "The new institutional economics: Taking stock, looking ahead". *Journal of Economic Literature*, 38: 595-613.

Williamson, O E. 1985. *The Economic Institutions of Capitalism: Firms, Markets, Relational Contracting*. New York: The Free Press.

Wong, P.K. 1988. "Technological Development through Subcontracting Linkages: Evidence from Singapore", *International Business Review*, 1:3, 28-40.

Wong, P.K., Yuen, P.H. and Erkko, A. 2005. "Entrepreneurship, innovation and economic growth: evidence from GEM data", *Small Business Economics,* 24:3, 335-350.

World Bank. 2012. *World Development Report 2012*, Washington, DC: World Bank.

World Bank. 2001/2006/2011. *World Development Indicators, 2001/ 2006/2011*, Washington, DC: World Bank.

World Resources Institute. 2007. *Annual Report 2006-2007*, Washington, DC: WRI.

Yandle, B. 1983. "Bootleggers and Baptists: The Education of a Regulatory Economist." *Regulation, 7:3,* 12.

Zhang, Y. and Duysters, G. 2010. "Entrepreneurship Development and the Role of Economic Transition in Entrepreneurial Activities in China", in Ying Zhang and Geert Duysters, United Nations University-Maastricht Economic and Social Research and Training Centre on Innovation and Technology, Maastricht: Keizer Karelplein.

Zilber, T.B. 2007. "Stories and the discursive dynamics of institutional entrepreneurship: The case of Israeli high-tech after the bubble". *Organization Studies,* 28: 1035-1054.

Zhou, Yu. 2007. "Chinese High tech industry and the World Economy, Zhongguancun Park", *Japan Focus*, Tokyo.

Zhou, Yu. 2005. "The making of an innovative region from a centrally planned economy: institutional evolution in Zhongguancun Science Park in Beijing", *Environment and Planning*, A, 37: 1113-1134.

Zucker, Lynne G. 1988. "Where do institutional patterns come from? Organizations as actors in social systems" in *Institutional Patterns and Organizations; Culture and Environment,* Lynne G. Zucker, ed. Cambridge, MA: Ballinger, 23-49.

Websites

http://www.tata.com/article.aspx?artid=XXjYqhPMSNM
http://www.tata.com/article.aspx?artid=XXjYqhPMSNM
http://www.india:jbs.cam.ac.uk/engagement/tataises/index.html
http://www.scribd.com/doc/27813353/Ratan-Tata-and-His-Enterprising-Skills
http://www.tatasteel100.com/people/index.asp
http://www.youtube.com/watch?v=HLYm4zF5soE (Reliance)
http://www.quora.com/Who-are-the-top-10-greatest-entrepreneurs-in-India
http://www.quora.com/Who-are-the-top-10-greatest-entrepreneurs-in-India

http://money.cnn.com/galleries/2012/news/companies/1203/gallery.greatest-entrepreneurs.fortune/11.html

http://en.wikipedia.org/wiki/List_of_Indian_entrepreneurs

http://network.nature.com/groups/india/forum/topics/2544 (biotech young Entre Scheme)

http://www.siteadvisor.com/restricted. html?domain =http:%2F%2Fwww.world colleges.info%2 Fhappenings_biotech.php&or iginalURL=381781429&pip=false&premium=false&client_uid=3653329488& client_ver=3.5.0.229&clie nt_type=IEPlugin&suite=true&aff_id=714-9&locale= en_us&ui=1&os_ver=6.1.1.0

http://en.wikipedia.org/wiki/List_of_social_entrepreneurs

http://www.youthkiawaaz.com/2011/01/top-10-women-entrepreneurs-and-leaders-of-india/

http://www.fiwe.org/

http://www.internationalentrepreneurship.com/asia/india/

http://www.schwabfound.org/pdf/schwabfound/SchwabFoundation_ProfilesBrochure2012.pdf

http://www.tata.com/article.aspx?artid=XXjYqhPMSNM

Afterword

Dr. Somu GIRIAPPA, a co-author of the book passed away on the 27 th of March ,2013, just before the manuscript went to the printer. A brief narrative will help the reader know our story of learning and human bondage that we endevored to enshrine during the past half a century , and between India and Japan.

In Memory of :
Our Eternal Joy of Learning and Human Bondage !
Ah, it's spring and time for *Sakura* merriment in Tokyo,
Those cherries were about to bloom en masse with extreme beauty.
On this moment, sad news of his death reached me,
Fading away cherry blossom as soon as they sprout and enchant
That' the spirit of life of eternal joy, know our worth,
I would say our relation blossomed at *Tambaram*,
Madras Christian College and *Mangalore University*
In our scholarly pursuits half a century ago.
Our collaborative work flourished to new heights culminating
In the publishing of a book on entrepreneurship.
But *Somu* is no longer with me. *Somu* would say,
'I wish my teacher cherry blossoms for ever',
As I would ponder over the blossom at my garden
To the eternal joy of learning and human bondage.
The good soul from the land of mangoes graced my family and me
At *Tambaram* half a century ago.

As I would say, ***thus far, no farther,*** *Somu* gifted me with his shadows

Of learning and human bondage that never extinguish from my memory.

May his soul rest in peace! Shine my family and me forever!

Noboru Tabe,
Professor Emeritus
Meiji Gakuin University,
Tokyo

Index

D